IDEAS OF LIBERTY IN EARLY MODERN EUROPE

Ideas of Liberty in Early Modern Europe

FROM MACHIAVELLI TO MILTON

Hilary Gatti

PRINCETON UNIVERSITY PRESS
Princeton & Oxford

Copyright © 2015 by Princeton University Press
Published by Princeton University Press
41 William Street, Princeton, New Jersey 08540
In the United Kingdom: Princeton University Press
6 Oxford Street, Woodstock, Oxfordshire OX20 1TR

press.princeton.edu

Cover image: Allegorical illustration of *Libertà* from Cesare Ripa,
*Iconologia overo Descrittione di diverse Imagini cauate dall'antichità,
& di propria inuentione* . . ., Rome, 1603, page 293.

All Rights Reserved

First paperback printing, 2017

Paper ISBN: 978-0-691-17611-6

The Library of Congress has cataloged the cloth edition as follows:

Gatti, Hilary.
Ideas of liberty in early modern Europe : from Machiavelli to Milton / Hilary Gatti.
pages cm
Includes bibliographical references and index.
ISBN 978-0-691-16383-3 (hardcover : alk. paper) 1. Liberty—History—
16th century. 2. Liberty—History—17th century. 3. Political science—Europe—
History—16th century. 4. Political science—Europe—History—
17th century. I. Title.
JC585.G365 2015
320.01′1—dc23
2014013540

British Library Cataloging-in-Publication Data is available

This book has been composed in Adobe Garamond Pro and Poetica Std

Printed on acid-free paper. ∞

Printed in the United States of America

Contents

Acknowledgments
VII

INTRODUCTION
1

CHAPTER 1
Political Liberty

Niccolò Machiavelli: Liberty and the Law
11

Niccolò Machiavelli: Liberty and *Fortuna*
16

Niccolò Machiavelli and Sir Thomas More
19

The Rule of the Prince
22

CHAPTER 2
Liberty and Religion

The Bondage or the Freedom of the Will:
Martin Luther and Erasmus of Rotterdam
31

"Of Our Own We Have Only Sin":
John Calvin and the Problem of Heresy
40

Inquisition: The Trial of Giordano Bruno
54

Religion as Dogma, or Religion as Debate?
Richard Hooker and Jacobus Arminius
65

CHAPTER 3
Libertas philosophandi, or the Liberty of Thought

Between the Prince and Parliament
81

CONTENTS

The New Drama: William Shakespeare
92

The New Science:
From Giordano Bruno to Francis Bacon
99

The New Science: Galileo Galilei
103

CHAPTER 4
The Freedom of the Press

The Problems of Writing History:
From Jacques Auguste de Thou to Paolo Sarpi
117

The Search for New Liberties: John Milton
133

John Milton: *Areopagitica*
140

The Virtues of Schisms and Sects
149

CHAPTER 5
Epilogue

Henry Neville, the Republic of Venice,
and the "Glorious Revolution" of 1689
159

CONCLUSION
175

Notes
177

Bibliography
193

Index
207

Acknowledgments

This book comes out of an unforgettable period of membership of the School of Historical Studies at the Institute for Advanced Study at Princeton in 2005. I am grateful to the philosophy faculty of the Università di Roma "La Sapienza," and in particular to the then dean of the faculty, Marco Olivetti (who is, sadly, no longer with us), for the sabbatical year that made that membership possible.

Among the numerous privileges accorded to scholars attending the Institute for Advanced Study is the extraordinary stimulus provided by discussion with distinguished members of faculty. I am particularly grateful to Jonathan Israel, director of the Studies in Early Modern History program, and to Heinrich von Staden for their lively interest in my work. A memorable conversation with Michael Walzer contributed significantly to chapter 2, "Liberty and Religion." Later on I received important encouragement from Quentin Skinner and Dan Garber that led to the completion of the project. Other scholars whose interest has proved an invaluable stimulus are Michael Wyatt, who shared with me numerous aspects of his wide knowledge of the Italian Renaissance; Ingrid Rowland, who shares my abiding interest in Giordano Bruno; and Marta Fattori and Lina Bolzoni, who have supported my studies in Italy in multiple and valuable ways. My thanks also go to Rens Bod of the UVA (University of Amsterdam), who allotted generous space for my work on liberty in his history of the humanities seminars. My two editors at Princeton University Press, Ian Malcolm and Ben Tate, have provided essential support during the publication process. Ultimately, however, it has been the constantly affectionate stimulus provided by my sons and daughter, Luca, Stefano, and Anna, that has brought this project to its final conclusion. To them and to my grandchildren I dedicate this book. May they live in a world that is peaceful and free.

IDEAS OF LIBERTY IN EARLY MODERN EUROPE

Introduction

I Defining Liberty

Since the second half of the twentieth century and beyond, the culture of the Western world has developed a remarkable inquiry into the meaning of the word *liberty*, with its multiple derivations: *liberal*, *liberalism*, *libertarianism*, and *libertinism*, not to mention its synonym, *freedom*. Many of the finest European and American minds of the last half century have devoted their attention to this inquiry, which has delved deep into the origins of these words, the conceptual contours of the ideas they express, their historical sources and the historical debates that have surrounded them, and the political structures that may be associated with them. Behind such a fervid and sustained activity may be discerned a concerted attempt to catch and hold onto the thing they attempt to define. Clearly related, in the first instance, to the aftermath of the systematic persecution and massacre of the Jews and the corpse-ridden wasteland produced by the dictatorial regimes that succeeded in coming to power in the first half of the twentieth century in some of the most civilized and refined cultures of the Western world, a literature has been produced on the liberty that was lost—and only arduously (and not always fully) regained—that is daunting both in its quantity and quality.

The impetus behind the production of such texts seems far from exhausted. Indeed it can be considered to have increased in intensity as the complicated processes of globalization that define our contemporary world render the discourse on liberty and human rights increasingly fraught with tensions, for the new global culture has made it clear that the values of individual and political liberty associated with the postwar democratic regimes of the Western world are energetically contested by many and diverse forms of explicitly antilibertarian political regimes and religious movements. So, once again, liberty has to defend itself against many enemies, sometimes publicly declared but at other times hidden dangerously underground or masked by a deceptive layer of affable libertarianism.

INTRODUCTION

One problem—a place from which it seems wise to start—is that the word *liberty*, like the thing itself, has not proved an easy one to deal with. One of the most prestigious participants in the twentieth-century discussion described above, Sir Isaiah Berlin, remarked in his now classic essay "Two Concepts of Liberty" that over the centuries the word has proved too porous to consider it semantically stable. Historians of ideas, according to Berlin, have recorded more than two hundred meanings of this protean word. So it may be useful to reflect on the fact that what is universally considered to be the key term of modern culture, society and politics, at least in the Western world, turns out to be so difficult to pin down in any but the most superficial and demagogic sense.[1]

Some of the words surrounding the concept of liberty have even become widely associated with pejorative rather than positive connotations. This is particularly the case with *liberalism*, which is often derided by those very people who claim to be the most ardent defenders of liberty. A number of commentators have pointed in succinct and at times disapproving terms to this downgrading of *liberalism* into a word of contempt, even within the confines of Western democratic society, where the word made its appearance only in relatively modern times.[2] Its meaning in Republican Party circles in the United States, for example, has become widely associated with what is seen as a deplorable preference for liberal governmental bureaucracy, and tolerance of such things as public support for those in need, the right of abortion and same-sex marriage. In Europe, on the contrary, it is associated with a wish for minimal governmental bureaucracy and maximum faith in the freedom of market forces: policies not loved by the political Left. This widespread pejorative use of the word *liberalism* on both sides of the political divide appears to some acute observers of political vocabulary to deny its roots in rational philosophy, where the word—which seems to have found its origin in the political philosophies of the European Enlightenment—has traditionally been associated with speaking up for individual rights and freedoms and with challenging the excesses of oppressive government and other forms of power. As for philosophical *libertinism*, a word associated with radical Enlightenment philosophies (above all, of French derivation), it has been the subject of an intense academic rather than political debate that, then as today, is met either by scandalized repudiation or by ardent as well as erudite apologetics.[3] In some ways it is a relief to remember that the English language offers the alternative, solid, Anglo-Saxon "freedom," more obvious both in its meanings and its practical applications and less subject to the slippery subtleties of its Latin counterpart.

In "Two Concepts of Liberty" Berlin raises the question of the best known and most intensely discussed linguistic and conceptual distinction in the liberty debate: that between "negative" and "positive" forms of liberty or freedom.[4] The idea of "negative freedom" derives, according to Berlin, from the answer to the question, "What is the area within which the subject—a person or group of persons—is or should be left to do or be what he is able to do or be, without interference by other persons?" The second—or "positive"—sense of the words *liberty* or *freedom* derives from the answer to the question, "What, or who, is the source of control or interference that can determine someone to do, or be, this rather than that?" This distinction was not invented by Berlin himself; indeed, he stresses that it is based on much historical precedent. Nevertheless, his discussion of this distinction, first delivered as a lecture at the University of Oxford in 1958, has become canonical not only for the finesse of his arguments but also for the intensity with which he proposes a subject that, as he explicitly reminds his readers, carried with it tragic memories of a still recent war.

It is rather the conceptual nature of the distinction that needs to be stressed here, however. The "negative" liberty being defined is clearly not a negative value as such but instead a space of indifference in which there should be no legal or social interference with the liberty of individuals to live their own lives according to their own choices. The "positive" liberty referred to is similarly not so much a positive value as such but instead the freedom of individuals to be moved by positive reasons, or by conscious purposes, that they claim the right to act on and realize in defiance of authorities in possible disagreement with such purposes. Berlin's way of articulating this distinction makes it clear that he values the idea of "negative" liberty, or the most complete possible lack of interference with the individual's thoughts and doings, more highly than the idea of "positive" liberty, which involves the evaluation of specific projects that the individual wishes to participate in freely but which may end up by being subject to undesirable forms of oppression and control. Berlin's profound admiration for the great nineteenth-century essay *On Liberty* by John Stuart Mill, which is the subject of another classic study in his volume, illustrates how highly he values Mill's central idea: that society or the law should interfere in the life of the individual only when there is danger of harm being done to others.[5]

Berlin's treatment of this distinction between "negative" and "positive" ideas of liberty—and in particular his distrust of the ambiguities involved in the idea of "positive" freedom—have been much discussed and at times subjected to criticism.[6] Here, however, attention needs to be given above all to some of those "historical precedents" mentioned by Berlin, although not pursued in his famous essay, and in particular to the question of whether such a distinction was already being made in the period covered by the present volume—that is, in the course of what is often called the long sixteenth century, or the period between 1500 and approximately 1650. The problem has rarely been examined with rigor, though in 1984 it formed the subject of a major essay by another prestigious political philosopher, Quentin Skinner, who asked whether such a distinction, as formulated by Berlin, could be applied to the idea of liberty developed at the beginning of the sixteenth century, and in particular to Niccolò Machiavelli.[7] The conclusion reached by Skinner is that the works of Machiavelli show how "negative" and "positive" concepts of liberty are not necessarily to be seen as in conflict with one another but may appear as complementary. According to Skinner there is no such distinction to be found in the works of Machiavelli, whose idea of liberty Skinner considers particularly complex and significant precisely because the concern with the liberty of the individual citizen is so closely interwoven with the interests of a free community.

A corollary to this conclusion, suggested by Skinner, is that the "negative" versus "positive" liberty distinction may not be a valid one in discussion of liberty in the early modern world—or at least not in the sixteenth century. It is usually thought to have been introduced in the middle of the seventeenth century by Thomas Hobbes in the chapter "Of the Liberty of Subjects" in his *Leviathan*, which anticipates Berlin in coming down on the side of "negative" liberty. Hobbes sees the most valid form of liberty as the right of noninterference by the community that subjects of any state should be able to claim in their individual concerns: that area of free action in which there reigns what Hobbes calls "the silence of the law." On the other hand, Hobbes points out that such liberty can be exercised by the subject only to the extent to which the constitution and laws of the state are willing to guarantee it. Furthermore, the subject's right to this "negative" liberty cannot, Hobbes points out repeatedly, justify criminal actions that the community as a whole considers as defying the natural or the civil law. Such a conclusion clearly puts the principal onus on the lawgiver; and accordingly Hobbes follows up his chapter "The Liberty of Subjects" with a chapter discussing the justice or injustice of the various "systems" of law governing the different kinds of commonwealth.[8] This chapter, titled "Of Systems Subject, Political, and Private," includes a careful analysis of one of the most delicate subjects that accompanies the debate about liberty in any time or place—that is, why and when single citizens or a group of citizens may be considered justified in opposing the sovereign will and laws of their community in the name of a liberty that is being denied them.

While it is important to emphasize the significance of Hobbes's analysis of "negative" liberty, it is equally important not to ignore a dense page in the fourth of the *Meditations on First Philosophy* by René Descartes, who in earlier years of the seventeenth century had developed a refined distinction between the freedom of the will in its capacity to pursue or to refrain from following its desires.[9] True liberty, according to Descartes, cannot be defined as simply an indifferent freedom of the individual to follow, or not follow, a chosen course of action (that is, in terms of a pure "negation" of constriction) but is correctly conceived only as the freedom of the will to decide in positive terms what is just and right, and to pursue them as its freely chosen ends. Contrary to Hobbes, and later to Berlin, Descartes thus expresses a decided preference for

INTRODUCTION

"positive" against "negative" liberty. Rather than Descartes's own personal position, however, what is of interest here is that at least by 1628, when Descartes wrote the *Meditations* in Holland (they were published in Paris only in 1649), the distinction between "positive" and "negative" liberty, which has played such an important role in recent debate, was already then being formulated. The earlier period of the long sixteenth century discussed in this book may thus be considered as culminating in such a distinction, but as not yet dominated by it.

II Liberty and Republics

While the discussion of liberty shows no signs of being exhausted in the beginnings of a new millennium, in the last few decades a principle subject of debate, which often involves the same voices as those raised previously to defend the value of liberty, has now become the question of republicanism. A long British tradition of conservative political thought sees in the events of the seventeenth century a close connection between liberty and the constitutional monarchy established, through a vote in Parliament, in 1660 in the person of Charles II. This was followed by the even more significant "silent revolution" of 1688 that ousted Charles's brother, James II, from the throne because of his fundamentalist and illiberal Catholicism, establishing the moderate Dutch Protestant, William of Orange, on the British throne in his place. Such events are viewed in this tradition as reestablishing British liberties within a popularly accepted monarchy closely monitored by parliamentary rule, while the previous if brief experience of a radically Protestant republicanism attempted first by the Long Parliament, established in 1640, and then by the quasi-dictatorship installed by Oliver Cromwell—with the support of a standing army after the beheading of Charles I in 1649—becomes associated with the idea of a militaristic oligarchy and the severe limitation of both political and religious dissent. "Republicanism" and "liberalism" are seen in this moderately conservative British context as opposing doctrines.

Such ideas, however, were severely questioned by the studies of Florentine republicanism in the early modern world conducted by Nicolai Rubenstein in the 1960s. Rubenstein showed how the "tyrannical" practices of the political oligarchy established by Cosimo dei Medici on his return from exile in 1434, reinforced by the even more severe "reforms" introduced by his grandson Lorenzo dei Medici in 1480, led to a situation in which "no magistrate dared, even in the smallest matters, to decide anything without first assuring himself of Lorenzo's agreement."[10] The Florentine anti-Medici coup of 1494 was studied by Rubenstein as an attempt to reestablish the old traditions of Florentine republican liberty that had inspired the Commune of Florence in the years of its great humanist chancellors such as Coluccio Salutati and Leonardo Bruni before the Medici takeover introduced more "monarchical" and personal forms of rule. Seen in a Florentine context, the republican idea became closely associated with the idea of political liberty, as it had been in the classical world of ancient Rome by writers such as Cicero.

These positive republican claims made in the context of Florentine historical events echoed the important studies begun, in a more Marxist environment, by Christopher Hill in the 1940s of what he called the radical underground movements in seventeenth-century England. Movements such as the Diggers and the Levellers, active during the brief period of the Long Parliament and Cromwell's commonwealth of the seventeenth century, were brought to the forefront of history by Hill, whose studies gave a new and more positive complexion to the evaluation of the republicanism that inspired the "English Revolution" itself.[11] A close connection between republicanism and political liberty has been taken up and developed in more recent years also by Quentin Skinner, in a number of significant and influential works that propose republicanism specifically as the political foundation necessary for the construction of a society in which liberty of the citizen is constitutionally ensured. The work of Skinner, and the many scholars who have been active in his wake, is based on a complex definition of a republic that does not necessarily deny the presence of a ruling figure as its head. The model republic finds its origins in the so-called mixed constitution as it was defined by the Greek historian Polybius in book 6 of his *Histories*: itself deeply influenced by the *Politics* of Aristotle. The best republic, according to this tradition of Greek political thought, is composed of interactive forms of government involving the powerful figure of a consul or some other type of head of state, an aristocracy or ruling class united in a senate, and a populace whose rights are assured through tribunal representation. The most successful model for such a republic, in the eyes of Polybius, was that of the ancient republic of Rome.[12]

Skinner's inquiries into the idea of a republic underline above all this neo-Roman basis of Renaissance and early modern republicanism, inspired by the works of Cicero, Sallust, and Titus Livy. His work inquires into the ways in which the various parts of Europe developed this classical inheritance: an inquiry carried out under the auspices of the European University in Florence that has made of the history of republicanism a major subject of debate in the new millennium. Traced in its various European and American manifestations, with their theoretical justifications, by scholars such as John Pocock in the United States and Skinner himself in England, this line of inquiry tends to find its early modern hero in the Machiavelli of the *Discourses on the First Ten Books of Titus Livy*.[13] The extraordinary prominence given to this republican Machiavelli, not only by Skinner but also by scholars such as Philip Petit and Maurizio Viroli, among many others, has left almost no page of the *Discourses* untilled. As for Machiavelli himself, he appears increasingly—according to this tradition—in the role of the new secular saint. His republican ideas, as these studies underline, were known to his contemporaries from manuscript versions of his *Discourses*; but after their posthumous publication in Rome in 1531 they also projected well into the future—above all into the seventeenth and eighteenth centuries. As Pocock has argued, they were then taken up and developed by the Dutch and English republicans, and later by the American and French revolutionaries.[14] Viroli, for his part, tends at times to take the whole discussion out of a historical dimension altogether in order to claim that Machiavelli's ethically inspired republicanism needs to become a more present and lively inspiration in Italy and the world of today.[15]

There have been some dissenting voices regarding this thesis. Victoria Kahn claimed some years ago that the Machiavellian hypocrite and crafty rhetorician were not simply naive Renaissance readings of his text, but reactions to a genuine dimension of his work that is confirmed by attention not just to its thematic but also its rhetorical aspects. This author concedes, however, that the deceitful Machiavel is not the only image of him present during the Renaissance. The Machiavel and the staunch republican are seen as "equally valid—and related—definitions of his work."[16] Moving in a different, although perhaps related, direction, it needs to be noted that a number of English-speaking historians of the idea of freedom—most particularly some American scholars—tend to see the liberty discourse as developing primarily in the Protestant world, and to characterize it as a specifically Protestant achievement.[17]

Perhaps the most influential proposal in this sense is closely associated with Richard Popkin, whose studies of Renaissance skepticism and the centrality of doubt in the freethinkers of the period of the late Renaissance and the European Enlightenment posited a strict link between a skeptical philosophical stance and the newly reformed theology, particularly in its more radical exponents. Popkin's studies were enthusiastically endorsed by a generation of Italian (but not only Italian) scholars who, in the wake of the pioneering studies of Delio Cantimori, had concentrated their attention on the Italian reformers who escaped to northern Europe to avoid persecution by the Roman Catholic Inquisition, only to find themselves in indignant disagreement with the new doctrinal orthodoxy of John Calvin and his followers in Geneva such as Theodore Beza.[18] Of particular importance in this context of the discussions of doubt and freedom in the northern European world of Reformed theology have been the studies of Antonio Rotondò.[19]

An influential proposal that defines itself rather differently from this cluster of theses has been developed by Jonathan Israel, who places seventeenth-century Dutch republicanism at the center of his discourse on liberty, with the work of Benedict de Spinoza as its principal inspiration. Citing Spinoza's *Ethics*, and above all his *Tractatus Theologico-Politicus*, Israel proposes Spinoza's thesis of secular justice and benevolence anchored in a rigorous concept of equality as passing through the eighteenth-century revolutionary movements in America and France to become the true inspiration of modern democracy.

A politics of democratic forms may thus be seen as a direct outcome of the Dutch Enlightenment. Concentrating on inspirational revolutionary figures such as Paul Henri Thiery d'Holbach and Denis Diderot in France, or Thomas Paine in England, Israel proposes what he calls a "radical enlightenment" founded on what he considers more fully defined and radical concepts of liberty. This idea is opposed to what Israel sees as the more moderate type of republicanism that was in his opinion dominant in early modern Europe. This moderate Enlightenment republicanism, deriving in Israel's opinion also from Machiavelli, is seen as inherently reluctant to allow the development of full forms of toleration and parliamentary democracy that would challenge in sufficiently radical terms the existing social and political hierarchies and privileges.[20]

It is not the purpose of this book to take sides with one or another of these theses that have done so much to form the ideas on the historical roots of the liberty discourse that dominate the culture of the Western world today. Its purpose is rather to pursue a line of inquiry of its own that underlines the importance of the late Renaissance culture of the sixteenth century as constituting an essential basis for the formulation of a modern idea of liberty. Machiavelli's political idea of liberty, elaborated at the very beginning of the sixteenth century, would only become fully influential during the seventeenth- and eighteenth-century republican movements in Europe and America. Well before this happened, the later years of the sixteenth century and the early years of the seventeenth saw radical upheavals not only in the political but also in the religious, scientific, and artistic fields of discourse that would have profound effects in inspiring a new and multiform formulation of the liberty discourse. The thesis presented here is that although the sixteenth century can only be characterized as one of the most oppressive and violent periods in European history—a dark moment of religious wars and inquisitions in which the unified structure of medieval Europe finally collapsed under the rise of a new religious divide and the political dominion of an increasingly absolutist concept of princely rule—it was precisely this historical situation that gave rise to a number of startlingly new claims for liberty, both political and individual. The violence and tumultuous wars that characterized this period inevitably meant that the juridical codification of liberty as a fundamental human right was still only obscurely foreseen and very infrequently implemented in the nations of a bitterly fragmented Europe. But it was an idea that began to circulate at this time, and cannot be separated from the liberty of conscience that was being ever more forcefully pronounced (not only in the Protestant world) as an inevitable consequence of the new religious pluralism.

The scope of this book is limited to what is often called the long sixteenth century, which led up to the Thirty Years' War in central Europe (1618–48). Without doubt, the Thirty Years' War represents a culminating point of the ferocious and destructive antagonism between Catholic and Protestant forces.

INTRODUCTION

Yet the violent religious struggles that dominated this period were not entirely negative in terms of the discourse on liberty. The new emphasis on the "interior life" or the "individual conscience," which the predominance of spiritual motives that characterized both the Protestant and the Catholic parts of Europe throughout the sixteenth century placed so much in evidence, provided a new dimension to the desire for liberty. Liberty of conscience became a more central theme than it had ever been before, providing new substance to the idea of political liberty as well. Furthermore, liberty of conscience was often associated with the republican values that were already beginning to gain support under the surface of a Europe where the masses were still largely silenced and oppressed. This book attempts to capture and give expression to some of those sixteenth-century voices that reach us from out of the violent convulsions of the Europe of those dramatic years. It includes Catholic voices as well as Protestant ones, and a number of radical, secular freethinkers of the period as well. It is open to various disciplines, to religious discussions, and to philosophical and political debates. It also pays attention to the dramatic developments in that period in the fields of the arts and the sciences, where the theme of liberty often became an issue of urgent importance.

This book carries the conviction that these multiple sixteenth-century voices were far from constituting an insignificant hiatus in the development of a modern concept of liberty. On the contrary, they can be seen as providing the foundational building blocks, of various shapes and sizes, that pave the way toward the future by proposing ever more mature concepts of liberty and human rights.

CHAPTER I

Political Liberty

Niccolò Machiavelli: Liberty and the Law

It is impossible not to begin with Niccolò Machiavelli, whose concept of republican liberty has been at the center of so much attention in recent decades.[1] With the advent of Martin Luther and the Protestant Reformation, the liberty discourse would take a brusque turn in direction, moving toward forms of liberty of the individual conscience that would often be belied by the militancy of the religious struggles of the period and the ferocious forms of oppression only too frequently used on both sides of the religious divide. The issue of political liberty, however, continued to be raised through the whole period covered in the present volume, posing the question of how and by what means the law should provide a guarantee for the liberty of conscience that rapidly became the fundamental issue of a Europe divided in the religious sphere as it had never been before.

Machiavelli himself seems to have been very little touched by the new religious struggles already taking place in northern Europe during his lifetime. Writing in the first two decades of the sixteenth century, he was by no means the first of the Renaissance Florentines to celebrate the republican idea of liberty. Indeed, his idea of liberty developed out of a complex Florentine political experience that had been much debated in the previous century, a century that had seen Florence involved in a series of dramatic changes of political regime when the governing body of the free city or commune, ruled in the early years of the century by chancellors of extraordinary prestige such as Coluccio Salutati and Leonardo Bruni, succumbed to a period of dominion by powerful and prestigious members of the Medici family, including Cosimo il Vecchio and Lorenzo il Magnifico.[2] Then, suddenly, in 1494, Florence took a different turn by initiating a new experiment in republican rule.

After an initial period of confusion, the new republic decided on the creation of the Great Council, a widely representative governing body that delegated its foreign policy to the smaller Council of Ten (the so-called Dieci di

Balìa).³ It was the Council of Ten that would employ Machiavelli on diplomatic missions after his election as second chancellor in June 1498 at the age of twenty-nine.⁴ Machiavelli's active political experience would come to an abrupt end in 1512 with the fall of the Republic of Florence, followed by the return of the Medici, who put the government of the city in the hands of another Lorenzo (grandson of Lorenzo il Magnifico), shortly to become Duke of Urbino as well. From that point onward, Machiavelli, in spite of repeated attempts to return to active service on behalf of his city, had no serious political role to play; he dedicated his attention to a theoretical study of politics that some scholars have seen as developing from discussions going back to the Middle Ages.⁵ Nevertheless, Machiavelli's contribution was a particularly distinguished one that—although at once much discussed, and often reviled as heretical with respect to Christian tradition—would prove to be extraordinarily influential in the centuries to come.

Paradoxically passionate at the same time as it is dispassionately detailed and precise, Machiavelli's treatment of the theme of republican liberty is to be found above all in his *Discourses on the First Ten Books of Titus Livy*. Nowadays considered an epoch-making book, and Machiavelli's greatest contribution to the discussion of the tensions between political power and the liberty of both the individual citizen and the community at large, the *Discourses* were too republican in spirit to be published in his lifetime, for not only Florence but the whole of Europe was witnessing the increasing entrenchment of princely and monarchical forms of power. The book would only be published four years after Machiavelli's death, in 1531, when two separate editions appeared in Rome.⁶ Nevertheless, Machiavelli's *Discourses* circulated widely in manuscript form in his time, and the work acquires its full significance only when read in the light of the dramatic Florentine events that inspired it.

"Happy to escape from the heat, we would go together to the most secret and shaded part of the garden, where some of us would sit down on the grass, which in that place is cool and fresh, some of us on chairs placed in the shade under the huge trees." With these introductory words to a later work, *The Art of War*, Machiavelli himself remembers conversations held with friends, in the years following the fall of the republic, in the Florentine gardens known as the Orti Oricellari.⁷ The *Discourses* were composed, probably for the most part in 1516–17, when Machiavelli decided to write up some of those conversations at the request of two of those friends, Zanobi Buondelmonti and Cosimo Rucellai, to whom he sent his text as a gift ("uno presente").⁸ In so doing Machiavelli underlines the importance of his political and diplomatic experience in the service of the recent Florentine republican councils. His book is not just a theory of politics but is based on actual political experience in the service of a republic: "here I am talking about things known to me, which I have learned through experience and much practice in the ways of the world."⁹

Machiavelli's *Discourses*, then, are founded on memories of the Florentine Consiglio grande, or Great Council, which had started to rule the city when Piero dei Medici, son of Lorenzo il Magnifico, had been expelled by the citizens of Florence in a popular uprising: "Now men began to collect in the Piazza, and in the *Pelagio* were heard cries of *Popolo e libertà*, whilst the bell was rung for a *Parlamento*," narrates Luca Landucci in his Florentine diary for Sunday, November 9, 1494.[10] Although immediately on the side of the new republican regime, Machiavelli would have to wait four years before being appointed to his prestigious political post, which he then lost with the return of the Medici in 1512. It was only in the aftermath of that return that a disheartened and unemployed Machiavelli sought solace in the gardens of the Orti Oricellari, where, with his friends, he commented on the Roman histories of Titus Livy in an attempt to define the contours of what he hoped would be a more robust republican system that looked back for inspiration to ancient Rome.

Some of those friends would be put to death or would flee to exile in 1522 for their part in an unsuccessful plot against the by then entrenched Medici rule in the person of the cardinal Giulio dei Medici; Machiavelli himself declined to take part in the plot and thus remained unharmed. A contemporary historian of Florence and its history of civil discord, Filippo de' Nerli, provides a clear account of the link between Machiavelli and this plot in a work titled *A Commentary on the Civil Events That Took Place in the City of Florence from 1225 to 1537*:

> A certain school of young men of letters, of the highest intelligence, used to meet in the Rucellai gardens during the lifetime of Cosimo Rucellai, who died young, and of whom there were great literary hopes.
>
> Among these was Niccolò Machiavelli; and I was one of his friends, as indeed I was a friend of them all, and often took part in their conversations. They were very active readers of literature and history, from which they learned many lessons, and it was they who persuaded Machiavelli to write that book of his about the Discourses of Titus Livy, as well as his book about the military arts. Then they started to think that, in imitation of the ancients, they ought to do something great, that would make them illustrious: and so it was that they had the idea of organizing a plot against the life of the Cardinal. In becoming plotters, they failed to pay due attention to the things said by Machiavelli about plots in his book of Discourses. If they had done so, they would not have carried out their plot, or at least would have gone about it with more caution.[11]

The manuscript of de' Nerli's book was donated to the Tuscan grand duke Francesco dei Medici in 1574 and published for the first time only in 1728. But it is of much interest in providing an objective contemporary account of what went on in those gardens. Machiavelli had indeed written at length of plots against tyrannical princes in chapter 6 of book 3 of the *Discourses*, claiming that "the observation made by Cornelius Tacitus is worth its weight in gold; for he claims that men must know how to honor the past at the same time as they obey the mood of the present. That is, they must desire good princes, but they must know how to bear with them however they may be. And truly, those who do otherwise more often than not ruin themselves as well as their country."[12]

These words can help in understanding how Machiavelli could write his *Discourses*, celebrating the liberty of republics, only shortly after he wrote *The Prince*. In *The Prince* Machiavelli had started out from a historical given: the arrival of the prince at the center of the power structure of most of the European nations of his time. Whether he liked the new prince or not was irrelevant. The return of the Medici to Florence in 1512, seen from Machiavelli's point of view, decreed the failure of the city's republican government to survive a general move toward monarchical rule, notwithstanding Venice's success in surviving as a republic in the same years and well beyond. That, however, was another story. From Machiavelli's Florentine viewpoint, the triumph of princely rule was quite simply what had come about; and *The Prince* is a study of what the new power structure would, and would not be likely to mean if, as he foresaw, it was to determine a large part of European history in the centuries to come.[13]

The Prince has become a famous text in the modern world above all for Machiavelli's claim that politics and ethics cannot easily be conjugated together. This chilling political realism was described famously by Benedetto Croce as "politics that lie on this, or rather on that, side of good or bad morals: politics that obey laws of their own, and against which it is useless to rebel."[14] More recently, Gabriele Pedullà has claimed that Croce's separation of politics from ethics is too clean and abstract. Machiavelli himself insisted rather on a perpetual conflict between the two that necessarily involves the good political leader in dire moral choices for which he cannot avoid taking full responsibility, both moral and political. If in *The Prince* Machiavelli can applaud the actions of princes such as Cesare Borgia it is because, to resolve certain specific problems, they have of necessity violated common justice and perpetrated massacres in the name of a common good (in Borgia's case, safety of the community at large from the dangerous ambitions of a power-mongering aristocracy) recognized as such by the majority of their citizens.[15] This does not mean that Machiavelli applauds massacres or cruelty as such. The desire for "good" rulers, by which he meant governors appointed by the city to rule in the interests of the city, remained his strongest and most deeply held wish. It is this desire that lies behind the urgency to the *Discourses*, where the analysis of the political history of ancient Greece and Rome is always subordinated to an explicit concern with the past, present, and future state of the city of Florence itself. A deep concern with the liberty of the city—above all that of the community at large but also of its individual citizens—lies at the heart of Machiavelli's *Discourses,* and most particularly its first book, which deals with the constitution of the best republics. There *liberty* becomes a keyword in almost every chapter.[16]

The most successful republics, according to Machiavelli, are those that adopt a mixed constitution like that proposed by the ancient Roman historian Polybius (one of Machiavelli's major sources); and he notes that a republican constitution like that of ancient Athens, which was founded primarily on the power of the people (*lo stato popolare*), has never lasted long (1.3.6).[17] The people in a good republic must collaborate with their prince and their nobles (*ottimati*), even if their interests are different and tensions and tumults often ensue. Much recent attention has been given to Machiavelli's insistence that conflicts and tumults within the state are to be seen as natural manifestations of the differing interests of the different classes of citizens, and are not to be considered as negative provided they are contained and controlled by institutions or *ordini* designed for that purpose, such as the ancient Roman Senate. For it is precisely from such internal conflicts that laws favoring the liberty of all those concerned will eventually emerge, as happened in the republic of ancient Rome (1.4.2).[18] The creation of tribunes in ancient Rome to represent the will of the people in the senate is praised by Machiavelli as one of the greatest conquests in the ongoing acquisition of freedom: the tribunes are the guarantee of the liberty of the people within the laws or the constitution (*ordini*) that bind the community together. For Machiavelli it is in this context of tribunal representation that the people become the guardians of the freedom of the community as a whole (1.5.2). He uses an example from the ancient world to point toward a modern concept of freedom through republican representation in a broadly parliamentary sense.

Later chapters of the first book of the *Discourses* are concerned with the problem of how to return to such a state of freedom once liberty has been lost to the interests of some selfishly dominant citizen or group of citizens who seize power only to pursue their own interests and ends. Machiavelli is pessimistic about the chances of such a return to liberty when the reign of tyranny has been long and brutal, for such forms of power tend to aim at producing a servile populace by reducing it to the state of beasts (1.16.1). A condition for reacquiring lost liberty is precisely that the people should not have become themselves corrupt, so that their conflicts with their ruling class, after they have succeeded in banishing their tyrants or corrupt kings, can lead to a positive outcome in the formation of a stable republic (1.18.1–2). Such a republic cannot be based on corrupt morals but must include, at all levels, a clear sense of justice ensured by laws that punish the selfish wrongdoer and award those who serve the community as a whole. The system of laws of a just republic, based on its constitution or *ordini*, must be observed if the liberty of the citizen is to be guaranteed and the community to live in freedom for any length of time; otherwise desolation and ruin will ensue (1.24.1). Machiavelli is nevertheless aware that the laws imposed even by elected magistrates can only too easily become antithetical to the idea of freedom. That is why the example of ancient Rome should be followed, for "they wrote down their laws on ten tables, and before confirming them they exhibited them in public so that everyone could read and discuss them, pointing out any defect and emending them before they were put into effect" (1.40.2).

Niccolò Machiavelli: Liberty and Fortuna

If bad laws conflict with the liberty of the republican citizen, another contradiction that Machiavelli pursues in the *Discourses* (as well as in *The Prince*)— and for which he is justly famous—is that between liberty and what he calls *fortuna*. In the pages of the *Discourses,* good luck or good fortune, in the sense of favorable circumstances, is primarily linked by Machiavelli to the question of a judicious use of military strength. Without a competent military, a republic remains exposed to the whim of its enemies, and blind *fortuna* only too easily wins the day. On the other hand, wise laws united to a wise use of the military tend to ensure good fortune and keep bad luck at bay (1.4.1). Later on, Machiavelli links the idea of fortune to that of religious faith, claiming that a wise use of religion by a ruler ensures long-lasting respect of the *ordini* of a just republic and a high level of moral life—both of them elements that tend to reduce the possibility of being destroyed by the fickle whims of fortune (1.11–12). Machiavelli cites here the words of two of the most famous citizens of Florence. First he refers to Dante, who in some verses in his *Purgatory* had "prudently claimed" that human virtue (*virtù*) is rarely sufficient of itself to ensure the long life of a community and should be considered instead as a gift from God.[19] Immediately after this literary reminiscence, Machiavelli refers to Girolamo Savanorola, the fiery Dominican friar whose sermons had roused the Florentine people to support the new republic of 1494, before he was cruelly burned at the stake by some who had become afraid of his hold over the city and its citizens. Machiavelli was notoriously ambiguous in his judgment of Savanorola, and in the *Discourses* refuses to say whether the Dominican friar was divinely inspired or not. He limits himself to noting that the Florentine people, whom he considers far from stupid, were content to believe that Savanorola's message came to them directly from God and that this helped to rouse them to virtuous action in a delicate moment of the city's political history.

Other pages of Machiavelli's works show how the influence of *fortuna* does indeed play an important role in the histories of cities: in a poem titled *Di fortuna* he writes of her immense and apparently arbitrary powers.[20] By and large, however, he wants to claim for *virtù* (meaning not only virtue but also wisdom and ability in the management of human affairs) the possibility of warding off the forces of circumstance and fate. Machiavelli's concept of *virtù* ensures the possibility of freedom of the will, even within a historical process in which the apparently inscrutable play of fortune, whether it is to be identified with the will of God or not (a subject on which Machiavelli tends to remain neutral), undoubtedly plays an important and at times a tragic part.

In the young Machiavelli this idea can be found expressed in a particularly dramatic formulation in the brief pages of one of his earliest works, written during his period of political activity on behalf of the Florentine republic. The text in question is a letter to which he gave the title *Capricious Thoughts*, addressed to Giovan Battista Soderini, a nephew of the Florentine republican leader, or *Gonfaloniere*, Piero Soderini.[21] Written during Machiavelli's period as the Florentine envoy to the court of Pope Julius II, between August and October 1506, the *Capricious Thoughts* take as their starting point the brilliantly successful attempt of this powerful and influential pope to carry out his ambition to chase the Venetians from the region of Romagna and to neutralize the power of the local princes in Bologna and Perugia by taking over government of these areas. This outcome was unfavorable to Florence, which now had a rigorously antirepublican ecclesiastical neighbor to deal with. The papal military campaign, which Machiavelli personally witnessed, included a famous episode in which Pope Julius entered Perugia with only a few soldiers and arms, given that the king of France had refused to come to his aid. This move effectively gave the lord of Perugia, Giampaolo Baglioni, a man with a long criminal record including incest and various forms of violent oppression, the opportunity of destroying—or at least much weakening—the papacy. It was an opportunity of which Baglioni nevertheless refused to take advantage, giving rise to sarcastic comments on his "pusillanimity" on the part of Machiavelli both in his letters of this period and later in the *Discourses*. Florence, whose free republic Machiavelli was then serving as their official representative at the papal court, had every reason to fear the substantial increase in the territorial and political power of the papacy that the takeover by Julius II of the nearby Perugia represented; and the success of the pope in fulfilling his mission, in spite of allowing his military weakness to be made publicly evident, stimulates Machiavelli to a series of reflections on the ways in which the *virtù* of princes fluctuates with circumstances, and can apparently either be capriciously thwarted or equally capriciously rewarded by *fortuna*.

The few pages of the *Capricious Thoughts* respond to this moment of surprising behavior on the part of Pope Giulio II—who had evidently judged correctly the psychology of his opponent—with an initial confession on the part of Machiavelli that he still can remain puzzled by political events (*non havere gustate né leggiendo né pratichando le actioni delli huomini et e modi del procedere loro*). The episode obliges him to reach the conclusion that different leaders can reach similar aims by following different means and making different choices. His classical examples are Hannibal and Scipio, the first of whom succeeded in introducing his armies into Italy through cruelty and perfidious actions while the second introduced his into Spain using piety and religion. His modern examples are Lorenzo dei Medici who succeeded in defending Florence by disarming the populace, and Giovanni Bentivoglio, who succeeded in defending Bologna by arming it. In the same way, similar tactics can be successful or a failure when used on different occasions.

Machiavelli is concerned here with trying to find a "rule" that will avoid admitting a situation of incomprehensible chaos and caprice in the political history of states. He finds this in two concepts. The first is that princes come with diverse characters and gifts, and each governs according to his particular abilities. The second—and less obvious—one is that, whatever their gifts and their methods, success in princes depends on a meeting point, or *riscontro*, between their aims and the opportunities open to them within their particular times: "he will be happy who allows his way of proceeding to coincide with the humor of his times, while, on the contrary, he will be unhappy who allows his actions to diverge from the humors of his times and the order of events." Machiavelli, however, does not stop there. The situation is made more complicated by his insistence that times change more rapidly than the characters of men; what gives rise to the victory of a prince one day can become the cause of his failure on another. The conclusion that can be reached is that rulers should always carefully study the changing signs of the times, for to do so with perspicacity will ensure lasting success. But because princes are unable to change their characters, which tend to be inflexible and fixed, it has to be recognized that fortune, in creating favorable or unfavorable occasions for a prince, dominates the political scene to an extent that Machiavelli finds disturbing, as he disarmingly admits (*la Fortuna varia et comanda ad li huomini, et tiegli sotto el giogo suo*). Later on, in *The Prince*, Machiavelli would claim, a little more optimistically, that half our actions are governed by fortune but the other half can be controlled by our own free choices.[22]

These pages have been the subject of an influential analysis by Gennaro Sasso, who points out that ultimately fortune cannot be seen in Machiavelli as either a goddess or a transcendental force (she is no longer, as in Dante, a "minister of God's will"), but instead as the limit imposed by historical circumstances on the freedom of human action. As such, fortune may be considered the founding principle of historical interpretation. In this way Machiavelli, who does not allow the universal centrality of humankind within the universe that the humanists had claimed, nevertheless—according to Sasso—keeps human action at center stage, for it is the changing relationships between men and their fortune, or the shape objectively assumed by their times due to the apparently capricious processes of history, both natural and political, that founds the possibility of giving a rational explanation of the historical process itself.[23]

Niccolò Machiavelli and Sir Thomas More

Commentators have discussed at length to what extent Machiavelli's *Discourses,* insofar as they outline the contours of the just republic, should be considered as pertaining to the genre of a utopia. The word *utopia* was coined by Sir Thomas More as he moved between the Low Countries and London on a diplomatic mission on behalf of the British king, Henry VIII, in just those years in which Machiavelli was beginning to think about his *Discourses.* More's word plays with ancient Greek, whose putative parliament, the Areopagus, he found a more stimulating model for his concept of liberty than Machiavelli's ancient Rome. *Utopia* means a place that is nowhere, signaling to the reader that More, who also had republican leanings, shared Machiavelli's disillusion with the princes of his time.

It is debated whether More's much admired and widely read *Utopia,* first published in Latin in 1516 under the supervision of his friend Erasmus of Rotterdam, was even read by Machiavelli, though it has frequently been compared with his *Discourses.*[24] Indeed, *Utopia* could well be considered as an extended comment on the reference to the "golden saying" of Tacitus so much admired by Machiavelli and quoted above, for More's book is structured as a dialogue between two voices corresponding exactly to the contrast that Machiavelli invokes. On the one hand More offers us an idealistic voyager to distant lands, Raphael Hathloday, who finally ends up in his utopia, a perfectly governed republic. He declares that from then on he finds it impossible to live under the tyranny of any of the monarchical regimes that dominate the Europe of his time. On the other hand More appears as a more mature persona, with his own name in his own work. His aim in the dialogue is to temper his utopian traveler's uncompromising idealism by advising him to bear with the modern European princes, however they may be, as only by doing so will it be possible to influence them to good. More's advice to his Utopian traveler is relayed through a pregnant theatrical metaphor:

> Whatever play is being performed, perform it as best as you can, and do not upset it all simply because you think of another which has more interest.... You must not force upon people new and strange ideas which you realize will carry no weight with persons of opposite conviction. On the contrary, by the indirect approach you must seek and strive to the best of your power to handle matters tactfully. What you cannot turn to good you must make as little bad as you can. For it is impossible that all should be well unless all men were good, a situation which I do not expect for a great many years to come![25]

CHAPTER I

Although More titles his work *Utopia* and confers on his idealistic voyager the status of its hero, the work remains, through the authorial voice of his experienced self, securely rooted in the reality of his time. Indeed, the whole of the first book of his text is composed of a description of the many elements of corruption and bad government that More sees in the England of his day. To call this work a "mere" utopia, in the sense of a naive dream of a perfect, political never-never-land, is thus to misunderstand the origin of the genre as it emerged in Machiavelli's time. The deeply desired utopian society, which in More's work too is republican in kind, acquires its meaning only insofar as it is compared with the unbridled ambition of the modern princes and their servile retinues. It seems equally meaningless to call Machiavelli's *Discourses* a "mere" utopia in this sense, particularly in the light of his own insistence that it was born of long political practice in the ways of the world. Indeed Machiavelli founds his republican vision in the *Discourses* in historical realities, equally as if not more securely than More. The period of republican Rome that lay between the early times of the Roman kings and the later experience of empire is often seen by Machiavelli through an enhancing glow of admiration and desire. Nevertheless, above all through the constant reference to Livy, it is always grasped in its historical outlines and frequently becomes most meaningful when it is seen as a prelude to more modern but not always successful experiences—particularly those concerning the Italian city communes and republics.

Machiavelli is even prepared to concede, as More does in the passage quoted above, that the contemporary "drama" recited on the political stage by the new prince may not always be of a totally negative kind. Apart from the possibility that the prince could be virtuous in the sense of governing in the best interests of his people (a possibility that Machiavelli also entertains at times, though with little real hope), there are special circumstances to be considered when a previously free and well-governed society has become thoroughly degenerate and corrupt. Although Machiavelli repeatedly claims that "the multitude is wiser and more constant than a prince" he nevertheless considers it impossible, or at least extremely difficult, that deeply corrupt cities should remain free republics or ever succeed in recreating themselves as such. He is even of the opinion that corrupt cities would do well to incline more toward strong princely rule than rule by the people "in order for those men whose insolence leads them to ridicule the law, rather than being corrected by it, to be restrained by a power of a princely nature" (1.18.4).[26] This passage seems to have been found of particular interest by the famous Florentine historian Francesco Guicciardini, a contemporary of Machiavelli's who, in his chapter-by-chapter comment of 1530 on Machiavelli's *Discourses*, remarks that "in similar cases [i.e., when cities become deeply corrupt] it may be necessary to stain one's hands with blood, but it would be better if such a necessity were never to arise."[27]

Far from authoring "mere" utopias, these were men who were desperately seeking ways of grappling with the overbearing, princely power structure that increasingly dominated their times. More, although clearly aware of the dangers of court life under the rule of a prince like Henry VIII, would agree to undertake the political career offered to him, rising to its summit in 1529 when he succeeded Thomas Wolsey as lord chancellor of England. The breaking point of his suppleness was reached, however, when Henry turned his back on the papacy, founding a national church whose authority in the religious sphere More was not prepared to accept. There had to be limits, and More knew when his had been reached. He disobeyed the king's command by refusing to swear an oath of faithfulness to the new Anglican Church in the name of his freedom to make his own religious choices. All that remained for him was to place his head on the executioner's block with dignity and determination.

More's death would not change the course of events, but the Catholic Church would recognize its value to their cause by making him into a martyr and a saint. Yet More was by no means a believer in religious freedom and toleration as today we understand it, and as he himself had praised it in his *Utopia*, where he claims it is essential that religion be peacefully discussed. In later years More reacted strongly against the beginnings of the Protestant Reformation, writing a series of anti-Protestant diatribes that made him into one of Luther's most bitter enemies. More is furthermore known to have approved of the physical and moral oppression of heretics to the Catholic faith. One commentator has written of "the exasperated and savage authoritarianism that makes the later More an uncomfortable and formidable exponent of the church's point of view."[28] The story of More's last years demonstrates how extraordinary fortitude and heroism in the name of one's own beliefs is something quite different from the recognition of the right of others to believe differently from oneself.

Machiavelli, for his part, by no means despised the power of religion to mold the moral habits and ethical seriousness of social and political communities. Indeed he praised those lawgivers, such as Moses, Numa, and Lycurgus, who had founded their societies on sound religious beliefs. He was, however, less severe and more flexible than More when it came to defining what beliefs should be considered acceptable and what should not. In a still much quoted essay, Isaiah Berlin found the modernity of Machiavelli precisely in his lack of interest in metaphysical or theological issues, considering him ultimately a pagan believer in the gods—rather than in God—as were Cicero and Livy, the ancient Roman writers by whom he admitted explicitly to have been inspired.[29] More recent studies of Machiavelli have tended to underline his place within the Christian and specifically the Catholic world. Maurizio Viroli goes so far as to claim that, according to Machiavelli, the good citizen must love his earthly country "in order to prepare himself for the heavenly country to come."[30] Whether this was the case or not, Machiavelli was destined to be harshly reviled through the centuries by the Roman Catholic Church, which he had mercilessly attacked in the *Discourses* as one of the major causes of the political chaos of his times. The church, Machiavelli thought, had favored the rise of the new princes and the consequent demise of republican freedom by dedicating too little attention to political arts and histories: for centuries "our religion has found the greatest good in humility, abjection, and in despising worldly things" (2.2.2).

Refusing, on the contrary, to abandon the sphere of "worldly things," Machiavelli himself would try unceasingly to find a way to serve the new Medici regime, however uncongenial he may have found their princely form of rule. The attempt was only a partial success. Although he eventually found the favor of cardinal Giulio dei Medici, who would later become Pope Clement VII, he obtained mostly commissions of an intellectual nature—above all an invitation in 1520 to write a history of Florence that he would publish as the *Fiorentine Histories*. This made him into a kind of official city historian but served only partially to bring him back to the center of Florence's political life. Indeed, his willingness to enter into dealings with the Medici led to him to being considered with suspicion by the remaining Florentine republicans, who managed to return briefly to power in the troubled year of 1527, which saw the sack of Rome. It is significant that Machiavelli was not reinstalled in his previous position of secretary to the Dieci di Balìa. He died later the same year.

In spite of the pessimism that pervades the vision of both More's utopian traveler and Machiavelli himself, there remained a deep conviction in both men that the *virtù* of a wise leader could prevail over the apparent caprices of fortune to give a rational meaning to the political history of states. When the new princes made this meaning politically void by cultivating only their own power and ambition, men with the education of a More or a Machiavelli could fall back on the power of the word, for rhetoric and eloquence, seen as essential tools of a virtuous public life, had already been cultivated by the European humanist movement for a century or more.[31] When Machiavelli's political career came to an end he knew where to look for the tools of a new trade: the study of ancient histories and the writing of new books in which to put forward alternative ways of organizing society and political power that would assure the survival of those republican liberties that the modern princes were threatening to trample underfoot.

The Rule of the Prince

The Florentine republic that Machiavelli served fell in 1512, when the Lega Santa (an anti-French alliance among Pope Julius II, the people of Venice, and Ferdinand II of Aragon) returned the city to Medici rule. Machiavelli's *The Prince*, written in 1513, is widely considered today—especially in the English-speaking world—to have been a handbook of political advice to the new

Medici. *The Prince*, however, is far more than a handbook of advice; it is more in the nature of a close analysis of the logic of a power structure which, as Machiavelli so clearly saw, was going to dominate the European scene for many years—even centuries—to come.

As with the later *Discourses* we have in Machiavelli's own words a celebrated description of the personal situation in which he wrote it. In one of the most famous letters in the Italian literary canon, dated December 10, 1513, Machiavelli wrote to his friend Francesco Vettori, Florentine ambassador to the papal court in Rome. The letter was written from Machiavelli's small farm just outside Florence, where he had taken refuge after the brief period of imprisonment and torture that he suffered in the immediate aftermath of the fall of the republic; Machiavelli had not only lost his post as secretary to the Dieci di Balìa but was also suspected (probably unjustly) of participating in a plot to assassinate the new Medici rulers. He was released in the general amnesty that celebrated in Florence the election to the papacy of cardinal Giovanni dei Medici, who became Pope Leo X.[32] Written while still aching from the pain of those recent events, the letter narrates in vividly realistic language how Machiavelli has been getting up early in the morning to catch plover using treacle as bait; how he expects to kill from two to six plover in a morning; how this pastime has come to an end because the plover have gone elsewhere, and how surprised he is to find himself missing such an uncouth activity, so far from his usual habits. Now all he has to do in the early morning is to go into his woods to converse with his woodcutters, who are usually immersed in some quarrel with their neighbors. Machiavelli's opinion of the countrymen in their commercial dealings is clearly less favorable than his opinion of the by now departed birds, and he decides not to sell his wood to anyone in the future.

In search of solace, he goes to a well to drink, and into a bower where he reads the love poems of Dante, Petrarch, Ovid, or Tibullus, thinking of his own past amorous passions. On the road once again, he passes by the village inn and speaks to those he finds on his way, taking note of their various moods and humors. Back in his house he lunches with his household on the simple fare that his small property provides. Then he returns to the inn, where he plays cards and dice with the meager company he finds there: a bird catcher, some millers, and a couple of men from the nearby kiln. The cards and games of dice give rise to furious accusations and quarrels. Machiavelli admits to participating in these humble conflicts with a kind of furious passion, finding in them some measure of relief as he imagines himself chastising the evil fortune that has struck him, in the hope of putting it to shame. Only with the arrival of dusk in the evening does he retire to his study and, wrapped in his ceremonial cloak, converse with the ancient writers on affairs of state.[33]

During a long winter of such days, Machiavelli tells his friend, he had written a little pamphlet titled *De principatibus*. Vettori might like to read it, and perhaps even present a copy to Giuliano dei Medici, Lorenzo il Magnifico's youngest son, to whom Machiavelli is thinking of dedicating it. In the event, Giuliano died in 1516, and *The Prince* was finally dedicated to the young Lorenzo dei Medici, a grandson of Lorenzo il Magnifico, who had been designated by the new pope as the governor of Florence. The Medici refused to respond to Machiavelli's request to continue what had been a distinguished diplomatic and political career in the previous republican regime. Nevertheless, Lorenzo became the leader seen by Machiavelli as a possible solution to Florence's institutional crisis, and even, in the famous rhetorical exhortation of the last chapter, the *redeemer* (the word is used by Machiavelli himself) of a newly unified state of Italy.

From the beginning, a large part of the Machiavelli discussion has centered on the problem of how to reconcile this famous (or according to some, infamous) book of advice to those concerned with wielding princely power, with the pervading republicanism of both Machiavelli's previous political experience and his later masterpiece, the *Discourses on the First Ten Books of Titus Livy*. Some critics have tried to solve the dilemma by underlining the tragic turn of fortune that had suddenly left Machiavelli destitute and without an occupation, so justifying the pragmatic realism with which he attempted to return to the world of politics through soliciting the favor of the new princes in power. In a well-argued essay that discusses Machiavelli's urgent personal need to return to active political service in the light of a project for the freedom and autonomy of the Italian Peninsula as a whole, Albert Russell Ascoli stresses the importance of chapter 15. The chapter represents a radical change of direction from the earlier chapters, which had tended to consider brute force and the possession of one's own arms as political priorities. It is here that Machiavelli stresses the importance of "real truth" (*la verità effettuale*) in political discourse rather than political fantasy (*stati che si sono immaginati*), underlining his own potential uses as a councilor precisely because he understands the realities of politics (*quello che si fa*) without wasting too much time on ideal possibilities (*quello che si dovrebbe fare*). The final pages of Ascoli's essay are of particular interest, for they contrast the dedicatory letter of *The Prince*—to Lorenzo and through him to the Medici pope Leo X, from whom Machiavelli is requesting an occupation in the political life of the times—to his later letter of dedication of the *Discourses* to Buondelmonti and Rucellai, who are not princes themselves though they deserve to be on account of their innumerable good qualities. Ascoli sees the Machiavelli of the *Discourses* as intent on avoiding his previous mistake in trying to talk to those who could have showered riches and honors on him because they actually govern a kingdom (although they are not really capable of doing it well) rather than speaking to those who do not govern anything (but would know how to do it well if only they were given a chance).[34]

Another thesis that posits some kind of change of heart between the desperate pragmatism surrounding the composition of *The Prince* and a later, more traditional republican stance is put forward by Robert Black, who considers the harsh political realism of *The Prince* as Machiavelli's most original contribution to the political discourse. It is in *The Prince* that Machiavelli theorizes his conviction that, especially in moments of grave crisis or corruption in the state, violence and even cruelty can become political necessities that the prince (who in any case, according to Black, is to be seen as tyrannical by definition) may have to resort to if he is to stay in power rather than repudiating them in the name of a traditional ethics. Usually translated into English as the famous "Machiavellian" dictum—"the end justifies the means"—this uncompromising insistence on the predominating importance of political realities over ethical values in affairs of state has given rise over the centuries to the myth of a diabolical "Machiavel." One way of avoiding the issue has been to concentrate attention on the *Discourses* rather than *The Prince*. According to Black, however, the excessive emphasis placed by many commentators on Machiavelli's later, more "virtuous" republicanism is to be deplored as a mistaken effort to whitewash away the most radically innovative aspects of Machiavelli's thought.[35]

Among Italian commentators, especially in the impressive amount of material published on Machiavelli in 2013 (five hundred years since the composition of *The Prince*), a somewhat different thesis has prevailed that sees no contradiction or hiatus between Machiavelli's lifelong republicanism and his analysis of princely power. Machiavelli's biographer, Gennaro Maria Barbuto, has written that there really is no "republican Machiavelli" who can be contrasted with a "monarchical Machiavelli," making him (in *The Prince*) into a turncoat concerned only with favoring his own personal fortunes. The sentiment is echoed by Gian Mario Anselmi in a luminous reading of *The Prince* presented in a dense volume published by the *Enciclopedia Italiana* to commemorate the five hundredth anniversary of *The Prince*. According to Anselmi, the contradictions and lacerations that some critics have seen between *The Prince* and the *Discourses* are to be considered as "methodologically outdated." Giorgio Inglese, one of the major experts on the textual problems relating to *The Prince*, considers the text as a "front door" leading directly into the *Discourses*,[36] for both principalities and republics were political realities of the early modern world, which (as precisely the recent example of Florence's failure to preserve its republican institutions showed) was clearly manifesting a tendency toward the disintegration of the republican city-states and a strengthening of the larger and more powerful monarchical nation-states. *The Prince* is a disenchanted analysis of this situation that undoubtedly removes Machiavelli's constant concern with the liberty of both states themselves and of their citizens from center stage. At the same time, however, the subject of liberty remains a subtext, occasionally emerging explicitly as an ideal that peoples subjected to princely rule never completely forget, something that the prince himself is advised to remember and respect.

CHAPTER I

One of the constant concerns that Machiavelli underlines in *The Prince* is the way, and the circumstances, in which a principality can or should preserve some form of participation of the citizens in the government of the state. The problem for the prince himself is how to allow his subjects some measure of political liberty, seen as an advisable means of ensuring their fidelity without allowing his citizens' ambitions and desire for power to subvert his own authority. The problem is made more acute by the fact that Machiavelli sees all states as divided between a class of powerful aristocratic citizenry (*ottimati*) and the common people (*popolo*) whose ambitions tend to clash. Rather than acting according to aims dictated by the common good, Machiavelli sees the *ottimati* as entirely engrossed in their own ambitious desire for power, wealth, and influence, thus creating a constant danger for the peace of both the prince himself and the mass of his people. The people, on the other hand, are more likely to be stirred up by a desire for their own peace and security that the *ottimati* are rarely concerned with satisfying and that the prince would do well to try to ensure so as to have the people on his side. As in the later *Discourses*, the inevitable social and political tumults caused by these conflicting desires of the different classes of citizens are not necessarily to be seen as negative for the well-being of the state provided they are safely contained within institutions or *ordini* created for that purpose. When the prince succeeds in giving his state such *ordini*, Machiavelli sees the tyranny of princely rule giving way to what he calls a *principato civile*, or a civil principality (chapter 9).

From the point of view of the prince, civil principalities present obvious dangers because they allow the various classes of citizen considerable freedom of expression, which can easily take the form of a challenge to his power. The wise prince, in this context, is thus defined as one who knows how to create a state with institutions that allow expression of the often conflicting desires of the citizens while at the same time establishing his own princely power as a necessary point of reference for maintaining peace and achieving glory. One of the most positive examples of such a principality in his own times, Machiavelli claims in chapter 19 of *The Prince*, is the French monarchy, for its leaders have known how to secure their own power and in the meantime substantially enlarge their territory, making France into one of the most powerful nation-states in Europe. Their success in doing this, according to Machiavelli, is due to their *parlements*, which act as arbiters in the conflicts between the *ottimati* and the common people, as well as ensuring the safety of the monarch himself from the excessive ambitions of those lords who envy him his power.[37]

Much recent attention has been dedicated to this awareness in *The Prince* of the fragility of the small Italian city-states, and the emphasis Machiavelli places on the more substantial nation-states that were consolidating their power in just those years.[38] It is this awareness that lies behind the remarkable prophetic rhetoric of the final chapter, in which he envisions a reunited Italy making its triumphant entry into a new world of free and autonomous nation-states. The visionary power of Machiavelli's rhetoric in this chapter has been an inspiration to Italian commentators from the time of the Risorgimento (the nationalist movement that would finally reunite the Italian Peninsula and make it into a free nation in the second half of the nineteenth century). A number of prestigious modern commentators, from Antonio Gramsci to Federico Chabod and from Luigi Russo to—more recently—Maurizio Viroli, have tended to read the whole text of *The Prince* in light of this remarkable prophetic climax.[39] Such a reading may lead to something of an oversimplification of the more harsh complexities of the book's earlier chapters. Nevertheless, it is clearly a reading that brings to the fore the theme of liberty, also in *The Prince*, that had seemed to remain submerged by the considerations on princely power within the state that had occupied Machiavelli's attention until he suddenly branched out into this famous rhetorical climax of his work. It is the freedom of a nation united and strong in its autonomy and independence from the "degrading stench" of foreign dominion that Machiavelli, in these famous final pages, urges the new prince to pursue. In this sense, it is undoubtedly possible to claim that *The Prince* leads seamlessly on to the *Discourses*, where—inspired by a reading of ancient Roman authors such as Titus Livy—princely rule dissolves into the republicanism that Machiavelli himself had previously served in fact, and continues to do in words.

The later years of Machiavelli's life saw the city becoming increasingly unquiet under a weakened Medici rule; with the election first of Lorenzo il Magnifico's son Giovanni as Pope Leo X and then of his nephew Giulio as Pope Clemente VII, the attention of the Medici had turned primarily to Rome. The republican forces still present in Florence were once again making themselves felt, especially in the period immediately following the death in 1519 of Lorenzo, Duke of Urbino, to whom Machiavelli had dedicated *The Prince*. The republicans would indeed manage to return briefly to power in 1527, before the Medici finally entrenched their long hold on the Florentine levers of power in the 1530s. One work of Machiavelli's in these years is particularly important for the theme of liberty in the state that is being considered here. Carrying the Latin title *Discursus florentinarum rerum post mortem iunioris Laurentii Medices*—although the text itself is in Italian—it is an officially requested report concerning the best way of governing Florence. The *Discourse on the Situation in Florence after the Death of Lorenzo dei Medici Junior* was requested from Machiavelli by cardinal Giulio dei Medici after the sudden death in 1519 of Lorenzo, to whom Pope Leo X had assigned the government of the city after the fall of the republic and to whom Machiavelli had dedicated *The Prince*. In the wake of that unexpected death, the cardinal had been asked by his cousin the pope to take the situation of Florence in hand, and he requested the advice of a number of his fellow citizens as to how the city should best be ruled.

Machiavelli's brief reply to this request by the cardinal assumes that there is no real hope of reestablishing a fully developed republic in Florence. The preceding Florentine republics are judged to have been founded on weak bases and therefore should be discarded as examples on which to construct a future. The only serious prospect is for a total renovation of the political structure of the city, taking account of a political situation that has to contemplate some kind of princely rule. Machiavelli outlines the new city councils as he would like to see them, contemplating several councils that come directly under the influence of the prince while at the same time attempting to maintain as much as possible of what he realizes is, under the circumstances, a necessarily limited republican prospect. The fundamental principle underlying this proposal is the necessity to reintroduce the Great Council of citizens that the Medici had abolished when they returned to power. The importance for Machiavelli of a new Great Council is expressed in a telling paragraph right at the center of his text:

> Without giving satisfaction to the whole population, no stable republic was ever founded. And the entire population of Florentine citizens will never be satisfied if the door of the council chamber is not reopened. So if the aim is to create a republic in Florence, it would be best to reopen this door and let the whole population in. Your Holiness should realize that those who might aim at taking the government of the state away from you, will want above all to open this door once more. So your best way of proceeding is to open it yourself, with decision and assurance. In this way you would deprive your enemies of the opportunity of opening it themselves, which in turn would lead to the ruin and destruction of your friends.[40]

Commentators on this text are fond of pointing to the sarcastic judgment of Alessandro Pazzi who, when in 1522 he was also questioned about the government that should be installed in Florence, noted that Machiavelli's proposal was too complicated and ingenious to be viable.[41] Nevertheless, Machiavelli did attempt to come to terms in this text with the reality of Medici rule by proposing a form of republic that would contemplate democratic councils while at the same time recognizing as its head the figure of a prince. Machiavelli sees the new prince as exercising control over the military and over the methods of justice, as well as giving final approval of the laws. Only over a long period of time would experience in republican methods hopefully lead to a final withering away of his princely power, giving rise to the triumph of the politics of democratic forms. For Machiavelli, even in his later years, the principal problem that always needed to be solved was that of the danger of tyrannical rule by one ambitious man, a situation that he tended to identify with unbounded princely or monarchical power.

For Machiavelli, then, right up to the end, there could be no question but that opposition to princely rule should be pursued through the establishment of the good "order" of good laws, conceived of as means of securing the liberty, and with it the well-being of the entire community. As he had already written in the *Discourses*, good laws justly applied are the foundation of the liberty of healthy republics, and the only protection against the rise of a tyrant: "And this is how most tyrannies arise," he noted; "either from the excessive desire of the people to be free, or from the excessive desire of the nobles to command. When they are not able to agree on making a law in favour of liberty, but rather one of the sides prefers to take the part of a single man, then we will see a rapid rise of tyranny."[42]

CHAPTER 2

Liberty and Religion

The Bondage or the Freedom of the Will: Martin Luther and Erasmus of Rotterdam

In the very years in which Niccolò Machiavelli in Florence was conversing with the ancients in his study on the question of political liberty, and the lessons to be drawn from the Roman republic, the Catholic Church that he himself criticized so strongly was being rocked to its foundations by the rise of a new form of Christianity. Machiavelli himself showed little interest in the new religious uprisings in the north; this may have been because some of the instances of religious and ecclesiastical reform that an obscure Augustinian friar named Martin Luther was announcing with vigor in Germany had already been anticipated in Florence by another friar, the Dominican Girolamo Savonarola, whose insistence on the active participation of rigorously virtuous citizens in the republican councils of Florence had found the approval of Machiavelli himself. The urban bounds of the already fragile Florentine republic, however, proved too narrow to contain Savonarola's exalted prophetic vision of a city chosen by God to further the ends of a divine destiny.[1]

According to Machiavelli, Savonarola had obtained a special power over the lives of the Florentine citizens, comparable to that of Moses over the Jews. This hold—following Machiavelli's own analysis of the friar's tragic end—proved to be the cause of a fatal envy on the part of rival factions, who succeeded in turning the citizens against him and, with the approval of the papacy, having him hung and then burned in 1498, only four years after the republic had come into being.[2] Luca Landucci's *Diary* narrates that some days afterward, certain women were found kneeling in the piazza out of veneration, on the spot where the friar had been burned.[3] It was not only with these devout women that the influence of Savanorola would remain an important memory in Florence, for he inspired many of the republicans who in the years to come would be opposing Medici rule.

CHAPTER 2

Martin Luther, on the contrary, survived, to the surprise of the Catholic authorities, who long underestimated his power and influence—to their own cost. Although Machiavelli himself seems hardly to have been aware of what was happening north of the Alps, precisely those events would contribute to overwhelm his name and works, giving rise to a widespread anti-Machiavellian cult that pervaded the second half of the sixteenth century in the Protestant parts of Europe as well as the Catholic ones. As Corrado Vivanti has pointed out, "Machiavelli's thought could no longer find a place in a society dedicated primarily to problems of a confessional nature, to the struggle between the Protestant Reformation and the Counter-Reformation. For those considerations left no place for other cultural problems, entwining themselves tightly as they did with the essential political issues of the time."[4]

Luther did not believe, as did Savonarola and many of the so-called Radical Protestants that Luther's movement eventually gave rise to, that one could speak directly with God.[5] Luther, however, believed that God's word was available to all through the Bible, which he proposed as a model for solving political as well as religious problems—indeed, as the authority to be followed in all walks of life. For Luther the biblical word defined a divine destiny whose decrees were not subject to influence by the weak and paltry efforts of the human will. Justification was by faith alone, and the salvation or damnation of the individual believer was in the hands of an all-powerful God and not of the believer himself. Catholic accusations that this deprived the power of the human will and works of all their efficacy were vigorously opposed by both Protestant contemporaries as well as later commentators. Good works were, on the contrary, an important part of Luther's scheme, but always as proof of the believer's salvation and never as its cause.[6] Even so, the question remained as to whether Luther's doctrines left any real scope at all for freedom of the human will, without which all forms of liberty—except that of God himself—become illusory and null.

At the end of 1520, after writing and publishing some of his most polemical texts, Luther composed a brief pamphlet titled *A Treatise on Christian Liberty* that he sent, together with a letter, to the Medici pope Leo X. It was, in many ways, the testimony of a rupture that had already taken place,; for the pope had just issued a sentence sanctioning the expulsion of Luther from the Roman Catholic Church. Whereas many other works by Luther are concerned with attacking the rigid hierarchies of the Catholic Church and its emphasis on works and worldly things ("the Holy Ghost does not concern Himself about red or brown birettas," Luther had written scornfully in the same year in *An Open Letter to the Christian Nobility of the German Nation concerning the Reform of the Christian Estate*), the *Treatise on Christian Liberty* is centered entirely on the question of faith.[7] In it Luther attempts to explain his insistence on the primacy of faith with respect to works with simplicity and clarity in a way that will make it available to the unlearned: "for only such do I serve." He starts by laying out a paradox concerning what he sees at the same time as "the liberty and the bondage of the spirit."

A Christian man is a perfectly free lord of all, subject to none.
A Christian man is a perfectly dutiful servant of all, subject to all.

The first proposition expresses Luther's sense of the freedom of the new Protestant Christian, for whom "no external thing, whatsoever it be, has any influence whatever in producing Christian righteousness or liberty." The apparently glaring contradiction represented by the second proposition, Luther points out, finds its source in the Bible in the words of St Paul: "Whereas I was free, I made myself the servant of all" (1 Cor. 9). The contradiction arises for Luther from the double nature of Christ, the Son of God but born of woman, and so at the same time in the form of God and in the form of a servant. Also, humankind has a twofold nature: spiritual and bodily, but primacy is to be given to the spiritual life: "Let us contemplate the inward man, to see how a righteous, free and truly Christian man, that is a new, spiritual, inward man, comes into being." Freedom for the Christian lies within, and derives from righteousness and a clear conscience. Works are extraneous to these things, for only the work of God concerns the spirit. Luther quotes Christ's own words as reported in John, chapter 6: "This is the work of God, that you believe in him whom he hath sent."

It is clear that what Luther calls "the Word," or the Christian message as it has been announced through the Bible, could be seen as threatening to limit the individual's freedom, for within the context of ideas delineated here, the believer is only free insofar as he accepts the Word. A modern reader might attempt to understand this apparent contradiction through a reference to what Sir Isaiah Berlin called "positive" rather than "negative" liberty, or what later commentators have thought of as an "exercise" concept of liberty rather than a purely "negative" acceptance of the right to choose in various ways.[8] Luther in the spiritual sphere, just as much as Machiavelli in the political one, obliges the modern reader to revisit the bases on which such a distinction is founded.[9] Just as for Machiavelli a citizen is no free citizen if he fails to place his virtues at the service of the public good, for Luther a Christian believer is no free believer if he fails to immerge his spirit in the words of God and so become the servant of all. Duties (in the case of Luther the religious duties of the truly faithful, and in the case of Machiavelli the civic duties of the true republican) are called on to complement rights, and only through fulfilling such duties is true liberty attained. There is clearly some confinement, in both cases, of an area of free choice, which Berlin feared—and not without reason. Luther for his part places precisely in the leap beyond the sphere of reason the ultimate form of liberty of the spiritual or inner being, which he celebrates in a vocabulary reminiscent of the mystical writings of the Middle Ages: "since these promises of God are holy, true, righteous, free and peaceful words, full of goodness, it comes to pass that the soul which clings to them with a firm faith is so united with them, nay altogether taken up into them, that it not only shares in all their power, but is saturated and made drunken with it."[10] Religious ecstasy and individual freedom coincide.

Critics of Luther, who consider him as looking backward to the middle-ages rather than forward to modernity, are at a loss to explain his long-lasting influence on the modern world. On the contrary, finding the locus of liberty within the spiritual life of the individual mind was a powerful idea, above all in a period when what Machiavelli called the "doors of the Council chamber," which republican liberty had kept open, were being systematically closed throughout a Europe caught ever more tightly within the power struggles of the new princes. It was an idea that does much to explain the extraordinary and rapid success of the Protestant Reformation, as well as its survival into the future. This new freedom of the spirit is considered by Luther in the final part of his treatise in its consequences with relation to works, or what he calls "the civil and human virtues." These are necessary only insofar as the true Christian can never live a life in idleness or wickedness, but they are not necessary for salvation, which comes only by faith. Consequently, because believers have no need of works to save their souls, the true believers, insofar as they are believers, also have no need of the law. They are above the law, which concerns only the bodily or outside being: "surely he [the believer] is free from the law, and it is true."[11]

Luther's words here refer exclusively to the spiritual aspect of humankind, and carry no implication that the laws of the land should not be obeyed by the newly reformed Christian in bodily or social life. On the contrary, Luther's own political theory, particularly as it would be elaborated in the early years by Philipp Melanchthon, tended to be one of passive obedience to the secular rulers and monarchs whose power the new Protestants often helped to entrench rather than to question.[12] With time, however, Luther himself started to ask when it would be dutiful for the believer to disobey what could be considered a wicked command by the prince; while the Radical Protestants, who were devising separatist groups with revolutionary programs of various kinds as early as 1521, would on occasion develop such pronouncements by Luther in an extreme sense by claiming that their faith placed them outside the laws of the land.[13] Luther himself, however, is not prepared to consider the liberty of the Christian in terms of revolutionary conflict with the political authorities of the time. He makes it quite clear in his treatise that he limits such liberty exclusively to the life of the spirit, for he writes of "that Christian liberty, even our faith, which does not indeed cause us to live in idleness or in wickedness, but makes the law and works unnecessary for any man's righteousness and salvation."[14]

Within the new and divided Europe to which Luther's new doctrines were giving rise, a pressing question at once arose as to what course would be followed by the major cultural figure of the day, the extraordinarily erudite and influential Dutch humanist Erasmus of Rotterdam. Erasmus, writing in a refined classical Latin that made his works available to all the European cultures of his time, had indeed already become a thoroughly cosmopolitan figure well before Luther appeared on the scene. Pressure was put on him at once both by the Catholics and the new Protestants to take their side, for a strong pronouncement for one or other contender in what was rapidly becoming a religious war was clearly to be considered a victory of no small importance for whoever obtained his allegiance. Erasmus corresponded directly with both Luther and his major cultural exponent Melanchthon, and had no difficulty in agreeing with much of the criticism they were directing against the Catholic Church. Indeed, Erasmus himself had in earlier days anticipated many of their objections, especially in his masterpiece of bitter satire "In Praise of Folly." There Folly herself, in woman's garb, became the only voice of reason in what Erasmus saw as a profoundly corrupt world, rapidly precipitating into the madness of unbridled ambition and excess. In that work of the early years of the sixteenth century, written in London in the house of Erasmus's good friend, Sir Thomas More, some of the most deadly arrows of his biting wit were directed toward the failure of the Catholic Church to provide that example of pious and simple spirituality that Erasmus himself saw as the primary lesson of any valid Christian faith.[15] Many thought that Erasmus would take Luther's side; and he seems to have been tempted by the new spiritual ardor to which the Protestant Reformation was giving rise. Yet Erasmus had nurtured himself primarily with the skeptical reason of the authors of classical Greece and Rome. He was a world away from Luther's blasting and often violent affirmations of the new Protestant creed; indeed, he accused Luther of causing a rift in European culture that it would take years, if not centuries, to recompose. Again and again Erasmus advised Luther to control his language, to soften the contours of his protest, to aim at dialogue rather than outright conflict, which could only end in war. In a letter to a friend of November 29, 1521, he exclaimed, "[W]hat results they have achieved! They have distorted humane studies with a burden of unpopularity, and every man of good will who is seriously attached to the truths of the Gospel is within range of perilous suspicions. They have opened a great rift which divides the world everywhere, which will last maybe for many years and get steadily worse. In return for a clumsy attempt at liberty, slavery is redoubled, to such a degree that it is forbidden even to maintain the truth."[16]

Erasmus never went over to the Protestant side; he preferred to remain loyal to the papacy in spite of his many reserves. He remarked bitterly in these years to the same friend to whom he had written the letter quoted above, "I, who have never supported Luther, except in so far as one supports a man by urging him towards better things, am a heretic to both sides."[17] Erasmus took many years to decide whether or not to enter into the religious disputes he so deeply deplored. Only in the early months of 1524, urged on by another Medici pope, Clement VII, did he finally sit down to write the work that attacked the central doctrine of the new religion, his *Discussion of Free Will*, which was published in early September of that year in Basel, Antwerp, and Cologne, with four more printings shortly following. Luther was roused to reply with one of his most uncompromising statements, recognizing that Erasmus had gone straight to "the crucial issue between us," which was "to investigate what ability 'free-will' has, in what respect it is the subject of Divine action and how it stands related to the grace of God."[18]

Luther titled his reply *The Bondage of the Will*; it was published in late 1525 in Wittenberg. Erasmus replied to this reply with his *Hyperaspistes: A Warrior Shielding a Discussion . . . against the Enslaved Will of Martin Luther*, published in two volumes in Basel in 1526 and 1527. With these works the sixteenth-century discourse on liberty took a new turn. With the discussion now only marginally centered on political liberty, or on problems concerning government of the city or the state, attention became focused primarily on what Luther called "the inner man" in his relationship with God.

Erasmus's *Discussion of Free Will* accepts without questioning Luther's already well-established challenge to take biblical texts as the correct ground with respect to which any discussion of such questions should be developed. This in itself proved quite natural for Erasmus insofar as he was without doubt the greatest biblical scholar of his age. Long before Luther, Erasmus had insisted on the necessity for the Christian to return to the purity of the biblical word, sloughing off the long tradition of Scholastic subtleties and ecclesiastical accretions that had finished by rendering the biblical word itself almost invisible to the simple and uncultured mind. In his preface to the facing Greek and Latin text of the New Testament that he had published in 1516, Erasmus had written that the Christian philosophy he was proposing lay in sentiments rather than in syllogisms, in life rather than disputes, in inspiration rather than erudition, in conversion rather than reasoning. Luther, together with many of his contemporaries, recognized with gratitude that aspect of Erasmus's inheritance; his own German translation of the New Testament was based on Erasmus's Latin translation from the Greek. Luther, however, would not accept that this gave Erasmus any advantage in the sphere of interpretation of the biblical word. On the contrary, he would accuse Erasmus of being a mere philologist and pedagogue, limited to applying what, in Luther's opinion, were inadequate humanist tools of textual scholarship to what for Luther himself were always primarily and quite literally the words of God. To whatever extent their respective attitudes toward the text, and their interpretations of it differed, the Bible was accepted unquestioningly by both contenders as the principal battlefield on which their conflict over the freedom or the slavery of the will was to be fought.

The metaphor of the battle is used by Erasmus himself in his brief preface to the *Discussion*, with an irony designed to defuse a conflict that he himself had done everything he could to avoid. He and Luther will surely appear before their readers as two "hired gladiators" fighting a wrestling match, comments Erasmus wryly, adding that "there is hardly a man less practised in the art than I, for I have always had a deep-seated inner revulsion from conflict."[19] The contest in any case seems to Erasmus a useless one from the outset, as he is not of the opinion that God always expressed himself in the Scriptures in ways comprehensible to the human mind. Luther may think that he has the key to their full meaning, but in that he is mistaken. To make his point Erasmus cites the examples set by skeptical classical authors such as Cicero and Paul's well-known dictum in 1 Corinthians 13:12, "we see through a glass darkly." Many things lie beyond the comprehension of the human mind, and are reserved for that time when the Lord will reveal his face and we finally behold his glory.

In an equally brief introduction, Erasmus raises the crucial question of who has the authority to claim himself the correct interpreter of biblical texts. Nodding briefly toward the authority claimed by the Catholic Church in such matters, he concedes that the church fathers and ecclesiastical councils constitute a long list of learned men approved by the consensus of many centuries. He and Luther are by no means lone contenders in this matter. He already knows how Luther will answer him on this question; he will say that the Catholic Church has always assumed an authority nowhere endorsed by the Scriptures themselves, that the only authority is that of the Spirit. Those who feel the Holy Spirit moving in them understand at once what the Scriptures mean, for they are simple and open to all who believe. Erasmus counters, "If Scripture is clear to those who have the Spirit, how do we know who has the Spirit?" He adds, ironically, "if Paul, in his own age, when this gift of the Spirit was flourishing, orders spirits to be tested whether they are of God, what ought we to do in this carnal age?"[20] The implication is that no one in his age would pass the test of uprightness and simplicity of heart, which is the only test of Spirit that Erasmus finds appropriate. To be effective, this argument would have to be supported by a vibrant attack on Luther's morals, which many of his enemies then and since did not hesitate to indulge in. The scrupulous Erasmus, however, appears to take all the wind out of his own sails by adding that he is making no reference to Luther here; and indeed in other places he had frequently conceded his recognition of what he considered Luther's pious and upright life.

The conclusion to these introductory pages is that Luther is admitted as a worthy antagonist. However, adds Erasmus somewhat slyly, neither of them is God; this is strictly a conflict of minds between two very human men. Erasmus then delineates his own strategy as one of a systematic consideration of the relevant biblical texts according to a careful division aiming at the fairest possible evaluation of their contents. He considers, in that order, passages from the Old Testament supporting free will; passages from the New Testament supporting free will; passages from the Scriptures seeming to oppose free will; passages already cited by Luther in his previous works to deny the existence of free will; additional passages that seem to oppose free will; and judgments concerning free will and grace. All this, however, requires a clear definition of free will on which such a survey can be based. Erasmus starts by supplying a characteristically brief and succinct one: "By 'free will' here we understand a power of the human will by which man may be able to direct himself towards, or turn away from, what leads to eternal salvation."[21] This definition refers back to the thought on the freedom of the will of St. Thomas Aquinas, which would influence so much of the philosophical speculation on the subject throughout the sixteenth and seventeenth centuries and beyond, for St. Thomas had claimed that the ultimate good, which he identified with Christian salvation, is the necessary goal of the will, which means that we have no choice of specification of such a goal. On the other hand, we do have freedom of exercise with respect to willing this universal good; that is to say, we have the power to avert our intellect from the pursuit of salvation in its Christian sense.[22]

Erasmus, however, prefers to conduct his investigation with reference primarily to biblical sources. Concluding his examination of the biblical texts concerned with free will, he feels himself nevertheless obliged to admit that the scriptures appear to contradict themselves on this subject in many places. In a detailed discussion of how Erasmus deals with such apparent ambiguities, Fiorella de Michelis Pintacuda has argued that Erasmus's fundamental inspiration derives from his *philosophia Christi*, which tends to dissolve such apparent contradictions by stressing the greatest contradiction of all: the incarnation of Christ.[23] The Christian is clearly obliged to recognize the primary importance of divine grace, which gives meaning to the sacrifice of Christ, the Son of God. For Erasmus, however, precisely the incarnation of God in Christ means that divine grace and the human will can cooperate in the making of ethical choices. The two parts involved, de Michelis Pintacuda insists, clearly cannot have for Erasmus anything but a very different weight; nevertheless, their collaboration can be—and is for Erasmus—a real one. Erasmus himself, in the final page of his *Discussion*, expresses what he calls a "moderate view" by forcing his own position as close to Luther's as he can, but then distinguishing himself quite clearly from Luther at the end:

> [A] moderate view will recognise the existence of some good work, admittedly imperfect, but on account of which man can claim nothing for himself; and of a certain degree of merit but such that its completion will be due to God. There is such a vast amount of weakness, vice, and villainy in human life that if anyone is prepared to examine himself he

will soon hang his head in shame; but we do not assert that man, though justified [by faith] is nothing but sin, especially as Christ calls him "born again" [John 3:5–8] and Paul calls him a "new creation" [2 Corinthians 5:17].[24]

That, for Erasmus, is why we—fallen creatures but with still something of our godliness remaining in us—can attribute some measure of our salvation to our free will. What significance would God's sacrifice of the Son have had if we do not? Erasmus uses the paternal metaphor as one of his final strategies to delineate the scenario known as the Happy Fall. God helps his creature to walk as if taking his first steps in the world, guiding and supporting his halting feet and showing him the apple or forbidden fruit. The child reaches up to eat and by his free act he brings sin into the world; yet that in the end is the most fitting outcome of the temptation as it prepares the erring child for the heavenly kingdom through the necessary incarnation of Christ the Savior. The final moment of salvation, though unthinkable for Erasmus without the intervention of God's grace, is constantly depicted in biblical stories as the crowning achievement of the erring sinner, the heavenly reward. "I do not see how, on these grounds," comments Erasmus, "they can posit the existence of a free will which achieves nothing." What sense does the cosmic story have if we use the deterministic metaphor preferred by Luther, that of God as the potter who molds our destiny entirely with his own hands as if we were nothing more than passive clay?[25]

Commentators have discussed at length Erasmus's use of patristic and Scholastic sources, many of which lie behind these arguments; this is why Luther, in his reply the following year, would accuse Erasmus of saying nothing new.[26] J. C. Margolin, on the other hand, has stressed in particular the importance for Erasmus of the new humanist optimism with respect to the creative and active powers of the human mind. Florentine Neoplatonists such as Marsilio Ficino were well known to Erasmus, but above all Giovanni Pico della Mirandola's vibrating *Oration on the Dignity of Man*—Margolin claims—can be heard echoing through Erasmus's text.[27] For Pico had stressed to the full the idea of humankind itself as a miracle of God's creation, able to assume heavenly powers or fall to hellish depths through its own autonomous choices and achievements within a wondrously vital and varied world. Margolin underlines how it is a similar sense of the responsibility assumed by the human will in its choices that informs Erasmus's attitude toward toleration, even in the case of the unbeliever. Accepting the new Lutheran insistence on the primacy of the life of the "inner man," Erasmus—unlike Luther—sees a space within the human mind that acts in freedom even with respect to God. However small such a space may be compared to the immense presence of the grace of God, for Erasmus it is a kind of mental sanctuary. Precisely for that reason no one's conscience should ever be forced by others.

CHAPTER 2

"Of Our Own We Have Only Sin":
John Calvin and the Problem of Heresy

The discussion between Luther and Erasmus concerning the freedom of the will was developed on the basis of differing interpretations of the Bible as a dispute within the Christian tradition. It concerned the measure of freedom to be attributed to the individual will in its choices with respect to a determinism that, on both sides, was identified with divine predestination and a Christian concept of salvation. The terms of the discussion would clearly change over the following centuries, especially when the principle of determinism tended to become associated—as it already was in Machiavelli—less with a divine will and more with the changing ways of fortune deriving from the historical process itself. Later on, the deterministic principle in the life of any individual or society would be increasingly identified—as, for example, in the theory of evolution—with a scientific reason or natural laws. But in whatever way the principle of determinism is stated, the question of the freedom of the will, its extension and its limits, remains fundamental. It was a subject that remained a major element of intellectual discussion throughout the period covered by the present volume.

It needs to be underlined that Luther's proposal of a complete determination of the human will by the decrees of a providential God offered a strenuous challenge to the traditional classical and religious thinking on this subject. His position gave rise to a debate that would become a major issue—perhaps *the* major issue—of the intellectual life of his time. The later years of the sixteenth century would witness even more extreme formulations of determinism in the theological thinking of John Calvin or of his followers, such as Theodore Beza, only to conclude during its final years with a less rigorous definition of divine predestination in the important, if much discussed, thinking of the Dutch theologian Jacob Arminius. To a large extent this intense debate on the freedom of the will took place within the newly Protestant parts of Europe, for Catholic culture remained faithful to the Scholastic and above all the Thomistic formulation of the problem that had been restated, in more modern and more humanistic terms, by Erasmus.

The center of John Calvin's thinking about the freedom (or rather the bondage) of the will is to be found in book 2, chapter 2, of his *Institutes of the Christian Religion* titled "Man hath now been deprived of Freedom of Choice and bound over to miserable servitude."[28] First published in Latin in 1536, and then in a definitive version in 1559, this work would play a fundamental and contradictory role in the history of the idea of liberty in northern Europe (as well as in the Protestant parts of the newly discovered American continent) throughout the long sixteenth century. On one side it would offer a radically extreme version of the bondage of the will already addressed by Luther, annihilating even more dramatically the spaces of free action traditionally accorded to the inner self; on the other side it would release new energies deriving from Calvin's conclusion that precisely this servitude of the individual will to the overarching will of God makes all humankind predestined to God's saving or condemning grace. For if all are in search of the light of the spirit, and all is darkness in the world of man, no one is licensed to govern over all, and even in affairs of the church every decision is best taken on the basis of consultation and a sense of community among those concerned. Calvin's attack on the hierarchies of government in both the political and the ecclesiastical spheres would offer a new stimulus to those who had lived for centuries under the yoke of lords and princes whose authority was now subjected to severe questioning. Of our own, Calvin wrote, echoing St. Augustine and including in his judgment all those in power, including the princes, the emperor and the pope, "we have nothing but sin."[29]

Such radical declarations undoubtedly stimulated on one side a newly egalitarian spirit that contributed to the overturn of many of the social and political—as well as ecclesiastical—hierarchies of the time. On the other side, however, it threatened to throw a cloud of deep and desperate pessimism over the spirit of believers, unable to offer even a minimal contribution to their own salvation—or, more probably, damnation—for Calvin was, in his own way, dogmatic and inflexible in the extreme: "Let no prating Pelagian allege that God obviates his rudeness or stupidity, when by the doctrine of his word, he directs us to a path which we could not have found without a guide. . . . No man can hesitate to acknowledge that he is able to understand the mysteries of God, only in so far as he is illuminated by his grace. He who ascribes to himself more understanding than this, is the blinder for not acknowledging his blindness."[30]

Many Protestants were disturbed by such a radical formulation of the doctrine of divine predestination, which seemed to threaten and mortify even the most minimal capacities of the human mind. Many were also disturbed by Calvin's intransigence, and the reintroduction into the Protestant world of the notion of heresy. Once Europe was separated by a religious divide unknown in previous centuries, accusations of heresy that sounded like declarations of war started to be hurled from one side to the other.

Erasmus, for example, in defending the Catholic position on the freedom of the will, knew that one of Luther's primary accusations against him would be that he was reviving the Pelagian heresy. The form of Christianity pursued by the monk Pelagius, born in England in the middle of the fourth century, glorified the energies of the human will, which he thought was only facilitated, or given support by, the word and grace of God. The English monk, however, came up against a formidable contemporary, St. Augustine, who objected that the definition of Christianity defended by Pelagius was too deeply imbued with classical belief in the powers of the human will, so conceding too little to the infinite grace and mercy of God. After much discussion within the early Christian church, Augustine's protests against Pelagius led to a declaration of the Pelagian position as an official heresy. With time, however, the position of the Catholic Church tended to become more lenient than Augustine's own. In line with the thought of St. Thomas Aquinas, it insisted that there must be freedom of the will, even if insufficient of itself to save the soul without the intercession of the grace of God. Thomas thus indicated a middle way, though Pelagianism remained an official heresy—and not only within the Catholic world. Luther and Calvin, both of whom took St. Augustine as their major authority on questions of theology, considered the Pelagian glorification of free will as misleading in the extreme.

It was inevitable that the humanist movement of the Renaissance, which consisted in a return to so much that was fundamental to the culture of the ancient Greek and Roman world, would be accused of tending toward Pelagianism; and Pico della Mirandola, especially, had often been accused in such a way. Erasmus, attempting a preventative defense of his position, tended to adopt what had long been known as a semi-Pelagian position. This consisted in claiming for the freedom of the will a space within the mind that was considered as important and real, at the same time as it was recognized as extremely limited and small, for the whole of mankind is stained and sinful, and so unable to achieve salvation without the infinite mercy of Christ. Erasmus's caution in defining this moderate position, however, was treated with little respect by Luther, who, toward the end of *The Bondage of the Will*, wrote on the subject one of his most powerful passages in praise of uncompromising assertion:

> This hypocrisy of theirs results in their valuing and seeking to purchase the grace of God at a much cheaper rate than the Pelagians. The latter assert that it is not by a feeble something within us that we obtain grace, but by efforts and works that are complete, entire, perfect, many and mighty; but our friends here tell us that it is by something very small, almost nothing, that we merit grace. Now, if there must be error, those who say that the grace of God is priced high, and account it dear and costly, err less shamefully and presumptuously than those who teach that its price is a tiny trifle and account it cheap and contemptible.[31]

Luther's scorn for Erasmus's caution and moderation runs through the whole text of his reply. In the very early pages, in his "Review of Erasmus's Preface," he derides an attitude toward biblical hermeneutics that says, "Here are problems which have never been solved." For Luther this amounts to a criminal misuse of God's words: "Scripture makes the straightforward affirmation that the Trinity, the Incarnation, and the unpardonable sin are facts. There is nothing obscure or ambiguous about that. You imagine that Scripture tells us *how* they are what they are; but it does not, nor need we know." These are, for Luther, not *problems which have never been solved* but the inscrutable mystery of God's omnipotence, before which humankind can only bow in passive wonder and obedience.[32]

Luther's contribution to the sixteenth-century discussion of liberty was thus extraordinarily complex and contradictory. On the one hand his indication of the inner human, or the individual conscience, as the ultimate locus of an ecstatic form of religious freedom can be seen as an immensely powerful and exhilarating contribution to the culture of the time. Its consequences were indeed liberating in the extreme, to the extent that it allowed large portions of the peoples of Europe to stand up and cast aside the deeply entrenched prestige and influence of the Catholic Church, which—often with authoritarian means—had dominated not only the religious but to a large extent also the cultural and political life of the medieval world. The word of the Bible suddenly became available to all, and the mediation of the priesthood no longer essential to communion with God. Erasmus's fears of what he thought were already the disastrous consequences of such a revolutionary move were countered throughout *The Bondage of the Will* by Luther's own exaltation in front of the new situation he had created. Coherently with respect to his theology of divine omnipotence, Luther imputed all that had happened to the will and word of God rather than to his own, explaining impatiently to Erasmus that God's word has always disturbed the world rather than placating it. Tumults and conflict are only proof that God's word is still with us; they have arisen in accordance with God's will and are going to increase rather than diminish, and they will only cease once all the enemies of the word of God have been stamped underfoot to mingle with the mud of the streets.

Such a violent conclusion of his argument illustrates perfectly the other side of the new Lutheran coin. His ringing reaffirmations of the essential Christian doctrines, even though freed from their traditional ecclesiastical scaffolding, were accompanied by a strict limitation of the process of liberation that he had set afoot to those who shared his own form of Christian faith. Indeed, Luther had no scruples in dragging along with him as obscure furnishings of the newly reformed churches of Europe the medieval visions of hell and eternal torment. If anything, they became even more terrifying to the sinful unbeliever insofar as they were now considered unavoidable by the illusory efforts of an enslaved human will: "Hell and the judgment of God await the wicked as a necessary consequence; though they do not themselves desire or conceive of such a reward for their sins, and indeed think it abominable."[33]

The heretic, then—a figure who had accompanied the Christian religion from the start—did not disappear from the scene with the Protestant Reformation. In an influential and still valid study of heresy, Roland Bainton, in his opening remarks on the early church fathers Lactantius, Chrysostom, and Jerome, expresses with admirable clarity the problem introduced by Christianity, especially after its official acceptance by the Roman emperor Constantine

CHAPTER 2

in the year 313: "The conviction of certitude is inherent in Christianity at the outset. 'I know him whom I have believed' (II Tim. 1:12). The skepticism of the late Academy was met by the ringing affirmation, *credo* (I believe). The content of that credo became ever more precise. The contest with the Gnostics led to the formulation of dogma, the closing of the (Biblical) canon, and the restriction of interpretation to the custodians of the tradition, namely, the bishops of the apostolic sees."[34]

In his pages on St. Augustine, Bainton considers him the first theorist of the Inquisition; while noting Augustine's early distaste for persecution, he concentrates on his final period and those Epistles that show how, under pressure from various heretical groups, he came to justify religious oppression through a theory of Christian love: "How can genuine affection suffer a loved one to die a death more tragic and real than that in the flesh? How can it permit him to commit a crime worse than murder, which destroys only the body whereas schism and heresy shed spiritual blood? In face of such peril, can love be scrupulous about methods? Christianity calls not for an absolute nonresistance, but for a benevolent disposition which makes its own choice of means. Constraint and love are not incompatible."[35]

Bainton notes the introduction by Augustine of a specific kind of imagery: the heretic becomes the wolf, the fox, the serpent, the thief or the robber. He concludes, "All these terms are found in Augustine . . . waiting to be used as justification for a policy more rigorous than any he would countenance." Bainton goes on to notice how such attitudes reflect on the administration of justice within the state. In *The City of God* (2.21), Augustine wrote there can be no genuine justice apart from the Christian faith. If the state promotes the faith, then it justifies its existence by serving the visible church. In spite of this hardening of attitudes toward heresy, however, St. Augustine never accepted the idea of the death penalty, seeing banishment as the ultimate punishment for the unorthodox. On the other hand, Augustine's 159th letter to Marcellius (included by Sebastian Castellio in his anthology of writings *Concerning Heretics: Whether They Are to Be Persecuted*) shows that he found no problem in extracting confessions of heresy by use of the rod.[36] This is justified as part of that "paternal diligence" that must characterize the Christian judge. St. Thomas Aquinas (in his *Theological Treatise* 2.2, question 11, "Concerning Heresy"), would add a note of greater severity by claiming that counterfeiting religious truth is worse than counterfeiting money—a crime that was then punishable by death. In the Middle Ages, heresy became to be considered from a juridical point of view as a more serious crime than treason against the state, because it offended not the temporal majesty but the divine one. All these attitudes, Bainton argues, can be seen as logical conclusions drawn from the fundamental initial premise of Christianity, that of the absolute certainty of its religious doctrines.

Coming to what he calls the "Protestant Persecutors" Bainton includes Luther himself as well as his follower John Brenz. Bainton sees Luther as following a trajectory similar to that of St. Augustine, passing from an initial distaste for religious persecution to a later endorsement of it: "Luther soon re-created the walls which he had demolished. A new institution, a new authority, and a new inquisition took the place of the old."[37] For Luther, humankind—what he calls "the children of Adam"—can be divided into two quite separate species: the saved, who are part of the kingdom of God under Christ, and the others, who are part of the kingdom of the world under the magistrate. The civil government has laws that extend only to bodies and goods on earth; nobody has the right to impose laws on souls, which are saved or not only by the word of God. In his *On the Scope of the Magistrate's Authority*, included by Castellio in his anthology of writings *Concerning Heretics* and translated here by Bainton, Luther wrote, "No one ought or can command the soul unless he is able to show it the way to heaven, but no man can do that, only God." He later adds, "However much they command and rave, they cannot force men to follow save with the mouth and the hand. The heart they cannot compel, though they burst themselves in the attempt. True is the proverb, 'Thoughts are tax free.'"[38] Castellio continues to quote from Luther, this time from his *Postills on the Gospel of the Tares for the Fifth Sunday after Epiphany on the Twenty-Fourth Chapter of Saint Matthew*, where Luther writes, "We learn from this text . . . how we should treat heretics and false teachers. We are not to root them out nor to put them to death. Christ makes this perfectly plain, when he says, 'Let both grow together.'"[39] These words exalting religious toleration, even in the case of the unbeliever, were written in 1525, the year that Bainton sees as the turning point in Luther's trajectory toward an apology of persecution.

The immediate causes of that change were the Peasants' War and the emergence of a far more radical form of Protestantism with the figure of Thomas Müntzner. Although the Peasants' War was short lived, and Müntzner himself was soon caught and executed, their influence—together with the development of the popular Protestantism of the Anabaptist movement—forced Luther into a position of violent defense. This was not surprising given the terms in which Müntzner had attacked him in his *Sermon before the Princes* of 1524, where Luther is derided as "Brother Fattened Swine." The theological bases of Müntzner's protests against the Lutherans regarded their conviction (unacceptable to Müntzner and his followers) that God no longer reveals himself through direct revelation to the faithful but only through the words of the Bible, as well as their persisting insistence on infant baptism. From a political point of view it was the Lutherans' passive attitude toward the secular authorities that came under attack. Convinced that he was spoken to directly by God, and that this gave him the authority to impose the gospel by force ("Let not the sword of the saints get cold"), Müntzner attempted to give rise to a revolutionary movement that aimed at freeing itself from the dominion of Luther and Melanchthon in Wittenberg while also aiming to bring the common people back into the picture as the real protagonists of the new religious reformation.[40] The ensuing persecutions of these revolutionaries were fully endorsed by Luther, including the total elimination of the group of Anabaptists who, in 1534, attempted an uncharacteristically violent institution of a communal form of a new Jerusalem at Münster, including not only the sharing of property but also the sharing of wives.[41]

John Brenz follows a trajectory similar to Luther's own, from extreme liberalism argued on the basis that the inner conscience of the believer cannot be subjected to human authority but only to God's, while finishing up by heading an organization for the prosecution of heretics. He justifies this change on the grounds that heretics are not to be seen as normal persons and therefore cannot be considered as having a conscience at all. Bainton is surely right in insisting that Brenz's position on this point raises a fundamental question as to whether those who define themselves as superior intelligences may coerce the subnormal toward what they consider their own good. The problems raised by the scorn for heretics assumed by Brenz, however, go far beyond such an already delicate issue, for Brenz is advocating as a fundamental assumption of the Reformed religion that only those who hold Reformed Christian views can be said to possess a conscience at all. That is an extremely serious assumption to make from the point of view of liberty; indeed, it virtually deprives of any value the idea of a newly inner faith that Luther had, in his early years, championed so triumphantly.

Calvin, as we have seen, can also be considered a profoundly contradictory figure with respect to a discourse on liberty. The delicate points of theological doctrine that united, and in some cases divided, Calvin from Luther or other major reformers are not of relevance for this study. What is important is Calvin's decidedly communitarian bias, which had as its consequence a greater insistence on the law. Calvin postulated the idea of a contractual relationship with the divinity through the concept of a covenanting community of righteous citizens. He attempted to establish such a form of Christianity in Geneva, through a renewed insistence on the law, by placing a special emphasis on the Old Testament as well as the New Testament. Calvin wished to bind the new believer to his faith both in the spiritual and the civil spheres. This religious program found its political expression in the covenanting oath he established at Geneva in 1537, which obliged all the citizens to promise that they would abide by the Ten Commandments. According to the Old Testament, these were the laws that had been handed down directly by God to Moses on Mount Sinai, against which there could be no appeal.

The communitarian bases of Calvin's program included a move toward egalitarianism and a repudiation of ecclesiastical and political hierarchies that would have a revolutionary impact in many parts of Europe throughout the sixteenth century and beyond. All the most radical forms of Protestantism that developed in Europe, as well as in North America, were deeply tinged with Calvinist communitarian doctrine, which has been and still can be seen as providing an important stimulus toward the development of democracy. On the other hand, Calvin's insistence on a communal duty to resist all those envoys of Satan who opposed his revolutionary form of Protestantism lent to his project a militantly oppressive dimension that limited the liberty of religious belief more emphatically than Luther had, at least initially, desired. Michael Walzer sums up the paradox succinctly when he writes of the Calvinist-inspired Revolution of the Saints: "In the world of religious office, conscience played a part very similar to its political role: it freed men from old loyalties, enforced a new sense of duty and required obedience to a wilful God."[42]

The extreme attitude of oppression at times inspired by Calvin's "wilful God" can be seen in an angry letter from the Scottish reformer John Knox during his exile from Britain under the reign of the Catholic Mary Tudor, in which he wrote, "And albeit that abominable idolators triumph for the moment, yet approaches that hour when God's vengeance shall strike [and] not only their souls but their vile carcasses shall be plagued. . . . Their cities shall be burnt, their land shall be laid waste, and their daughters shall be defiled, their children shall fall on the edge of the sword, mercy shall they find none because they have refused the God of all mercy."[43] This was written a year after Calvin himself had given his full approval of the burning in Geneva of the Spanish theologian Miguel Servetus in 1553, for questioning the doctrine of the Trinity. Not all the newly reformed Protestants, however, were prepared to accept such a logic of oppression, even unto death. The burning of Servetus caused widespread distress among many in the Reformed areas of Europe who had already found themselves in a position of dissent with respect to Calvin's insistence on an unqualified public acceptance of what he considered to be the fundamental doctrines of the Christian faith.

Undoubtedly the most important and influential work to be published in the aftermath of the execution of Servetus was titled *Concerning Heretics, whether they are to be prosecuted and how they are to be treated: A collection of the opinions of learned men both ancient and modern*, which was first published in Magdeburg in Latin in 1554 as an anonymous work said to be written by one Martin Bellius. We have already considered this work in its English translation by Roland Bainton, published in a volume that contains many important considerations on the persecution of heretics in the sixteenth century by Bainton himself. *Concerning Heretics* is nowadays attributed to Sebastian Castellio, perhaps aided by Celio Secundo Curione and possibly also by Lelio Sozzini. All these men were Protestant refugees from Italy, and they were together in Basel shortly after the burning of Servetus in Geneva a year earlier. Their criticism of Calvin's intransigence with respect to Servetus—a prestigious theologian whom they much admired—commanded a considerable and important hearing within the culture of sixteenth-century Europe. It was particularly influential in Holland during the struggle in the Low Countries for new forms of republican liberty; it has also been an inspiration to modern historians concerned with the problem of heresy. Roland Bainton's introduction to the English translation of this text turned into a book-length consideration of heresy within the entire Christian tradition, while one of the major twentieth-century Italian historians, Delio Cantimori, dedicated a still famous book to these and other Italians who made a choice for the Protestant Reformation, thus condemning themselves to permanent exile from Italy herself. Cantimori underlines the profound influence these figures had within northern European culture and history with respect to the themes of toleration and religious liberty.[44]

Castellio and Curione were professors at the University of Basel. Castellio himself was a native of Savoy, the region separating Italy from France, and in French was called Châteillon. He had originally gone to Geneva, but was in disagreement with Calvin on certain points of biblical interpretation. When he was refused ordination he left for Basel, where he worked on biblical texts. Castellio's protest against the burning of Servetus comprises a series of extracts from writers of various ages who expressed themselves in defense of toleration; they are not placed in chronological order, and include some passages taken from Castellio himself as well as from Curione and Sozzini. Of Luther and Brenz, among others, Castellio included only passages written in defense of toleration, ignoring their later change of mind. Considerable space is dedicated to passages written by the German Lutheran Sebastian Franck presented under the pseudonym Augustine Eleutherius, including this passage: "Today if ten men listen to the same sermon they are no sooner out of the door but they debate as to what was said and there are as many opinions as heads." Franck concludes that systematic persecution of heretics by all the religious authorities in the world would eventually eliminate the human race, and reminds his readers that Christ himself and his disciples were also considered as heretics by the Jews.[45]

The passage included by Castellio himself comes from his preface to the Bible dedicated to the English king Edward VI (Basel, 1551). Meditating on his times Castellio writes, "We exercise cruelty with the sword, flame, and water and exterminate the destitute and defenceless. We declare that we are not allowed to kill anyone, yet we deliver men to Pilate and if he releases we say that he is no friend of Caesar. And what is worse we declare that all this is done through zeal for Christ and at His command and in His name. Thus we cover the cruelty of the wolf with sheep's clothing. What a time! We are bloodthirsty through zeal for Christ, who, rather than shed blood, poured forth His own."[46] Castellio's dedication of his work to Duke Christophe of Württemberg picks up St. Thomas Aquinas's metaphor of the gold coin to reelaborate it in very different terms. Aquinas, it should be remembered, had claimed that anyone counterfeiting the true coin of Christian truth must be punished even with death. In Castellio's handling of the metaphor it is written, "Likewise in religion let us use the gold coin which is everywhere acceptable no matter what the image." He adds, "Until now this money has had many different imprints and images according as men disagreed with one another with regard to the Lord's Supper, baptism, and the like. Let us bear with one another and not readily condemn the faith of someone else, a faith which is based on Jesus Christ."[47]

Castellio, writing within a bitterly divided Christian community, is clearly echoing Erasmus. Like Erasmus, he is primarily concerned here with the rupture caused within European culture and society by the unexpected success of the Protestant Reformation. Heresy, however, is clearly not a problem that finishes at the borders of Christianity, as the extracts from Sebastian Franck in Castellio's work had underlined. Divergences between Christianity and other religions could be—and often were—equally fierce and damaging to all concerned, added to which the humanist return to classical cultures such as those of ancient Greece and Rome had given rise to a pervasive return to pagan cults, particularly on the part of the new natural philosophers of the late Renaissance. The problem of how religious discussion could or should be carried out in such a diversified situation of conflict, and often of terror, was a dramatic one to many of the major cultural figures of the time, and they attempted to devise various solutions to the problem. The French polymath Guillaume Postel proposed a return of the Catholic Church to its universal origins as the spiritual mother of all Christians, bitterly attacking the new Protestants for the ruptures they had caused. At the same time, he proposed an intensely mystical formulation of the Christian message, deeply tinged with Kabbalistic motives, which he hoped would accommodate all those who believed in the essential doctrine of Christian love: God loves all men everywhere, and hates nothing he has made. Postel had made a detailed study of Islam, whose doctrines he outlined at length to his contemporaries, thus making an important contribution to the culture of his time. He was not, however, prepared to tolerate anything and everything; at times he attacked the aggressive character of the Muslim religion that was threatening the borders of Christian Europe in the East, claiming that it should be contained by missionary crusades.[48]

Postel was far from being alone in this period in urging a return to the fundamental spirituality of the Christian faith. Indeed, the studies of Delio Cantimori, followed by many later distinguished Italian historians of religion and philosophy, have underlined the importance in this sense of a numerous group of Italian exiles who abandoned their original Catholicism for Protestantism, but ended up by repudiating the new Protestant dogmatism with equal fervor. These men were often influenced by anti-Trinitarian tendencies imbibed from Lelio and Fausto Sozzini as well as Servetus himself.[49] Italian historians of religion tend to underline the enduring importance of the Renaissance humanist tradition for these Italian Protestant exiles, including the defense by Erasmus of the freedom of the human will. They were men who tended to find themselves in a dangerously isolated position within the culture of their time. This numerous group of Italian exiles—which included such thinkers of note as Francesco Pucci, who eventually died burned at the stake as a heretic in Rome in 1597; Giordano Bruno, also burned at the stake in Rome, in 1600; and Giulio Cesare Vanini, executed as an atheist and blasphemer in the French town of Toulouse in 1619—often sought a safe haven in England, where many of their major works were written. But their presence in cultural centers such as London or Oxford was often far from welcome, and on more than one occasion they found themselves expelled from the religious communities in England that brought together the Protestant exiles from foreign lands.

A particularly significant case in point is the figure of Jacopo Aconcio, whose major work of 1565 titled *Satan's Stratagems* was written during a visit to England from 1559 to 1564. Aconcio, who was a native of the northern Italian town of Trent, had slipped over the Alps to avoid persecution by the Roman Catholic Inquisition and had met up in Switzerland with many of the foremost Italian religious exiles gathered there, such as Celio Secondo Curione and Bernardino Ochino. In England he frequented the circle of Sir Robert Dudley, uncle of Philip Sydney; Sydney was later to be praised by Giordano Bruno for his hospitality to Italian visitors to the British Isles. In England, Aconcio carried out important work on fortifications, of which he had expert knowledge, but he also entered into bitter conflict with the English branch of the Reformed Church of Holland, which he attempted to frequent, but which expelled him from its midst for what were considered excessively radical religious views tinged with anti-Trinitarianism.[50] Book 2 of Aconcio's *Satan's Stratagems* replies to his critics by outlining a project for religious tolerance based on a strictly rationalistic ideal—not without a certain amount of skepticism—that would ensure his continuing influence right up to and including the European Enlightenment of the following century.[51] It is known, for example, that John Locke had a copy of *Satan's Stratagems* in his library.[52]

According to Aconcio, the religious disputes of his age and the ensuing oppression of heretical opinion should be understood as a subtle strategy of Satan designed to bring out the worst human passions of hatred and contempt: "It is Satan's object from one quarrel to make an infinite number, to kindle wrath, to divide the church into factions, to store up seditions, to set up tyrannies; in a word, he is plotting no less than general conflagration and destruction."[53] The only remedy, in Aconcio's opinion, is a return to behavior based on "that excellent reason, whereof Satan is not the author, but the Holy Ghost." Oppression by cruel chastisement creates only further evils, such as the bloody story of the Anabaptist occupation of Münster. Accordingly, the vocabulary of Aconcio's text is full of words rare indeed in the literature of the period, pleading for virtues such as "kindness," "tact," "gentleness," "goodwill," and "charity." Religion should be part of the inner self only, founded on a few fundamental spiritual values acceptable to all and not on dogmas or doctrines about which it is possible to wrangle indefinitely to no useful end. The fundamentals, however, are not to be relativized or disputed. For Aconcio they are bright lights of indisputable truth, perceived by a logical process of thought similar to a geometrical theorem. His rationalism (Aconcio wrote a discourse, *On Method*, that is said to have influenced René Descartes) leads him to praise as models for the religious life the mathematicians, who "furnish the best established and most convincing demonstrations."[54] Aconcio's pre-Enlightenment optimism allows him to believe firmly that all reasonable men and women will eventually be persuaded to follow the light of such demonstrations. Behavior of an inquisitorial kind will thus become superfluous. Aconcio despises religious inquisition, noting bitterly that it is often fostered by the accumulation of wealth, ambitions of high office, fat benefices, and other similar desires.

Another important work on liberty in the sphere of religion to be produced in Europe in the latter half of the sixteenth century came from the Catholic side. It was written by the Frenchman Jean Bodin, who had elaborated in his major publications one of the most powerful and influential definitions of monarchical power to be written before Hobbes. This may make Bodin seem an unlikely author of a work on freedom in the sphere of religion, yet he was deeply disturbed by the effects that violent religious confrontation could have on political and social stability, and he was looking for a way of discussing religious differences without having recourse to conflict and war. Bodin's *Colloquium of the Seven about Secrets of the Sublime* is a dialogue among men of seven different religious persuasions. Probably completed by 1588, it has long been recognized as one of the major statements on liberty in the field of religion elaborated in sixteenth-century Europe and has been brought to the attention of English-speaking readers through the translation, with accompanying comments, by Marion Leathers Kuntz.[55]

Coronaeus represents the Catholic viewpoint that was Bodin's own; Salomon, the Jewish; Toralba, the philosophic naturalist; Fridericus, the Lutheran; Curtius, the Calvinist; Senamus, the skeptic; and Octavius, the Islamic. Book 1 places the discussion in the Venetian house of Coronaeus, starting off with praise of Venice as "the only city that offers immunity and freedom from servitude." It then describes Coronaeus's "pantotheca," a construction of olive wood based on the number 6 and made up of 36^2 (i.e., 1,296) small boxes containing all the materials of the universe. This is an interesting expression of a widespread Renaissance perception of the number 6 as imbued with special meanings, a perception that probably derives ultimately from astronomical

CHAPTER 2

considerations concerning the revolutions of the planets. Coronaeus's pantotheca seems to be a latter-day version of Giulio Camillo's Theater of Memory, which was also associated with Venice; it involved a wooden theatrical construction divided into numerous boxes in which all knowledge was supposedly stored according to a preencyclopedic structure.[56] There is already a statement here of the encyclopedic spirit that would later dominate the European Enlightenment, seeing in the progress and storing of the knowledge of all things a foundation of the liberty of the human mind.

In Bodin's text a possible suspicion of materialism is immediately warded off by a harsh attack on Epicurus by the natural philosopher, Toralba, who says of Epicurus that he "was so unjust towards immortal God that he snatched all justice from Him."[57] At the same time, in order to underline his belief in the soul, Coronaeus has the narrator read to him Plato's *Phaedo*. Bodin does not elaborate on the fact that this is the dialogue in which Plato tells the story of Socrates's death at the hands of Athenian authorities who were not prepared to allow him freedom to philosophize as he wished. Rather, Bodin emphasizes the passage in Plato's dialogue describing how Egyptian cadavers are preserved with such skill that they escape putrefaction for an incredible length of time. This sparks off reminiscences of a sea voyage in which Coronaeus had attempted to bring back to Venice such an Egyptian cadaver but had had to throw it overboard because of a violent storm. Clearly Coronaeus thinks of this as a symbolic act of recognition that salvation cannot be achieved through pagan rites and rituals. So Bodin seems to be dissociating himself from the ancient theology admired by so many Renaissance intellectuals and strongly endorsed by Giulio Camillo, who, together with many Renaissance Neoplatonists, had privileged a pagan theology by declaring himself a disciple of the ancient Egyptian sage Hermes Trismegistus. Bodin, on the contrary, seems intent on conducting his reader toward a more modern theology. In fact, during the storm, all the travelers call on a monotheistic God to save them. The problem is that not all of them are imploring mercy of the same God. This inspires Coronaeus to ask, "[W]ith such a variety of religions represented, whose prayers did God heed in bringing the ship safely into port?"[58]

Bodin's text next devotes many pages—indeed, all of books 2 and 3—to a discussion of nature, demons, the spiritual world, and whether or not angels exist and are powerful enough to work miracles. Only in Book 4 does he return to the vexed problem of the variety of religions. Senamus the skeptic introduces the discussion by saying, "I think these discussions about religion will come to nothing. For who will be the arbiter of such a controversy?" Fridericus the Lutheran immediately replies, "Christ the Lord! For he said that if three were gathered together in His name He would be in their midst." Senamus objects to this, noting that "the point of disagreement among Christians and Jews as well as among Mohammedans and Christians is whether or not Christ is God." Curtius the Calvinist, intent on transforming religious reform or even revolution into the law, intervenes to say, "We need suitable witnesses and references to confirm this." Senamus, however, objects again: "It is doubtful what witnesses are reliable, what records are trustworthy, what bondsmen are secure in determining a certain and sure faith." Coronaeus the Catholic then tries to clinch the matter by saying, "The church will be the judge. Augustine said: 'I would not believe the Gospel unless the church also confirmed it'." But Senamus will not allow this conclusion either. "An even more serious problem is what is the true church?" he asks. "The Jews say their church is the true one, and the Mohammedans deny it. On the other hand, the Christian makes a claim for his church, and the pagans in India say their church ought to have preference over all others because of its age. And so the very learned cardinal Nicholas of Cusa wrote he must represent nothing about the Christian church, but by positing the foundation that the church rests on its union with Christ, he assumes that which is the chief point of debate."[59]

As all the participants in this discussion, with the possible exception of Senamus the skeptic, are readily assuming that which is the chief point of debate (that is to say, the rightness of their own religious beliefs) there is a sense in which Bodin's dialogue, as Senamus had anticipated, reaches no final conclusion at all, for all the speakers—after long and impassioned discussion concerning a large variety of theological and philosophical problems—remain faithful to their original positions. Yet conclusions of an important kind are reached about the ways in which such diversity of religious belief should be negotiated. One of these is the necessity of curbing inflammatory reactions when one's own religious position comes under attack; only by listening with courtesy, and control over the emotions, is liberty of speech on the part of other believers to be assured. This necessity is emphasized by Coronaeus the Catholic himself, partly it would seem as a question of courtesy in his role as the Venetian host to the discussion. When Salomon the Jew indulges in a particularly vehement attack on religious ceremonies, Coronaeus, a stalwart defender of Roman rites, deliberately restrains his instinctive impetus to give a harsh reply, saying quietly, "I think I should defer to another time, lest I seem to have hampered anyone's liberty of speaking." This leads ultimately to the conclusion of the whole work, at the end of book 6, on a note of Pythagorean harmony. The religious problem has not been solved; on the contrary, religious diversity remains as marked and emphatic as it was at the beginning of the discussion. However, an atmosphere of harmony has been established precisely through the ability that the participants in the discussion have developed to talk about their differences without resorting to either physical or linguistic violence. There have been some areas of tension and difficulty, but these have been successfully navigated. A harmony is thus finally established that rests on the recognition that diversity should be seen as a source of cultural richness rather than conflict. This final image is summoned up by Bodin in suggestively tangible terms: "Coronaeus bade me to summon the boys to whom he offered the song: 'Lo, how good and pleasing it is for brothers to live in unity,' arranged not in common diatonics or chromatics, but in enharmonics with a certain more divine modulation. All were most sweetly delighted with this song, and they withdrew, having embraced each other in mutual love."[60]

In the bleak European scenario of the 1580s Bodin's dialogue opens a window on a more serene and enlightened world in which acceptance of the diversity of religious opinions—or what John Rawls in our own time has called an "overlapping consensus"—appears momentarily in reach of achievement.[61] It is interesting to note that Rawls was influenced by Bodin's *Colloquium*, and wrote in his *On My Religion* that "friendly and sympathetic discussion of our beliefs is accepted [by Bodin] as an important part of our religious life, argument and controversy are not."[62] The fragility of Bodin's vision, however, is evident in the fragility of the means by which such a peaceful consensus is seen to be obtained. All appears to depend on the open-minded hospitality of the Venetian host, the reference to Venice being essential in this context, for the republican government of Venice—less popular and more aristocratic than that of Florence—had survived the prevailing tendency toward ever more personal and oppressive princely rule and would continue to do so for many years to come. Venice, indeed, would continue to be associated with values of republican freedom right up to its eventual demise as an independent republic at the end of the eighteenth century.[63] Yet Bodin himself had been theorizing a form of government that had decidedly monarchical characteristics to it; and he never makes clear by what means the Venice in which he situates this dialogue—his final work—would or could guarantee the advanced form of religious pluralism his text is sanctioning. Although it was undoubtedly true that the seaboard location of Venice—looking out toward the east—led to the accommodation of a large number of different cultures and religions, the city itself nevertheless decided to remain within the Catholic world. It was thus obliged constantly to negotiate its political and cultural autonomy with the ecclesiastical authorities in Rome who were consistently antagonistic toward its libertarian tendencies. Significantly, Bodin himself, in the last few words of his *Colloquium of the Seven*, firmly shuts the window he has so tantalizingly opened, declaring in the words of his Catholic mouthpiece, Coronaeus, that the religious discussion has been illuminating but that there will be no more of such discussions in the future. The Counter-Reformation wins the day over liberty, advising Coronaeus and his friends to submit to the prevailing cultural climate of the times.

Inquisition: The Trial of Giordano Bruno

Giordano Bruno, born in Nola, Italy, in 1548, was sent to nearby Naples to study and heard there the preaching monks of the imposing and important

Monastery of San Domenico. They seemed to him immensely impressive in the way they wielded a cultural and religious authority that, for the young man from the more rural Nola, opened up an exciting and prestigious new world. He not only succeeded in becoming one of them, entering into the monastery as a novice in 1565, but he went on to complete the rigorous course in theology and to become a preaching friar. Whether or not Bruno's religious calling was a genuine one is difficult to gauge given his reluctance in his later years as a philosopher to refer to that early period of his life. In any case, his monastic experience came to an abrupt end when he was found reading the life of St. Jerome with the comments of Erasmus, which he had to thrust down the convent privy before fleeing north to Rome and beyond.[64]

Before investigating what had happened in the Catholic world to the reputation of Erasmus since the year 1524, when we saw him being personally invited by Pope Clement VII to support the Catholic cause by responding to the heresies of Luther, it can be instructive to take a brief look at the volume Bruno was reading that caused his dramatic rupture with the Dominican order. Erasmus's edition of the works of St. Jerome was the first and most important of his many editions of the fathers of the church. It was originally published in nine folio volumes in Basel by Johann Froben in 1515, and was reprinted in revised editions throughout the sixteenth century. As well as the saint's letters and other writings, the edition contained a letter of dedication by Erasmus to William Warham, archbishop of Canterbury, under a still Catholic Henry VIII; the life of Jerome; prefaces to some of the volumes, and detailed commentary and notes. Erasmus is eloquent in his admiration for Jerome, which leads him to express a clear preference for Jerome with respect to St. Augustine, whom he saw as the more dialectical of the two. Augustine, he claims, was more of the theologian, with less eloquence and purity of faith. On the other hand, Jerome's monasticism, which often took him for long periods of prayer and vigil into the desert, was exercised, according to Erasmus, with pristine purity of a very different sort from the modern monasticism Erasmus so disliked: "Nor was profession as a monk at that time anything else than the practise of the original, free, and purely Christian life."[65]

Judgments such as these clearly expressed bitter criticism of the modern church. Erasmus, indeed—like Lorenzo Valla and others before him—interpreted his humanist vocation as an editor and commentator of classical and Christian texts as an exercise that went well beyond a purely linguistic philology to assume an often critical stance seen as synonymous with liberty itself. The humanist scholar, through his thorough investigation into the original words lying behind corrupted and doubtful texts, became a purveyor of truth in an obscure and fallen world. His tools were those of a classical and skeptical reason that Erasmus celebrates in one of his prefaces to the works of Jerome with a reference to a favorite classical author: "Thus Pliny firmly believes that a book has given pleasure only if some displeasing elements have been dis-

CHAPTER 2

cerned in it. So strong is his conviction that approval can only be *critical* approval."⁶⁶ The humanist thus uses his philological tools to define a space for critical comment on human culture and history that requires ample autonomy and freedom of speech. The fact that the churchmen of the fifteenth and early sixteenth century often, if not always, admired the achievements of the major humanists of their time is a sign of how far the humanist ethos had penetrated within the churches themselves. Until well into the 1520s Erasmus could rely on a special relationship with the highest levels of ecclesiastical power and prestige, both in Catholic and Protestant Europe, that he attempted in vain to use in order to reestablish order and unity within an increasingly ruptured world.

The extent of the rupture caused by the Protestant Reformation, as well as by the failure of the Catholic Church to contain or control it, became evident to all when the idea of a general council seeking reconciliation was abandoned and the Catholics started meeting at Trent in a council of their own. The Council of Trent (1544–63) initiated a vigorous period of internal reformation and reorganization of the Catholic Church whose ramifications were to prove of long-lasting religious and historical importance throughout southern Europe and beyond. The aspect of that movement that is of interest for a study of the early modern development of a concept of liberty is the emergence of the Inquisition as one of the major instruments by which the Catholic Church attempted to solve the problem of the new heresies, for the Inquisition amounted to a concerted and extraordinarily well-organized attempt to repress all forms of thought and expression except those admitted under the careful and vigilant control of the Catholic authorities themselves.

The Inquisition was not a new phenomenon within the history of the Catholic Church. It came into being in the thirteenth century when the theological debate was assuming a number of particularly complex characteristics that the church was eager to control. It then had a Spanish ramification beginning in 1478, largely as a way of dealing with the question of the Spanish Jews. The modern Inquisition, however, was founded by the papal bull *Licet ab Initio* of Pope Paul III announced on July 21, 1542, specifically as a way of dealing with the new Protestant heretics. The bull created a centralized Congregation of the Inquisition in Rome, where the major inquisitorial trials were held, though local inquisitions continued to operate throughout Italy as well as in other areas of the Catholic world. As John Tedeschi, who has done much to further the serious study of the Inquisition in the English-speaking world, has pointed out, "Like other sixteenth-century monarchs, he [the pope] reshaped a previously existing governmental function as part of a program to centralize authority."⁶⁷

This process of centralization was a gradual if relatively rapid one. It has proved possible to consider the first years of the new Inquisition as a period in which the inquisitorial authorities attempted to mediate with heterodox forms of thinking rather than to adopt a full-scale policy of oppression. On the other hand, an increasing severity becomes apparent in the later decades of the sixteenth century as a direct outcome of the Council of Trent.[68] With two bulls, *Cum Quorundam Hominum* (July 22, 1556) and *Cum Ex Apostolatus Officio* (February 15, 1558), Pope Paul IV established a class of crimes involving heresy against the central doctrines of the church that called for the death penalty even when the accused was neither relapsed nor impenitent. In 1588, Pope Sixtus V reorganized the Curia, or the central organs of the ecclesiastical government in Rome, making the Holy Office of the Inquisition into the first among the fifteen congregations into which papal government was divided.[69]

Besides the Holy Office or the Congregation of the Inquisition itself, the Council of Trent decreed on February 26, 1562, as one of its most formidable instruments of ideological control the Congregation of the Index, whose function from its official institution in 1571 onward was to impede the diffusion of heretical publications. Undoubtedly the bitterness of the strife that accompanied the development of the Protestant Reformation was in a large part due to the fact that it happened to coincide with the massive development of the new printing industry and the realization of its full potential in the sixteenth century. It has been estimated that "between 1517 and 1520, some 300,000 copies of Luther's works were sold; while thirty years later, when the religious conflict was revived by the Calvinist offensive, Geneva became the printing capital of Europe and its presses were capable of producing 250,000 books annually."[70] These were impressive numbers indeed in a culture in which literacy was still limited to a small part of the population. The book began to be considered by the Catholic Inquisition as "the silent heretic," and the effort to limit and contain the diffusion of those books considered dangerous by the Catholic Church turned rapidly into the most remarkably articulate and mercilessly oppressive exercise in censorship known to modern times. A measure of the importance accorded to the Index of Prohibited Books by the Catholic Church is demonstrated by the fact that it survived the eventual demise of the Inquisition at the end of the eighteenth century and was formally suppressed only in 1966.

Like the Inquisition itself, censorship and indexes of forbidden books had existed in the Catholic world well before the Council of Trent. Local indexes associated with such places of Catholic orthodoxy as the Sorbonne in Paris or the University of Louvain in the Low Countries had been quick in condemning what they considered printed forms of heresy; and these academic centers had already indulged, during Erasmus's lifetime, in harsh criticism of his free-ranging humanism. The Germans, too, had reacted early on to the dangers of the new printing presses, instituting inspection of the books exhibited at the Frankfurt book fair as early as 1486. Savanorola in Florence was one of the first to denounce books for their heretical potentialities in Italy, and during his brief period of ascendancy in the city there were a number of book burnings that he instigated. The problem in Italy was not so easy to solve, as Renaissance humanism had given rise to an intense study of the pagan past as well as to a widespread curiosity with respect to creative ideas wherever they were to be found. The many examples that could be cited of the wide range of humanist study need not be limited to such irreverent pagan authors as Lucian (some of whose satirical works were translated by Erasmus together with Thomas More) but would have to include the extensive interest of the humanists in the Hermetic texts and in the Jewish Kabbalah, in the Aristotelian commentaries of the Arabic philosophers of the Middle Ages, in the natural philosophy and magic of the ancient world, and in the work of classical historians and poets. It is not surprising that the first attempts of the newly founded Inquisition in Rome to promulgate indexes were a failure, involving the withdrawal of a number of unsuccessful early drafts. It was only with the election of Giampietro Carafa as Pope Paul IV in the summer of 1555 that the Counter-Reformation exercise in book censorship got seriously underway. Paul IV could count on the support of a formidable grand inquisitor, cardinal Michele Ghislieri, who, according to the carefully documented account by Paul Grendler, "skilfully played the political and spiritual cards at his disposal" to obtain the enforcement of a new index, promulgated in early 1559, throughout the Italian Peninsula.[71]

From the beginning, the new exercise in censorship had caused widespread distress among booksellers and publishers—especially in Venice, where an exceptionally flourishing printing industry created inevitable protests against what was immediately seen as a major economic as well as cultural setback to their trade. The problems created by censorship, however, went well beyond the inevitable economic ones to address questions such as the relationship between book and author, and between the single volume and the *opera omnia*. An interesting petition of the Venetian booksellers and publishers submitted to the Inquisition against the first unsuccessful indexes in 1554–55 raises problems that were to trouble the exercise in censorship throughout the sixteenth century and beyond. Illustrating their point with a long list of prestigious authors who were being forbidden, the petitioners pointed out that many of them had written numerous works that had "nothing to do with religion or with ecclesiastical affairs, but only with the law, with medicine, philosophy, or translations of other authors who were not prohibited."[72] So what was being censored, exactly—the author or the single work? And must all these fields of study suffer because in the single matter of religion some authors were not as orthodox as the church desired? Notably, the list of authors named in this protest included Philipp Melanchthon, the major intellectual figure behind Luther's reform and a personal friend of Erasmus. The petition lists his works on rhetoric and grammar, as well as his influential commentaries on Aristotle, implicitly suggesting to the inquisitors that, as many modern historians have since claimed, proceeding down the road of a blanket censorship would lead to the Counter-Reformation destroying the European Renaissance altogether.[73]

Pope Paul IV and Cardinal Ghislieri, acting together, turned a deaf ear to these protests; their only concern was with eradicating the heretical tendencies that the circulation throughout Italy of books published in the north by the reformers had encouraged to an alarming degree in the 1540s and '50s. Their 1559 index clamped down ruthlessly on nearly 550 authors whose complete works were banned, including all of the works of Machiavelli and Erasmus as well as authors writing in the vernacular in terms that were considered to be not so much formally heretical as immoral and obscene. These included Pietro Aretino, François Rabelais, and a large part of Giovanni Boccaccio's *Decameron*. Also included in this index were all printings of the Bible in the vernacular, the number of which had increased due to the combined work of Erasmus and Luther. The new index even went to the extent of forbidding the entire production of nearly sixty publishers from Protestant Europe, including one from Venice itself; this was Francesco Brucioli, brother and publisher of Antonio Brucioli, one of the major Italian reformation authors of the 1540s.[74] The 1559 index was a sign that the Counter-Reformation did not intend to make subtle distinctions between the person of an author, his works, or his publisher; wherever a suspicion of unorthodoxy was discerned, it was simply to be stamped out. This brings us back to the figure of Giordano Bruno, in the monastery of San Domenico in Naples, intent on thrusting Erasmus's commented edition of the *Works of St. Jerome* down the privy before fleeing north on a journey that would take him to most of the major capitals of learning in Europe, from Paris to London to Wittenberg to Prague.

It was, in fact, in Prague in 1588 that Bruno published a book titled *One Hundred and Sixty Articles against the Mathematicians and Philosophers of our Times* that criticized the modern mathematicians and philosophers of his age; it contained the major statement he made on the subject of liberty in his published works. Bruno's life north of the Alps had not been easy; taking up a position outside the Christian culture of his time, he ended up being considered—somewhat like Erasmus—a heretic to both sides. Unlike Erasmus, who never abandoned the Christian faith, Bruno dedicated his attention above all to natural philosophy. His gradual conviction that Copernican heliocentricity had reshaped the world in its true form, added to his extension of Copernicanism to an infinite rather than a closed universe—which Bruno saw as populated by an infinite number of heliocentric systems involved in eternal processes of evolution—would gradually be further developed to contemplate an atomistic concept of matter. These were Bruno's major contributions to the new science, not unmixed with elements of natural magic deriving from his faithfulness to a Neoplatonic concept of a world soul, or universal intelligence, which he saw as pervading all things and animating them with unfathomable forms of energy and life.[75]

The ultimate locus of life, which Bruno calls divine, is identified with the monad, or an ultimate unity or one. The metaphysical status of the monad remains uncertain within his philosophy given that he often follows Aristotle in repudiating Plato's transcendental ideas. The subject has caused—and continues today to cause—heated debate among Bruno's commentators, divided between those who interpret him as the last in a long line of Renaissance Neoplatonists, deriving ultimately from Plotinus, Nicolaus Cusanus, and Marsilio Ficino, and those who stress the immanent nature of his intuition of divine unity.[76] The issue is perhaps destined to remain unresolved, as passages can be found in Bruno's works comforting both sides of the argument—which should perhaps suggest that attention is best placed elsewhere. Undoubtedly, in his atomistic poem *On the Triple Minimum* Bruno identifies the source of life within his infinite universe in the nucleus of his atoms, which confer on matter an active and vital nature, involving the whole in an overwhelming process of vicissitude that defies the limited capacities of the human mind. Bruno thus distrusts the modern mathematicians and logicians who wish to reduce to the certainties of mental order what in his opinion remains unknowable—at least in a complete and ultimately certain way. As recent commentary has emphasized, Bruno's own mathematics tend toward approximation, not without contemplating the possibility of alternative mathematical concepts to the classical ones that dominated the science of his day—for example, geometrical propositions of a non-Euclidean kind.[77]

Bruno was aware that his physics and mathematics, as well as his metaphysics and religion, were not those officially sanctioned by the culture of his time. He had indeed been hounded out of most of the European capitals he had visited, including Oxford, Paris, and Wittenberg, and had evidently gone to Prague in the hope of finding favor with the Catholic emperor Rudolf II, well known as a scholar interested in esoteric and unorthodox inquiries. In his dedicatory letter to the emperor for his *One Hundred and Sixty Articles*, published in Prague in 1588, Bruno develops his argument in favor of liberty for the philosopher by starting out with a denial of innate ideas.[78] Rather, he denies the existence of an innate faculty of judgment that would give the human mind the capacity of knowing intuitively what is certain and true. If this capacity of judgment were innate, Bruno argues, we would all know what is right, and there would be no conflict of opinions such as that which all generations have experienced—particularly his own. Given that there is no innate capacity of judgment that indicates with certainty what is true or false, there are no people so vain as those who think their ideas are the only right ones. Among these Bruno lists provocatively those who believe in a revealed religion, convinced that God has illuminated only them while leaving the rest of humanity in the dark. It would be enough, writes Bruno, to consider the different number of revealed religious beliefs, which are all equally firmly held, to understand that this is only a way of dividing humanity up into inevitably

LIBERTY AND RELIGION

warring sects. It is interesting to see Bruno in Prague writing along lines so close to those of Bodin and in exactly the same year.

Bruno, however, pushes his argument much further than does Bodin. Based on what he calls "a pact with nature," he sees the differences in religions as an anthropological concept rather than a theological one. Nature has decreed which religion is best for each country, continent, and race; it is when the missionary zeal of what Bruno ironically calls "Mercuries sent from Heaven" breaks the pact with nature in the name of a universal God that war and conflict break up the original state of natural peace. Bruno is far from sharing Michel de Montaigne's concept of the noble savage; civilized peoples must nurture their cultural heritage by distancing themselves as far as possible from the habits of "brutes and barbarians." The means of doing this are seen as based on love and respect for difference rather than on hate and war. Bruno is deliberately keeping the terms of his argument vague in this passage; it is never specified who exactly the "Mercuries sent from Heaven" are. They could be read as the new Protestants, breaking up the ancient unity of the Catholic Church, or the Spanish Jesuits pursuing the conversion of the natives of the South American continent in the colonializing experience that Bruno deplores.[79] He claims that his own religion precedes the modern era of conflict and oppression, and is to be identified with the deepest beliefs of his country of origin. Again, this could be read as a statement of fidelity to his original Catholicism or taken further back to the pagan religions of Italy in the ancient world. As in so many works written in this period of ferocious censorship, the surface of the text remains deliberately opaque.

A more explicit statement comes in the following paragraph when Bruno speaks of his true subject in this letter, which he calls the "free intellectual disciplines." In order to be a truly free intellectual, Bruno argues, it is essential not to follow passively in the paths traced out by one's teachers or parents. What adds up to the normal common assumptions of one's environment or one's age can also be deceptive. Philosophy requires a more rigorous foundation, which Bruno finds in skeptical reason. This must develop a process of systematic doubt, both of those things that seem abstruse and absurd and of those that seem certain and self-evident. All forms of intellectual submission are to be avoided, including a blind allegiance to such established authorities as Aristotle or others of his kind. The pursuit of intellectual truth can only be founded on what, in Bruno's opinion, can be justly called innate. This is not any form of absolute certainty concerning what is true or what is false but instead what he calls "the eyes of sense and intelligence" with which to pursue the truth as far as the human mind can reach. The true philosopher will push these limits ever further toward the light of pure truth in what Bruno sees as the only acceptable form of war: the war within the individual psyche, where the mind struggles against falsity and deception in order to assure the victory of reason in that mental republic or city that Bruno calls "the soul." A significant step is already taken here toward Descartes's *cogito ergo sum* (I think, therefore I am). Bruno clearly sees this new emphasis on the workings of the individual mind as the path philosophy must follow in the modern world. For this to be possible, he insists, philosophy must be guaranteed against all forms of legislation forbidding discussion and free thought.

Toward the end of 1591, for reasons that have never been fully explained, Bruno took the decision to return to Italy, again via Venice, which Bodin had described as "the only city that offers immunity and freedom from servitude." Giovanni Mocenigo, a nobleman, had invited Bruno to attend him in his Venetian palace and to teach him the arts of memory. It was a subject on which Bruno was expert and had written copiously; but the experiment was not a success. What exactly happened in Mocenigo's palace is not known, except that on May 23, 1592, Mocenigo imprisoned Bruno in his room and turned him over to the Inquisition.[80] In Venice the Catholic inquisitors were a mixed body of state officials and ecclesiastics, and were reputed to be relatively moderate.[81] The Venetian trial was brief; Bruno attempted to outline his philosophical doctrines to inquisitors whose main concern was to see him kneeling down to ask forgiveness for whatever unorthodox opinions he may have held. In a final hearing of July 30, 1592, Bruno did kneel down and publicly declared his willingness to submit to the opinion of his judges. The trial seemed set to terminate with his release. Then Rome intervened, stressing that Bruno was a citizen not of Venice but of Spanish-dominated Naples, where inquisitorial proceedings had already been initiated against him. Furthermore, the pope himself, Clement VIII, personally desired that Bruno be extradited and tried again in Rome. On February 19, 1593, Bruno arrived in the prisons of the Holy Office in Rome; he would only leave seven years later, when his sentence to death was publicly announced and he was handed over to the secular governor of the city to be burned at the stake. On that occasion Bruno is known to have declared that his judges feared pronouncing their sentence against him more than he feared receiving it. On February 17, 1600, Bruno was burned alive in Rome's Campo dei Fiori as an impenitent heretic, his tongue held in a brace to prevent him from speaking his mind. All of his works were immediately placed on the Index of Prohibited Books.[82]

The earliest comments on Bruno's trial were made by his nineteenth-century commentators, who only had the Venetian documents to work from; a summary of the Roman part of his trial would only be found and published in 1942. The principal concern of these early commentators was to explain Bruno's apparently contradictory behavior in Venice, which consisted of giving remarkably frank answers to the inquisitors about the contents of his philosophy while at the same time repeatedly declaring his willingness to recant. Already in the crucial third session of the trial at Venice, Bruno had admitted that he considered the universe infinite and eternal, populated by infinite worlds, and governed by a universal providence identifiable with nature herself. He confessed to doubts about the incarnation of Christ and about the Trinity, and declared that he believed in a world soul according to the doctrine of Pythagoras. It is interesting to note that Bruno called on the ideas of St. Thomas Aquinas himself about the creation to claim that universal being may either have been created or be eternal; in both cases it was to be considered as dependent on a first cause so that nothing was ever random or independent.[83] A few days later in the trial Bruno was on his knees, declaring that he would do or think nothing that might dishonor the religion he once served as a monk.

In his biography of 1889, Domenico Berti accompanied the recent publication of these documents with a suggestion on how to read them. He pointed out that the sixteenth-century discussion of Aristotle's idea of the soul, particularly as it had been conducted at Bologna University by Pietro Pomponazzi, had developed a concept of "double truth" that was important in protecting the neo-Aristotelian natural philosophers of Bologna and Padua from interference on the part of the church. This theory reelaborated the claim already made in the Middle Ages that it was possible to argue "philosophically" for theses such as Aristotle's concept of the soul—which Pomponazzi thought was mortal, and not immortal as St. Thomas Aquinas had declared—while at the same time remaining faithful to Christian orthodoxy at a "theological" or "religious" level of truth. Berti called on this double theory of truth to explain Bruno's behavior at Venice, pointing out how Bruno himself constantly stressed to the inquisitors that, when he was explaining what he himself called the "impious" aspects of his thought, he was speaking specifically "as a philosopher and according to the principles of a natural light."[84] Later, in the early years of the twentieth century, Giovanni Gentile considered Bruno's strategy at Venice as based on a reading of Machiavelli, who clearly shared Pomponazzi's Renaissance theory of double truth.[85] In Gentile's opinion, Machiavelli's idea of religion as necessary politically to ensure the moral and social cohesion of community life is what allowed Bruno, the philosopher, to behave as he did. Thus Bruno never compromised his philosophical conscience at Venice; on the contrary, according to Gentile, his behavior was "a coherent practical demonstration of his philosophical integrity."[86]

With the publication of a *Summary* of the Roman trial in 1942, discovered in the archives of the Holy Office by Angelo Mercati, it became clear that Bruno's strategy of alternating remarkably frank admissions of the Christian unorthodoxy of his philosophy with a willingness to abjure it publicly was never abandoned.[87] Rather, it became particularly prominent in the final stages of the trial. These were characterized by an event that all commentators agree was decisive: the appointment at the beginning of 1597 of the Jesuit Roberto Bellarmino as the official adviser to the pope on matters relating to the Inquisition. (Bellarmino would himself formally become an inquisitor in 1599.) The *Summary* indicates Bellarmino as becoming the dominating figure for the prosecution at Bruno's trial, dating from a crucial hearing held on January 18, 1599, when the accused was finally handed a list of eight heretical propositions culled directly from his works. Bruno now had to decide if he was prepared to deny them—that is, to deny his essential philosophical creed.

Unfortunately this list appears not to have survived, though commentators have succeeded in plausibly reconstructing it. It is probable that it included Bruno's Copernicanism and his doctrine of an infinite universe, while it is certain that it included his idea of the soul as a pilot in a ship. Bruno saw the individual soul as unable to survive the dissolution of the body, both of them returning at death into the infinite ocean of universal being. This had serious consequences for his moral philosophy, which he had also made clear to the inquisitors. Bruno's philosophy did not contemplate judgment of the individual after death, or the idea of hell, though in the fourth Venetian session of the trial he had declared his willingness to profess these beliefs "when speaking as a good Catholic."[88] Clearly, however, his doctrine of the soul was a crux marking the distance between his philosophy and Christian theology; and the part of the *Summary* dedicated to the ideas culled from Bruno's books dwells at length on the subject. Bellarmino was quick to see the heretical implications of Bruno's explicit definitions of the individual soul as no more than a fragmentary reflection within the great universal mirror or a passing voice mingling with the infinite voices of universal being.[89] Bellarmino rigorously held Bruno down to these ideas when he started vacillating again, attempting to abjure anything and everything except for his doctrine of the soul. Bruno, for his part, ultimately realized (and had probably known all along) that he could not be flexible all the way down without denying the ideas that he had elaborated into a philosophy during a lifetime of exile and remarkable creativity. In a dramatic last stand he stood firm, claiming that he had nothing to retract because there was nothing that he needed to retract. From there, events proceeded to their cruel and tragic conclusion.

Bruno's position with respect to the cultural and religious authorities he was addressing, both in his work and in his trial, was based on an eloquent use of rhetoric in the cause of liberty as an essential intellectual and civic value in the hope of bringing about a change of heart on the part of those in power. There is little sign in his works of the attitude of Machiavelli earlier in the sixteenth century, and of the apologists of the republicanism that would come later (in the seventeenth century and beyond) who argued the necessity for institutional and legal guarantees as a condition for ensuring liberty equally for all citizens, irrespective of the goodwill of the governors concerned. Bruno's essentially rhetorical strategy would nevertheless become the norm among the natural philosophers of the beginning of the seventeenth century, the principal examples being Francis Bacon's eloquent letter of dedication of *The Advancement of Learning* addressed to James I and Galileo Galilei's much celebrated "Letter to Madama Christina Lorena." At the same time, as a fierce critic of Bruno, Marin Mersenne acutely noticed that Bruno would become an inspiration for the *libertins erudits* of French derivation who in the seventeenth century attempted to further an advanced form of *libertas philosophandi* often with direct reference to the new science of the time.[90]

Bruno is often considered a harsh critic of the Renaissance humanism that in his time was giving way to new inquiries, interests, and intellectual movements. Bruno's behavior at his trial, however, can be thought of as coherently in line with the example of Erasmus, whose works had given rise to Bruno's exile in the first place. Bruno was endorsing the humanist choice to use the persuasive powers of rhetoric in an attempt to move the political and ecclesiastical authorities to adopt more open-minded and liberal attitudes. His reasoning and his rhetoric were directed toward establishing a culture of dissent in the hope of being able to have a dialogue with those whose ideas differed from his own. His efforts were doomed to failure even more emphatically than were Erasmus's own. The post-Tridentine Roman Catholic Church had no place in its inquisitorial system for the religious liberty and pluralism that Bruno was proposing. Its laws decreed for him the silence of heresy and a cruel death.

Religion as Dogma, or Religion as Debate? Richard Hooker and Jacobus Arminius

During his difficult but productive exile from Italy, Giordano Bruno had visited England between the spring of 1583 and the autumn of 1585. He had arrived from Paris carrying letters from the French king, Henry III, to his ambassador in London, Michel de Castelnau, Lord of Mauvissière, and had stayed on as the ambassador's gentleman attendant. This position took him to the English court, where he seems to have met Elizabeth I. His admiration of the English queen was, in any case, a constant theme in his philosophical dialogues written in Italian and published in London with the printer John Charlewood.

In the first of those dialogues, *The Ash Wednesday Supper*, Bruno praises Elizabeth I as the finest political mind of his time, superior in wisdom to her contemporary male counterparts—praise for which Bruno was to be sharply questioned by the Roman Catholic inquisitors during his trial.[91] This generic praise would become more specific when in the last of his London dialogues, *On the Heroic Frenzies*, Elizabeth I appears as the chief English nymph, presiding over the peacefully flowing waters of the River Thames; here she appears to assume some kind of divine power that defines her as the guardian of England's religious as well as political estate. Bruno's Italian text works cautiously through metaphorical allusion and prophetic imagery rather than explicit discourse; but an increasing amount of recent comment is claiming that what Bruno is praising in these pages is the politico-religious solution represented by the Anglican Settlement.[92] If that is correct, it is praise from an outside observer, as Bruno appears to have made no attempt to approach the Anglican authorities directly. His attitude may be defined as Machiavellian insofar as it expresses objective approval for a religious authority whose autonomy from Rome is seen as investing it with a special power to install a harmonious political relationship between church and state.

Before he started writing his philosophical dialogues in London, Bruno had twice visited the University of Oxford, where he participated in some academic debates and later gave a series of bitterly disputed lectures. Although Bruno appears to have approached Oxford with friendly intentions, his lectures there were—by all accounts, including his own—a disastrous failure. Among other things, he appears incautiously to have challenged the dominating authority of Aristotle within the academic culture of the time by proposing a defense of the new Copernican cosmology, which had not yet been accepted by the universities of Europe. Our knowledge of what actually happened during Bruno's lectures at Oxford remains fragmentary and incomplete, as no text of them has survived.[93] It is known, however, that they were attended by a number of young scholars destined to become prominent figures of the Anglican Church in the years to come. Among these were the future archbishop of Canterbury, George Abbott, who some years after Bruno's death still remembered those lectures with indignation and scorn. It is Abbott who mentions their Copernican content, although it is not clear how much of it he understood. Abbott seems to have disliked Italians anyway, as he reports scornfully that Bruno had a barbarous way of pronouncing Latin with a Neapolitan inflection.[94]

Another promising and still youthful Oxford scholar who seems to have listened to Bruno was the future commentator and theologian of the Anglican Settlement, Richard Hooker. It is not clear how much he understood of what Bruno was trying to say; sometime after Bruno's visit to Oxford, Hooker wrote a letter to his more radically Protestant friend John Rainolds. In a passage referring sarcastically to a somewhat obscure apocalyptic writer, Hugh Broughton, whom Rainolds disliked, Hooker called him "an English Jordanus Brunus"—a remark that has puzzled Bruno scholars. Although Bruno also at times used prophetic and apocalyptic imagery, his mind-set could hardly have been further away from Broughton's Judeo-Christianity, which was founded on a conciliatory reading of the Bible that claimed to find all the truths of the New Testament already embedded in the Old Testament prophecies and especially in the book of Daniel. Such misunderstandings of Bruno at Oxford are paradoxical, for Hooker's later defense of the Anglican Settlement in his massive *Laws of Ecclesiastical Polity* of the 1590s has many things in common with Bruno's praise of Elizabeth I in his philosophical dialogues written and published in London in 1584.

Richard Hooker was born at Exeter in 1554, nephew to John Hooker, alias Vowell, who had been associated with Peter Martyr Vermigli. One of the most prestigious of the sixteenth-century theologians, Vermigli was an ex-Augustinian Italian monk who converted to Protestantism; he later developed a strictly predestination theology of salvation that went well beyond Luther in its symbolic view of the Eucharist.[95] On Henry VIII's death in 1547, Vermigli was called to England by archbishop Thomas Cranmer and took up a prestigious chair at the University of Oxford, where Hooker would later be a student. Hooker was also a protégé of bishop John Jewel of Salisbury, so he had impeccable Anglican credentials; he became a fellow of Corpus Christi College, Oxford, in 1579, remaining there until he was appointed master of the Temple Church in London in 1585. He gave up his place at the Temple in 1591 to begin work on his *Laws*. The preface and the first four books were published in 1593, and the fifth book in 1597. Hooker died in 1600, and the remaining books 6 and 7 were published much later, in 1648, while an eighth book was published only in 1661; these last three books are in the form of unfinished drafts. Hooker's work was never translated into Latin, and though at once recognized in the English-speaking world as the major sixteenth-century defense of the Anglican Settlement, it has not had a comparable influence on the wider European stage.[96]

Attitudes of commentators toward Hooker have greatly changed in recent years. Considered for many centuries a balanced and impartial commentator of the religious conflicts of his times, he is now more often presented as a deeply engaged controversialist intent on making a political statement in the interests of the British monarchy and Elizabeth I's Anglican Settlement of 1559. Hooker's relationship with proponents of a "further reformation" (that is, the radical Protestants, or Puritans, who were challenging the authority of the Episcopal Anglican Church) passed from a sympathetic attitude corroborated by his friendship at Oxford with the radical John Rainolds to open hostility when he reached the Temple in London. There his reader was Walter Travers, who unsuccessfully contested Hooker's nomination. Travers's *Full and Plain Declaration of Ecclesiastical Discipline* of 1574 was a major exposition of the Calvinist-inspired, Presbyterian system of church government; it challenged the power of the royally nominated bishops in the name of elected elders of the church who would directly represent the religious interests of the community.

In his introduction to Hooker's text, Arthur Stephen McGrade points to the importance of book 5 of the *Laws,* where Hooker defends a religious life that finds its major point of reference not in a biblical theology but in Archbishop Cranmer's *Book of Common Prayer* of 1552, issued in its final form, after consultation with Peter Martyr Vermigli, in 1563.[97] Hooker sees the *Book of Common Prayer* as an expression of a public devotional theology of a Christian community identifiable with the nation. This communal religious life is founded on more than the *Book of Common Prayer* itself—which is, rather, its principal instrument. At the foundation of the religious life as it is perceived by Hooker is "the law," which is the subject of the crucial book 1 of his treatise. Law, according to Hooker, results necessarily from the condition of human nature, which originally is without knowledge or in a state of "utter vacuity." Civilization requires political association of these unformed minds, which—after seeing to their own basic wants—look toward higher things such as worldly wisdom and virtue. Ultimately these more civilized minds will look for union with God based on faith, hope, and charity. This progression toward a civilized community and, beyond it, an active devotional life can take place under the direction of a prince—in Hooker's opinion—only if such authority is derived either directly from God or from the consent of those persons on whom his laws are imposed; otherwise there will be tyranny. Royal power is therefore limited for Hooker by both divine and natural law, and further by a basic human right to some form of communal consent.

McGrade emphasizes the importance of Hooker's thought for its repudiation of the idea that all rules of religious as well as political life derive directly from the Bible and therefore require necessary consent. Hooker attacks the Calvinist claim that "in Scripture there must be of necessity contained a form of church polity, the laws whereof may in nowise be altered." Later, in the final years of the seventeenth century, John Locke, in chapter 2 of his *Second Treatise of Government*, would refer to Hooker in support of his own conception of morality as based on natural human equality without political subordination of one person to another: "this *equality* of Men by Nature, the Judicious *Hooker* looks upon as so evident in it self, and beyond all question, that he makes it the Foundation of that Obligation to mutual Love amongst Men, on which he Builds the Duties they owe one another, and from whence he derives the great Maxims *of Justice* and *Charity*."[98] McGrade thus feels that he can speak of Hooker's fundamentally republican conception of the Anglican Settlement, for Hooker's emphasis is on the whole body of the community as the source of the political and religious power of the prince in Parliament.

For Hooker, the parliament is "the body of the whole realm," the true body politic. It is clear that this definition of republicanism does not deny the power of a king when defined as the king-in-parliament. This concept derives from the formulation of the Anglican Settlement in religion as it had been originally conceived by Henry VIII and had been reestablished by Elizabeth I in 1559. Both Henry VIII and Elizabeth I had insisted that the Anglican Settlement be approved by parliamentary consent. McGrade's emphasis on Hooker's republicanism can thus be connected to the important paper by Harkku Peltonen, "Citizenship and Republicanism in Elizabethan England," which questions the traditional view expressed by Thomas Smith in his *On the English Republic* that "the prince is the life, the head, and the authority of all things that be done in the realme of England."⁹⁹ Peltonen's carefully documented study shows how this view, which deliberately creates a dichotomy between an active monarch and an all-obedient subject—denying the English man or woman of the sixteenth century any real identity as a citizen—fails to correspond to a widespread sense of civic life and citizenship in Elizabethan England that was especially evident in the local administration of the newly thriving urban centers. Peltonen admits that Smith himself qualifies the above statement by claiming that the power of the prince should be underwritten by "a multitude of free men collected together and united by common accord and covenauntes." Peltonen, however, thinks that the Elizabethan sense of republicanism went well beyond such a statement. He underlines the importance of the English translation of Cicero's *De officiis* (*On Moral Obligations*) in 1534 by Robert Whittinton, who urged not only princes but also "priuate persones and cytezyns" to read his volume with care.

Peltonen's survey of Elizabethan England in this unusual light of a concept of active republican citizenship gives particular emphasis to the essentially republican administration of London, where elections to office, both ecclesiastical and civil, tended to involve the common as well as the chief citizens of the city in regular rotations of office and administrative prestige. Once himself in London, Hooker, as we have seen, was not prepared to endorse the Presbyterian views of those such as Walter Travers. The Presbyterians were already pressing for election of radically Protestant elders by the individual religious congregations as a form of popular religious rebellion against what they saw as the essentially aristocratic hierarchies of the Anglican Church. Travers was reacting against what Peltonen himself admits to have been often an "underlying notion of aristocratic citizenship" present in sixteenth-century England. The English may have been more sympathetic to the Venetian aristocratic model of republicanism than to the more popular Florentine formulation of a republic proposed by Machiavelli. Nevertheless, Hooker's traditionalist stance, as the major apologist of the Elizabethan settlement in religion as well as in politics, can also be defined as "republican" to the extent that he saw the merits of the Anglican Settlement to derive not from a monarchical principle in any absolutist sense, but from the primary importance of the law as enacted in Parliament.

In his preface to the *Lawes of Ecclesiaticall Politie*, Hooker is above all intent on defining the Anglican Settlement as a happy mean between the rigors of the post-Tridentine Catholic Church in Rome and the equal rigors of Calvin's Presbyterian discipline in Geneva. Although recognizing Calvin as without doubt the wisest man that the French church ever enjoyed, and praising him for his diligence in writing his *Institutes*, Hooker is ironic about Calvin's insistence on the necessity of conforming to his own religious dictates: he considers Calvin's theological intransigence to be no less than that of the Church of Rome, so that members of the reformed churches are judged to be more or less perfect according to how skillful they are in interpreting Calvin's writings. His books already form a canon according to which both Christian doctrine and discipline are supposed to be judged. Hooker is as skeptical as Erasmus was about the power of the Spirit that the radical reformers were invoking to justify their own reading of the Scriptures, and he refers disparagingly to "the kind of spirituall regiment" under which the Calvinists live. He is equally skeptical about the requests being put forward by the English radical reformers to hold a conference or disputation about the question of whether or not to replace the royally appointed bishops with regularly elected elders. Such disputes, Hooker claims, cannot be decided in any other forum than that of a national parliament, and he advises those involved in such disputes to: "doe that which wise men, who thinke some Statute of the realme more fit to be repealed, then to stand in force, are accustomed to doe before they come to Parliament where the place of enacting is; that is to say, spend the time in re-examining more dulie your cause, and in more thoroughly considering of that which ye labour to overthrow."[100]

The force of this statement would clearly have been greater if the English Parliament of the time had been less subject than it was to royal control. For Hooker's advice to the radicals to have been valid, the possibility of their voice being heard in Parliament would have had to be a real one. This was clearly not yet the case at the end of the sixteenth century. Nevertheless, the principle announced here by Hooker is one of the greatest importance within the context of the religious struggles of the time. In theory, at least, it opened up religious heterodoxy to the possibility of parliamentary debate and legal negotiation. Hooker's thought here, if only cautiously, is reaching out toward solutions of the sort that a few years later would be successfully established in France through the Edict of Nantes, which would offer legal guarantees to the French Protestants to practice and discuss their religion freely within a still largely Catholic community.

The breadth and independence of Hooker's attitudes to some of the crucial religious debates of his time are further illustrated in book 1, chapters 8.7–8.9 of the *Lawes*, where he discusses the "natural law" in terms that broach the delicate subject of the freedom of the will. It is noteworthy that his discussion of this vexed subject is more in line with that of Erasmus than with either Luther or Calvin. Within a Christian concept of God's all-seeing providence, Hooker concedes a considerable measure of freedom to the individual will.[101] He thus denies the strict predestination theologies of Luther and Calvin, noting that "it cometh to pass that even of good actions some are better than other some, whereas otherwise one man could not excel another, but all should be either absolutely good, as hitting jump that indivisible point or center wherein goodness consisteth; or else missing it they should be excluded out of the number of well-doers."[102] This inclusion/exclusion policy of absolute preordained separation of the saved from the damned is exactly what

Luther and Calvin were proposing with their doctrines of the elect. Hooker's repudiation of their concept of predestination is of the greatest importance for an understanding of the Anglican Settlement and the religious tone of Elizabethan England. Notably, Hooker never cites Luther or Calvin in this section of his work, nor indeed Erasmus. The sources he explicitly mentions on the freedom of the will, however, are the same as those called on by Erasmus; as well as the same biblical texts, we find mentions of Aristotle and St. Thomas Aquinas, with, nearer his own times, Nicolaus Cusanus, Marsilio Ficino, and Bernardino Telesio—that is, classical, Scholastic, and early modern neo-Aristotelian or Neoplatonic humanist authors rather than the great Protestant theologians who were so influential at that time.

If Hooker's pages never caused the bitter disputes that followed the publications of Erasmus on the subject of free will, it is perhaps because he was more cautious in taking issue with Luther or Calvin. It seems to have been precisely this caution on the part of Hooker that inspired the praise by the later Enlightenment philosopher, John Locke, when, in chapter 2, section 5, of his *Second Treatise of Civil Government* he appreciated the level tones of the "judicious Hooker." According to Locke, Hooker's was a voice of tolerant reason raised in the name of an ecclesiastical policy based not only on a considerable measure of freedom of the individual will but also on the freedom of parliamentary discussion, guaranteed by law.[103]

A voice not dissimilar to Hooker's, particularly in the desire to solve theological differences by discussion and debate, was raised only a few years afterward in Holland where, toward the end of the sixteenth century, there was a lively republican ferment in the political field. Among the theological issues debated at that time was Calvin's extreme doctrine of the bondage of the will, which was subjected to a stringent examination. The questioning of it by the Dutch theologian Jacobus Arminius became an issue of both national and international concern whose echoes would resound well into the century to come.

Jacob Harmensz, more widely known as Jacobus Arminius, was a Dutch Reformed theologian and pastor. Although he studied in Geneva under Calvin's successor Theodore Beza from 1581 to 1586, Arminius seems never to have accepted Beza's strict Calvinistic doctrine of predestination. He remained an orthodox Reformed theologian in his belief that salvation was by grace alone and that human works could never be the cause of salvation. Nevertheless, Arminius insisted that the free human will was able to determine whether to accept or to refute the saving grace of God. "God makes man a vessel," he wrote, whereas "man makes himself an evil vessel." Arminius was worried by the fact that strict predestination theologies tended to make God the source of evil and damnation. In a critique of the English Calvinist William Perkins, he wrote, "To fail to restrict evangelical grace to sinful man is to make God the author of sin."[104]

CHAPTER 2

Arminianism thus became the name for a theology that refutes the total depravity of humankind and its absolute reliance on divine grace, underlining rather the human capacity to answer either positively or negatively God's offer of salvation. This revaluation of the powers of the human will was accompanied in Arminius by a revaluation of the powers of the human mind, and the capacity to approach, at least partially, the mysteries of faith by reason.[105] These ideas conflicted with the orthodox Calvinism of Beza and his many Dutch followers, and caused widespread discussion and debate, above all in Amsterdam and Leiden, the two Dutch towns in which Arminius preached and taught. Although he himself always remained within the Reformed Church, and objected to being considered unorthodox, in the minds of many of his contemporaries Arminius became associated with the Dutch freethinkers of this period such as Dirck Volckertszoon Coornhert, a humanist critic of Calvinism who had reacted strongly against the oppression of dissenting ideas and in particular against the death penalty for heretics.

Arminius himself was distressed by the tumults his theological ideas were giving rise to, and pressed for a council or synod in which they could be publicly debated and the issue of free will resolved. He died in 1609 before the Dutch authorities had managed to satisfy his request. The Synod of Dort was finally convened only in 1618–1619 by the states general. This would have pleased Arminius, who was of the opinion that the civil magistrate should be called on to negotiate the religious disputes that disturbed so many of the societies of the time. But whereas Arminius himself had wished for a synod that would discuss objectively the conflicting views of predestination and free will that his theology had given rise to, the Synod of Dort convened with the specific purpose of expelling the followers of Arminius from the Dutch Calvinist church.

By the time of the Synod of Dort, the followers of Arminius were called the Remonstrants after the name of a declaration in five articles drawn up by forty-four of his followers in January 1610, after Arminius's death, and discussed at a conference in The Hague in 1611. The synod did not condemn the theses of Arminius himself, whose collected works were not published until 1629, but it condemned the theses drawn up by the Remonstrants, and did so with a vengeance. The Remonstrants were not even allowed to be seated during the synod and were treated as conspirators. Open accusations of treachery through conspiracy with Spanish Catholic forces were made against the Remonstrants' principle supporter, the influential Dutch statesman Johan von Oldenbarnsveldt. Although he denied these accusations, Oldenbarnsveldt was tried and executed in 1618. The Remonstrants were forbidden to preach or to worship in public places on pain of banishment, and many of them were forced to flee the country. The most famous of the followers of Arminius, the expert on international law Hugo Grotius, was imprisoned, though his wife organized a colorful escape by smuggling him out of prison in a book chest.[106]

Grotius managed to reach Paris, where in 1625 he published his major work, *The Law of War and Peace*, in which he bitterly criticized the "frenzy" of uncontrolled violence of those involved in the religious wars of his time.

The Synod of Dort was extended to delegations from other Protestant countries, including Britain, which sent a group of theologians approved by King James I. James himself does not seem to have been unsympathetic to the theological opinions of Arminius, but he had political reasons for supporting the authority of the states general, and above all of the Dutch Calvinist prince Maurice of Nassau. James conducted affairs at the synod primarily through his ambassador, Sir Dudley Carlton, who had instructions to support the Calvinist cause. In the event, however, many of the British theologians sent to Dort sympathized with the greater role given by Arminius to the freedom of the will. John Hales, for example, who had arrived at the synod as a moderate opponent of the Remonstrants, sympathized with them ever more closely until finally, after an address by one of the most prominent Remonstrants, Episcopius (Simon Bischop), he exclaimed, "There I bid John Calvin good-night!" On their return the British delegates contributed to arousing widespread sympathy with the remonstrant position. English Arminianism was a highly ambiguous phenomenon; on the one hand it was seen by some as reinforcing the position of the established Church of England because it advocated the supremacy of the state over the church. On the other it was associated by many of the more radical Puritans with a notion of freedom of conscience in matters of faith, on the basis of which they felt justified in opposing the national Anglican Church. It exerted a strong influence on John Wesley, the founder of Methodism, one of the principal seventeenth-century dissident movements with respect to the established Anglican Church.[107]

One of the principal recent commentators of Arminianism, Keith D. Stanglin, has written that "the crucial difference between Arminius's doctrine of predestination and that of most of his Reformed contemporaries was his belief that predestination is conditional on a person's free acceptance or rejection of God's saving grace." This means that, for Arminius, the individual is free to chose either Christian faith (and subsequent salvation) or unbelief. Clearly Arminius condemns those individuals who reject the offered grace of a Christian god. Nevertheless, what Arminius is defending is a conditional nature of predestination in which the individual believer is no longer entirely subject to the already predetermined will of God but assumes some degree of responsibility for his own salvation or damnation.[108] It would clearly be absurd to claim that Calvin's presence in Reformed Europe was entirely eclipsed by Arminianism, which continued to flourish in spite of the Dutch Calvinists' efforts to eliminate it from the scene. Nevertheless, without doubt the Arminian influence was such that the issue of free will began to be widely considered in terms less harsh than those in which Luther or—even more radically—Calvin had presented it. The voice of Erasmus, which the northern humanists had never entirely forgotten, began to echo once again in many of the foremost exponents of the culture of the Protestant world. Precisely for this reason, however, many reacted strongly against Arminianism, fearing that it could become the prelude of a reconciliation of the Protestant parts of Europe with the Catholic Church.

Recent discussion of Arminianism tends to place it contextually within the theological issues that were often being violently debated in the Reformed parts of early modern Europe and to concede little importance to the Erasmian and humanistic influences that seem to have played their part in the Arminian challenge to strict Lutheran and Calvinistic ideas of predestination. Yet the Erasmian discussion of free will, and the humanist ethos on which it was so largely based, do seem to have had some influence on the more latitudinarian position assumed by Arminius on the vexed question of predestination. The catalog of his books put up for auction after his death does not contain Erasmus's original plea for the freedom of the will, but it does contain (among several other important works by Erasmus) the *Hyperaspistes* or *A Warrior Shielding a Discussion . . . against the Enslaved Will of Martin Luther*.[109] This, as we have seen, was the lengthy reply by Erasmus to Luther's *Bondage of the Will*, in which all of Erasmus's principal arguments in favor of free will are repeated with added emphasis. Furthermore, the library catalog also contains a work listed as *Opera Ioh. Pici Mirandulani duobus vol.* (1572), in which Arminius would have found Pico della Mirandola's famous *Oration on the Dignity of Man*, a text that Margolin has claimed as one of Erasmus's major sources. Pico had given eloquent expression to the humanist faith in the dignity of the human mind and its capacity to rise toward divine power and knowledge or to sink to the deepest depths of hellish evil according to the dictates of a perfectly free will. Margolin demonstrates convincingly that echoes of Pico's *Oration* can be heard clearly in Erasmus's text, and surely it is possible to hear a further echo in Arminius as well. Erasmus, as we have seen, was immediately accused of the heresy of Pelagianism, and inevitably Arminius was as well.

So strong and widespread was the accusation of Pelagianism against Arminius and his followers that in London in 1626 a small anonymous volume appeared titled *Pelagius redivivus. Or Pelagius raked out of the ashes by Arminius and his Schollers*. It was written by Daniel Featley, a prominent disputant and preacher, noted for his attacks on Roman Catholics and their doctrine. The greater part of the pamphlet consists of a parallel table giving the opinions of the Pelagians alongside similar quotations from Arminius and his followers. However, the author is aware that Arminius never proposed a full acceptance of the freedom of the will, so the accusation of Pelagianism is soon watered down to become *Demipelagianisme*.[110] This had been Luther's scornful accusation against Erasmus. Demipelagianism is a more moderate theory than Pelagius's own heresy; it concedes a large space to God's predestinating will but nevertheless insists on a small space in the mind in which the believer can accept or refuse the saving grace of God. In the English pamphlet, even Demipelagianism is considered to be a dangerous beast with many heads: in the first place it claims that God only "Predestinated" in the sense that he foreknew, or decreed to elect, those who would believe. This means that an act of faith on the part of the believer comes before election by God: a doctrine that limits God's powers of predestination. As a consequence of this introduction of acts of free will that qualify God's predestined order of the elect, the Demipelagians and Arminians claim (heretically, in Featley's opinion) that the final number of those elected to be redeemed is at any time uncertain, whereas strict Calvinism holds that the number of those predestined to redemption is decreed by God at the beginning of time and cannot be increased or diminished. The last page of this virulently anti-Arminian tract somewhat naively furnishes a congenial glimpse of Arminius himself in polemic with his antagonists by revealing to the reader, "When *Demipelagianisme* was objected against *Arminius*, he ingeniously answered, that it *might be a good* Quaerie, why Demipelagianisme *should not be accompted true Christianisme*."[111]

Arminius had every chance to absorb currents of thought deriving from the Renaissance humanists, who were still very much alive in Italy in spite of the strenuous efforts of the Counter-Reformation to stamp them out. In 1586, still in his student days, Arminius left Geneva for what one of his commentators calls somewhat dismissively "his Italian trip."[112] It in fact only lasted a few months, but it took Arminius to one of the principal cultural centers of early modern Europe, the University of Padua, as well as to a short stay in Rome itself. In that time Arminius seems to have learned the language, as the catalog of his books left at his death contains a considerable collection of works in Italian as well as a number of volumes in Latin by authors of the Italian Renaissance. Arminius had more than one copy of the Italian works of the father of Renaissance writers, Francesco Petrarca, as well as a thoroughly mundane poem such as Ludovico Ariosto's *Orlando furioso*. He possessed Latin works by humanist authors such as Angelo Poliziano, Girolamo Cardano, and Francesco Patrizi, as well as a reading of the Psalms by the fiery Florentine Dominican friar Girolamo Savonarola. He also had works of the Protestant Italian exiles who had brought humanist ideas of toleration and freedom of the will to northern Europe, such as Bernardino Ochino, Celio Secondo Curione, and Jacopo Aconcio. The library contained an equally impressive collection of French humanist texts, including more than one copy of Michel de Montaigne's *Essais*. Although there can be no certainty as to whether and which of these texts Arminius actually read, it amounts to an impressive collection that surely denotes more than a cursory knowledge of, and interest in, Renaissance humanism.

Arminius is known to have attended at Padua some lectures by the Aristotelian philosopher Giacomo Zabarella. This was a significant choice. Padua University was, throughout the Renaissance, one of the principal centers of

CHAPTER 2

the Aristotelian tradition, and a university to which students arrived from all over Europe, including the Protestant countries of the north. Situated in the Venetian territories, it was relatively free from interference from the Catholic authorities in Rome, and a numerous community of German-speaking students continued to study there throughout the sixteenth century, protected by the university authorities. When Arminius arrived in Padua in 1586, Giacomo Zabarella, a famous professor of philosophy, had recently been promoted to the second chair in natural philosophy, which he would occupy until his death in 1589. Although he never questioned the Paduan tradition of a rigorous Aristotelianism, Zabarella was open to the new humanistic influences that privileged direct textual exegesis over the medieval commentaries, and also in his insistence that he followed Aristotle only insofar as Aristotle himself established things on the basis of reason. So, according to Charles Schmitt, for Zabarella "reason, not Aristotle, is the final court of appeal."[113] Students arrived from all over Europe to hear Zabarella, above all for his lectures on logic and scientific method, and admired him for his rigorous rationalism albeit still linked to Aristotelian syllogistic demonstration.[114] Zabarella limited his teaching of Aristotle to the logic and the philosophy of nature—that is, to what Francis Bacon would shortly be defining as *secondary causes*. In Zabarella's opinion not only theology but even metaphysics lay outside the sphere of a strictly philosophical discourse. This was probably one of the causes of Zabarella's popularity with students from both sides of the religious divide.

Arminius may have learned from Zabarella something of the art of clear reasoning and exposition, which would give rise to the definition of Arminius—on the part of a number of commentators—as essentially a pre-Enlightenment thinker. Nevertheless, Arminius's own work as both teacher and author was about to concern itself with precisely those areas of theological dispute that Zabarella avoided so studiously. Dispute and violent dissent were, however, not at all loved by Arminius, who did everything he could to contain the theological issues that his teaching addressed within the bounds of civil discussion and debate. For the purposes of this book, Arminius's major text is his *On Reconciling Religious Dissensions among Christians*, the farewell oration delivered when he ended his term as *rector magnificus* of the University of Leiden in 1606. The English translator of the works of Arminius, James Nichols, himself a convinced Arminian, describes it as the oration in which Arminius "develops those sound principles of religious liberty which were espoused and defended by his successors, and on account of which the Dutch Remonstrants acquired the best portion of their just celebrity."[115]

In the opening part of his oration Arminius claims that no discord is more shocking and hideous than that about religion: "Every one thinks that his life, (that is, his spiritual life) and the liberty which is proper for that life, are included in religion and its exercise." What has happened instead is that "[r]eligion itself, through the vicious corruption of men, has been made a cause of dissension, and has become the field in which they may perpetually exercise themselves in cruel and bloody contests." Arminius continues in a lighter vein, claiming that religion in his time "experiences almost the same fate, as the young lady mentioned by Plutarch, who was addressed by a number of suitors; and when each of them found that she could not become entirely his own, they divided her body into parts, and thus not one of them obtained possession of her whole person. This is the nature of discord, to disperse and destroy matters of the greatest consequence." The lighter vein does not last long. Like Jacopo Aconcio before him, Arminius sees the religious wars of his time as the work of Satan, "that most bitter enemy of truth and peace, and the most wily disseminator of falsehood and dissension." But Satan acts through the minds of men, corrupting them through blindness, anger, pride, and a hatred of peace or concord. For Arminius, it is a false remedy for this condition to prohibit all controversies respecting religion. On the contrary, the remedy is "*an orderly and free convention of the parties that differ from one another.*" It should be held in a place "free from danger and violence, and secured against all surprise and ambuscades, in order that those who are summoned may come to it, remain in it, and return to their homes, in perfect safety." The action to be adopted in the synod must be "a regular and accurate debate on the matters in controversy; mature consultation concerning them, and complete liberty for everyone to declare his opinion." Above all, Arminius insists, the synod must not attempt to obtrude by force upon others those resolutions that may have found the most consent: "For this reflection should always suggest itself,—'Though this Synod appears to have done all things conscientiously, it is possible, that, after all, it has committed an error of judgement.' Such a diffidence and moderation of mind will possess greater power, and will have more influence, than any immoderate or excessive rigor can have, on the consciences both of the contumacious dissidents, and of the whole body of the faithful; because, according to Lactantius, 'To recommend faith to others, we must make it the subject of persuasion and not of compulsion.'" The oration ends with an eloquent appeal: "The God of Peace, who dignifies the peacemakers alone with the ample title of 'children' (Matt. V. 9), has called us to the practice of peace."[116]

The discussion over Arminianism was to be far from peaceful; it was extremely tense and complex, and involved most of the major religious figures of the early seventeenth century. We can take, for example, Marco Antonio de Dominis, a Croatian who became the Catholic archbishop of Spalato (the modern town of Split). In 1616 he fled to England after bitter criticism of the papacy and the Catholic Church. In London, de Dominis was persuaded by the then archbishop of Canterbury, George Abbott, to take up the side of the orthodox Calvinists in the disputes held at the Synod of Dort. De Dominis himself, however, resented such pressure being put on him, and shortly afterward he left England for Rome where, in spite of a public return to his original

Catholic faith, he was soon imprisoned and tried by the Inquisition. He died in prison before his trial finished, which did not prevent the Catholic authorities from condemning him as an impenitent heretic and burning his dead body in the Campo dei Fiori in Rome.

Widely considered by both sides of the religious divide in his own times as a traitorous turncoat, concerned with furthering his own personal interests, de Dominis has recently been revalued as one of the last major figures of post-Tridentine Europe to have seriously contemplated a religious reunion of the warring Christian faiths.[117] As far as the Arminian question was concerned, in many ways de Dominis sided with the Remonstrants. He thought, echoing Arminius himself, that decisions on religious questions directed toward the public peace should be taken by the temporal rather than the religious authorities. He contrasted with Arminius, however, insofar as he was against the very idea of public disputes over the niceties of religious doctrine, claiming that they render even harsher the hatred and divisions among the common people. Both sides, he claimed, in a text titled *In Expectation of the Golden Age*, should embrace each other in a spirit of charity and union in religion, thus achieving stability and rendering the people stable also by establishing for them the essential articles of religion.

It is clearly significant that the Synod of Dort of 1618–19 coincided (even if the coincidence was largely fortuitous) with the publication in London in 1619 by the king's printer, John Bill, of the first Italian edition of Paolo Sarpi's *History of the Council of Trent*. This remarkable and much discussed text shows an extraordinary capacity on the part of Sarpi to illustrate, with the help of an impressive display of documentary evidence, the complex proceedings of the Catholic Council, whose meetings between 1542 and 1552 had been surrounded by considerable secrecy. It also revealed how the council, which had originally convened as an attempt to resolve the religious disputes of the sixteenth century together with the new Protestant churches, had by mutual discussion and consent developed and concluded as a formidable statement of the absolute power and dominion of the Catholic world and within it of the papacy and the Roman Curia.[118]

Sarpi understood the Council of Trent—and disapproved of it—as a declaration of war on all those forces hostile to the Catholic cause, calling it with critical asperity "the Iliad of our century." His *History of the Council of Trent* was far too critical of papal absolutism to be published in the Catholic parts of Europe, even in the relatively tolerant Venice; the manuscript was smuggled to England, where it was published in London, aided by de Dominis himself, who wrote for it a strongly anti-Catholic preface addressed to the English king James I. Sarpi, through his Servite friend Fulgenzio Micanzio, criticized this preface as too openly antipapal and aggressive, considering it to be largely responsible for the bitter reaction to the book in Rome, where within a few months it was placed on the Index of Prohibited Books. But beyond the vexed question of how Sarpi's text came to be printed in London, and to what extent Sarpi approved or disapproved of the mode of its printing (questions that will be taken up and developed in chapter 5 of this book), there were clearly analogies in the mind of de Dominis between the uncompromisingly Calvinist outcome of the Synod of Dort (an outcome of which Sarpi himself tended to approve) and the uncompromisingly papal outcome of the Council of Trent (an outcome of which Sarpi, too, disapproved). In both cases de Dominis was concerned with underlining "the relativism and selective choices, often of a political nature, that lay behind the production of and disputes over religious dogma."[119] Sarpi himself may not have agreed with de Dominis about the outcome of the Synod of Dort, but he was certainly in agreement with the statement cited above. Both men saw religious dogma, so often rooted in primarily political concerns, as the foremost danger of the Europe of their times—a danger that, if peaceful solutions were not forthcoming, would inevitably lead to bloodshed and war.

By 1619, however, both de Dominis and Sarpi had become hostages to fortune. As they themselves had tirelessly testified, the geographical and dogmatic boundaries between the Catholic and Protestant worlds had been deeply engraved on the map of Europe in the course of the previous century, and were predictably about to be fought over and contested with unprecedented violence and merciless massacres. The Thirty Years' War had just begun and would hold vast areas of Germany and central Europe groaning in its iron grip until more than one generation had perished in a seething sea of blood. Only in 1648 would the exhausted armies of one of the world's most disastrous wars of religion finally agree to the Peace of Westphalia. This consigned to Europe a profoundly modified power structure within which the modern nation-states could at last begin to develop, each with their own specific religious characteristics. But by that time, all the figures we have been concerned with in this chapter, whose warning voices had not been heeded, were long since dead.

CHAPTER 3

Libertas philosophandi, or the Liberty of Thought

Between the Prince and Parliament

The course taken by both the political and religious discussions of the sixteenth century has demonstrated how a series of tensions were born in the wake both of the new humanist movement of the early Renaissance in Italy, with its rigorous return to the pre-Christian cultures of ancient Greece and Rome, and then of the rise of the Protestant Reformation in northern Europe. Although very different in their characteristics and aims, both of them were movements that broke up the compact and unified culture of the European Middle Ages, articulated within a Christian world picture characterized by the dominion of a Catholic or universal church. The breaking up of that picture would have dramatic and long-lasting effects on the search for new and more stable forms of liberty. On the one hand most of the new princes of the time, including the pope and his papacy, moved rapidly and incisively toward an entrenchment of centralized and often programmatically oppressive forms of power that severely limited, where they did not annihilate altogether, all those forms of newly autonomous inquiry to which the humanist movement and the Reformed religions had given rise. The Protestant reformers, above all, were constantly obliged to fight for their continued existence against the violent reactions of the authorities of the time. In many cases this lead to the new religious communities themselves assuming apocalyptic and militantly aggressive tones that were not immediately conducive to a concept of liberty beyond that of the survival of the group concerned. On the other hand, a new insistence on the individual conscience as the ultimate locus of any meaningful form of religious liberty was powerfully expressed in the reformation theology itself. An analogous insistence in the dimension of rational thought was starting to turn into a new philosophy of mind centered on the individual thinker rather than on universal precepts. So it is hardly surprising to find, in the final decades of the sixteenth century, a renewed concern with the problem that Niccolò Machiavelli had raised so incisively in its early years—that is, how these new liberties of thought and expression were to be guaranteed against those who wished to suppress them.

An inward-looking concern with "conscience" was no invention of the sixteenth century; it went back, in classical times, to the enigma of the sibyl: "know thyself." It was in the Middle Ages that it became associated specifically with religious faith, particularly among the medieval mystics. Then the Protestant movement gave a new impetus to concern with conscience, and particularly to the right of the individual to follow the dictates of conscience in making decisions regarding faith. As we have seen in considering the figure of John Brenz, however, this new insistence on conscience could have a negative outcome with respect to the concept of liberty, for if conscience was considered as the voice of God within the individual, its dictates became, by definition, indisputable. Those who held what were considered by the reformers as mistaken beliefs could end up being thought of as having no conscience at all. Such extreme conclusions, however, were by no means universally accepted. Donald Kelley, in a study of what he considers the "rise of ideology" in the sixteenth century, above all in the wake of the disputes caused by the new multiplicity of religious doctrines and beliefs, notes the positive dimension of the new insistence on "liberty of conscience." He quotes from Martin Luther's *Table Talk* Luther's reported boast, "I don't understand law, but I am an authority on matters of conscience."[1]

It was nevertheless inevitable, as Kelley points out, that the concept would pass from the private sphere of faith and become politicized. Both the political and ecclesiastical platforms of the French Reformed Huguenots in the 1560s, which gave rise to the French civil wars of religion, were founded, as the Prince of Condé declared from Orleans, on "the holy liberty of our consciences."[2] On the other hand, it was not long before a realization became widespread that the churches of the period (or "denominations" as the Protestant historiography of the period has preferred to call them) were—all of them, in their various ways—intent above all on survival in a profoundly disrupted and intensely violent world. It was hardly likely that the churches themselves would be either willing or able to function as guarantees for any kind of general principle of liberty of conscience or of thought, for throughout the various communities into which they were fragmented they were attempting above all to impose their own faith.

It is debatable how much of a distinction needs to be made with respect to such a statement when referring to what has become known since the 1960s as the Radical Reformation. Certainly important claims for a "liberal ferment" of ideas are made by modern historians who come from within such religious denominations as the Anabaptists or Mennonites when studying their own sixteenth-century origins. A case in point is the close attention to themes of religious liberty and toleration on the part of George Huntston Williams in *The Radical Reformation*, especially the pages he dedicates to the Waterland congregations of Dutch Anabaptists. In 1581, with the political support of William of Orange and inspired by the writings on religious toleration of the freethinker Dirck Volckertszoon Coornhert, the Dutch Anabaptists, according to Williams, instituted a degree of religious liberty that was remarkably advanced for that time. Not all historians of the early modern world, however, have accepted this claim. Antonio Rotondò, writing on Williams's volume some years after its publication, sounded a note of caution by pointing out that such claims tend to derive more from a historical perspective that can take account of future developments such as the English Revolution and the American War of Independence than from a coherent awareness of such themes on the part of the early radical reformers themselves. Throughout the sixteenth century not only the Catholic Church but also the ever increasing variety of Protestant churches, sects, and denominations were all fighting for survival in a bitterly conflicting situation of doctrinal ferment and dissent.[3]

The princes or monarchs of the time could in some rare cases be more convincingly appealed to, though nothing guaranteed that an illuminated prince would pass on his libertarian views to his successor. Giordano Bruno arrived in Prague after having been obliged to leave Wittenberg, where he had been successfully teaching philosophy for two years at the university under the protection of a tolerant Lutheran prince. After that prince's death, however, a more intransigent Calvinist regime was not prepared to accept the services of a freethinker such as Bruno. The tolerant and broad-minded prince rarely passed laws guaranteeing liberty in his domain and, when he did, such laws could always be changed by a less tolerant successor or at times even by the same prince, who would predictably come under pressure from the authoritarian voices in his territory. For example, the remarkably liberal Edict of Beaulieu, issued by the French king Henry III in 1576, granted considerable liberty of worship to the warring French Protestants, even instituting for the first time in France special courts of appeal to ensure the judicial implementation of such rights. Soon, however, Henry came under pressure from the increasingly powerful ultra-Catholic Guise faction. The noble family of Guise had obtained considerable power in France in the first half of the sixteenth century, and maintained a strong influence throughout the century by adopting an extreme position of fidelity to the Roman Catholic Church and fomenting war on the new Protestants. It was not long before Henry passed another edict virtually canceling all the new liberties for Protestant citizens that he had so recently conceded.

The attention of many of the most reasonable and perceptive spirits of the time thus became directed toward another, rather different kind of institution: the parliaments or general councils inherited by the sixteenth century from both the classical and the medieval worlds. It was there, according to Machiavelli, that liberty could and should be guaranteed not by ordinary laws but by the *ordini*, or constitutional laws, that formed the foundation of the community concerned.

The idea of a parliament, in the broad sense of a civic council of elected citizens involved in an activity of decision making and debate, derived ultimately from models supplied by ancient Greece and Rome. The Greek Areopagus on the one hand or the ancient Roman Senate on the other were considered in the Renaissance as the original models for such institutions; and we have seen Machiavelli proposing a reading of the Roman history of Titus Livy as the most appropriate preparation for the formulation of modern republican councils in Florence. Medieval parliaments, however, had to a large extent transformed the classical picture by introducing as their major point of reference the feudal monarch or prince, whose parliament in many cases originated as a means of containing the overbearing arrogance of the barons. The medieval parliaments were also obliged to take account of ecclesiastical power organized, after the official acceptance of Christianity by imperial Rome, in structural forms previously unknown to the classical world. Throughout the continent of Europe, parliaments developed with certain constant characteristics; all of them originated as an exercise in representation of the orders or estates of the medieval world: the nobility and gentry, the clergy, and the commons. The European parliaments, however, developed from these common origins on a national or often a regional level with a bewildering variety of forms.[4]

Some of these parliamentary histories have assumed a particular significance for many observers, not only within the culture of the time but also in the work of more modern historians and commentators. The violent struggle between the republican councils of Florence and the Medici family, with its ambitions for princely rule—which Machiavelli introduced us to—has assumed a central role in the study of more modern democratic institutions in works such as John Pocock's *The Machiavellian Moment* and the studies of his many followers.[5] However, the survival of the Venetian republican councils, analyzed by Gasparo Contarini in his widely read study *The Commonwealth and Government of Venice* (1543), also attracted much attention in both early modern Europe and beyond. In 1656 James Harrington, outlining to Oliver Cromwell the principles of government on which he had based his utopian *Commonwealth of Oceana*, referred frequently to the constitution of republican Venice, which was formed, in his opinion, on lines not dissimilar to those of ancient Rome: "Venice consisteth of the *pregati* proposing, and sometimes resolving too, of the great council or assembly of the people, in whom the result is constitutively; as also of the doge, the signory, the censors, the *dieci,* the quaranties, and other magistrats executing."[6] Contarini considered Venice the only city in a violent and blood-stained Europe that maintained the "quiet safety" of its citizens, for it combined a government of the nobility with popular authority in such a way that they remained equally balanced and content.[7] Venice became renowned for a tolerance of free thought and discussion that attracted many early modern intellectuals to its shores. The ability with which republican Venice (in contrast to Florence) maintained a remarkable degree of independence right up to the advent of Napoleon Bonaparte at the end of the eighteenth century was an extraordinary achievement in a period dominated by the absolutist ambitions of the princes, and it was widely admired by other European cultures that often tried to emulate its governmental skills. Even so, liberty of thought and expression was only relatively free in Venice, which never renounced its fidelity to the Roman Catholic Church and was obliged to institute in its territory both inquisitional courts and the new Indexes of Prohibited Books, though their authority tended to be enforced with less severity than in Rome.

A great deal of specialized attention has also been dedicated in recent years to the French situation, and to the ways in which the French *parlements*, both locally and at the national level in Paris, faced up to the religious crisis of the sixteenth century and to the pluralism of thought to which it immediately gave rise. The French Estates-General were divided into three chambers representing the three medieval estates: the Catholic clergy, the nobles, and the commons. In France the Roman Catholic Inquisition never became sufficiently organized to stamp out the Protestant Reformation in the same way it succeeded in doing in Italy. This was to a large extent due to the fact that the Reformed Christians of France, known as the Huguenots, included some of the major intellectuals and legal experts of the period; they were sufficiently strong to unite in a movement that, although always a minority, achieved in the sixteenth and early seventeenth centuries significant forms of official recognition, if only at the cost of civil war. The French wars included one of the most ferocious religious massacres of all times. Carried out on St. Bartholomew's Night in 1572, the massacre, ordered by the French king Charles IX under the sway (so it was widely rumored) of his Italian mother, the Medici queen Catherine, saw many thousands of Protestants killed in a few hours, and deeply wounded the consciences of the entire Protestant world. Whether the massacre diminished the influence of the Huguenot movement or gave it a new lease of life through the theme of Protestant martyrdom is still a subject of debate today.[8]

What is more directly of interest here is the way in which this traumatic event encouraged the Huguenots to think of drafting republican constitutions for the cities in which they dominated, constitutions that—it has been observed—demonstrate an interesting combination of Calvinist piety and Spartan virtue. It has been claimed that the author of one such document owed much to the classical ideal of the city-state and to Machiavelli's ideas for the reform of Florence.[9] The document calls for an end of the afflictions of the persecuted Protestants by instituting political elections of the chief citizens of the town, whose results must be announced in a public place so that the new commander can govern both in the case of peace or war "in the interests of civil life and good order." Further developments of this Huguenot interest in electoral procedures extend them to bodies envisaged as governing at a national as well as at a local level. In one document it is specifically stated that whether the elected representatives of this larger council agree or disagree on a policy, "the assembly will record their views, and read them out" so that everything is clear to all the participants as correct custom requires.[10] These documents illustrate the widespread Protestant dissatisfaction with the French Estates-General, and the official *parlements*, most of which remained firmly under Catholic influence and largely subject to royal control.

Apart from such empirical attempts at an institutional level, a number of major theoretical political treatises emerged from the French Protestant struggles of the sixteenth century, which would have a considerable influence on the development of parliamentary institutions in the centuries to come. Francis Hotman was a distinguished professor of law and a humanist scholar. His *Francogallia*, published in 1573, applied humanist scholarship to a study of ancient forms of Franco-German parliamentary councils, presented as models for solving the political and religious crises of his time. In chapter 11 of his treatise, titled "On the Inviolable Authority of the Public Council and the Kinds of Things Decided There," Hotman claims that their powers consisted of "deposing kings; then, the power of deciding on peace or war, of making public law, of conferring high honours, governorships, and regencies." Finally he concludes that they had "power over all things that, in the usage of the common people, are called 'affairs of state.'"[11] These were radical claims indeed, in a period when Hotman's Catholic countryman Jean Bodin was theorizing absolute monarchy in terms precluding any possibility of a division of powers. Another distinguished French Protestant of noble lineage, Philippe du Plessis-Mornay, had close ties with the English nobility and above all with Sir Philip Sidney. Du Plessis-Mornay is commonly thought to be the author of a treatise titled *Disputes against Tyrants* published in 1579 under the pseudonym Stephano Iunio. It is concerned with whether it is right to depose a tyrannical ruler, if necessary by force, if he should violate his oath or fail to convene a council. Medieval authorities such as Baldus de Ubaldis are called on to justify such action, even in the case of the pope, for "who can possibly doubt that the public council may depose a tyrant and deprive him of his kingdom?"[12]

Radical voices such as these gained only a very limited hearing in terms of reforming the parliamentary councils in the France of their time. When the Protestants did finally achieve an important recognition in 1576, it was Henry III who conceded a considerable measure of freedom of worship to the French Huguenots with his Edict of Beaulieu. It can be debated whether this concession was made on the basis of a principle of freedom of conscience or instead as a question of political calculation. In his essay "On Freedom of Conscience" (1578), Michel de Montaigne bitterly criticized the "inordinate zeal" that had inspired the defenders of Christianity in the early years of its affirmation, claiming that such zeal had "caused more harm to literature than all the fires started by the Barbarians." He further went on to defend from contemporary attack the figure of the Roman emperor Julian, who had attempted to stamp out the new Christianity from the Roman Empire. Julian, according to the best historical sources, was a morally exemplary and valiant emperor—even if as an orthodox Catholic believer Montaigne is constrained to recognize Julian's pagan religion, based on animal sacrifices to the gods, as "vicious." When Julian did finally concede some freedom of belief to the new Christians, according to Montaigne, he did it in the hope that their internal disagreements would finish by destroying the new religion itself. Montaigne subtly suggests that a similar hope probably lay behind the recent concession by the French monarch, inspired more by empirical political considerations than by moral concerns. Montaigne's essay leaves the reader with the suspicion that it would be hypocritical and naive to think that the recent edict was inspired by noble principles of freedom or tolerance of free thought.[13]

It is a debated question whether Montaigne himself was the author of the passionately radical tract titled *On Voluntary Servitude*, which he praises with eloquent admiration in his essay *On Friendship*.[14] Montaigne tells his reader that this tract had been written by his close friend Étienne de la Boétie. Montaigne claims that he had wished to publish this text as part of his essay, but was unable to do so as it had only recently appeared from the workshop of a Protestant publisher who had used it incorrectly to further his own success. La Boétie, who had written this text in his youth, had died some years previously, but Montaigne continues to consider him as a soul mate with whom he claims to have lived a "seamless" relationship. Although La Boétie's tract is far less subtly ambiguous than Montaigne's own writings on the subject of liberty, some commentators think that Montaigne chose this way as a kind of ruse that allowed him (using La Boétie's name) to write about liberty from tyrannical rule far more directly and openly than his public position as a mature local councilor would have allowed him to do.

Whether or not *On Voluntary Servitude* was written by Montaigne or by the young La Boétie himself, it undoubtedly represents a remarkably radical and overt statement against any kind of monarchical rule. Sometimes known with the title *Against One-Man Rule*, it virtually brands every kind of monarchical rule—whether achieved through popular election, force of arms, or dynastic succession—as inevitably condemned to culminate in tyranny. When power resides in a single figure, many are willing to become slaves, and voluntarily to bond themselves in servitude in order to achieve wealth, influence, and reflected glory. To break this voluntary bond of servitude requires courage: "it is remarkable to hear about the courage that liberty puts in the hearts of those who defend it," declares the author of this fiery pamphlet.[15]

Various ways of restoring liberty from tyrannical rule are suggested in this tract. At times it seems enough simply to disobey the tyrant, for that will quickly reveal the fragile bases of a power that will thus remain naked and undone. Yet this is rarely achieved, as all peoples fall into forgetfulness of liberty, and tyranny encourages cowardice and despondency. Furthermore, tyrants pretend to act as tribunes of the people, when in fact they are inflicting evils on them. The people allow themselves to be so deceived, especially when the tyrants use the force of religious belief as an instrument of power. Like Machiavelli, the author of this tract compares tyranny to a disease in the body that grows and spreads until the whole kingdom is affected. When that happens it becomes very unlikely that liberty will ever be restored to that kingdom, and for this reason tyrants and their accomplices, in their afterlife, deserve a special place in hell.

It is usually conceded that Montaigne was one of the councilors who advised the Protestant prince Henry of Navarre, who converted to Catholicism when he inherited the French throne upon the death of the childless Henry III in 1589. As Henry IV of France, Navarre granted major concessions to the French Protestants in 1598, allowing them freedom of worship through the Edict of Nantes, which was issued by royal command rather than by parliamentary concession. The French parliamentary councils, however, were called in to acknowledge and support the new measures. The important degree of toleration granted to the Protestants by Henry IV's Edict of Nantes included the formation of Chambers of the Edict, which were special law courts attached to the local estates or parliaments wherever the Protestants were numerous enough to create problems of a legal nature. These had accompanied the previous measures of toleration of 1576, but had proved inadequate to their task. The remarkable novelty of the Edict of Nantes was precisely that it contained firm and secure legal guarantees allowing the Protestants not only to exercise their religion freely but also to take legal action where such a right was denied them. This gave more strength to the central articles of the Edict, such as Article 6, which reads, "We allow those who follow the religion known as the reformed one to live and reside in all the cities and places in our kingdom, and all those areas that obey our laws, without being subject to enquiry, being vexed, molested, or constrained to do anything with respect to religion that goes against their conscience, or for that reason to be searched for in their houses or wherever they wish to live."[16] The Edict of Nantes led to a long period of much needed peace in France. In the course of the seventeenth century, however, the Estates-General gradually succeeded in eroding the privileges accorded by the edict to the Protestant faith, until finally Louis XIV abolished it altogether in 1685; the Huguenots were obliged to flee into exile or convert back to the Catholic faith.[17]

This only partial success story in terms of a parliamentary recognition of freedom of thought and expression was counterbalanced by the remarkable success obtained by the parliamentary assembly of the Low Countries where, in 1581, the people suddenly found themselves with a republic as their governing body. A full consideration of this event would require a specialized study of the particular circumstances that gave rise to it, which would go well beyond the terms of our subject in this book.[18] However, it is clear that the unusually frequent meetings of this assembly, which met regularly between 1499 and 1576, usually in Brussels, would have given the citizens involved an extraordinary experience in the handling of parliamentary procedure unknown in other European countries at this time.[19] After negotiations by the parliament of the Low Countries with a number of European princes invited to assume the government of their territory had proved unsatisfactory, they issued a declaration of independence on July 26, 1581, that, it has been claimed, "gave the cue for the English parliamentary war, and the English Revolution, to the American Declaration of Independence, to the better side of the French Revolution, and to the public spirit which has slowly and imperfectly recovered liberty from despotism."[20]

The declaration of independence is above all concerned with justifying the sloughing off of monarchical authority in favor of parliamentary rule. It does this by claiming that when a prince fails to govern wisely "and instead of defending his subjects oppresses them, denying their ancient privileges and customs, and commanding them as if they were slaves, he should no longer be called a prince but a tyrant and need not be recognized as their ruler." This is only justified, however, when the decision to liberate the country from tyrannical rule is made in the parliament by the estates of the country concerned.[21] There was little possibility at this stage of European history for such a parliament to govern alone for any length of time, and both in the wealthy northern province of Holland, where the House of Orange was to continue its rule, and in the southern province, where the Spanish attempted an abortive absolutist coup at Antwerp in 1583, monarchical presence remained to be reckoned with. However, in both provinces the institution of the estates survived, held together by the Union of Utrecht. This ensured that the Low Countries were saved from the absolute monarchical rule that was to afflict so many parts of Europe in the seventeenth century and later. Indeed, Holland in particular would become internationally considered in the seventeenth-century Enlightenment as the European center of libertarian culture and publishing and a haven for many radical intellectuals and *philosophes*—including René Descartes—who were unable to live and work peacefully elsewhere.[22]

The English Parliament of the sixteenth century experienced no such revolutionary success as that achieved by the Dutch. It did, however, succeed in being confirmed as an indispensable instrument in the monarchical rule of the Tudor dynasty, not only under Henry VIII but also during the long reign of Elizabeth I. Some of the experiences consumed during the not infrequent sessions of the sixteenth-century Parliament in London would provide a crucial

CHAPTER 3

foundation for the dramatic upheavals of the seventeenth century, which would ultimately see the British Parliament emerge as the major center of political power and debate within the history of modern Britain.

The first significant parliamentary victory of the sixteenth century in England was due to the political acumen of Henry VIII, who realized that the deeply disturbing rupture caused by his decision to cut Britain off from its traditional ties with the Catholic Church in Rome and to create a national Anglican Church would be accepted by the population only if it were ratified by Parliament itself. The result was the Statute in Restraint of Appeals passed in 1533 decreeing that "the Appeles in suche Cases as have ben used to be pursued to the See of Rome shall not be from hensforth had ne used but within this Realme." The act justifies this change, in conservative rather than revolutionary terms, with an appeal to those old authentic histories and chronicles in which it is expressly said that "this Realme of Englond" is an empire, or a body politic composed of all sorts and degrees of people for whom both the spiritual life and earthly justice is to be determined within the realm and not from outside.[23]

The problem that this and many succeeding parliaments would have to face was that the act also represented a decided entrenchment of the monarchical power of the king himself, and of "the Dignitie and Roiall Estate of the Imperiall Crowne of the same." The "Queen's Speech" of Elizabeth I, on her first summoning of Parliament in 1559—actually pronounced for her by an official representative in her stead—makes the veiled threat that "divers things that are to be done here in Parliament, might by means be reformed without Parliament." Only then does it go on to lay down for the members what areas of lawmaking they will be expected to debate, making it clear that a principal duty will be to "supply and relieve" the financial losses that have of late happened to inflict the Crown. Elizabeth's frequent scolding of her parliamentary members for not always respecting the royal prerogative, her "great disliking" when the Parliament of 1580 decided on a public fast of the members in the Temple Church in London without requesting her consent, and her constant reproofs to Parliament for those speeches that "dealt more rashly in some Things, than was fit for them to do" were always counterbalanced by her "most hearty thanks unto both Houses for their great and good Care of her Highness's Safety" and by promises that another Parliament would soon be convened.[24] Throughout the sixteenth century, the English Parliament met and debated, but it remained firmly under royal control.

Parliament's major achievement during the century was the prominence it gave to the problem of free speech. When in his famous address to Henry VIII of 1523 the speaker of the House of Commons, Sir Thomas More, petitioned for freedom of speech, he made it clear that the value he was defending was not to be seen as one of many but instead as the essential condition for genuine parliamentary proceedings to take place. For More it was a necessity "for every man to discharge his consciens, and boldlye in every thinge incident among [us] to declare his advise; and whatsoever happen to any man to say, [that] it may like your noble maiestye, of your inestimable goodness, to take all in good parte, interpreting every mans word, howe uncomingly soever they be couched, to proceed yeat of good zeale towards the profit of your realme." Precisely because the lower house, the House of Commons, contained representatives of the common people, More found it imperative to pay attention also to those who lacked an elegant rhetorical style. So he explained to Henry VIII that "it often happeneth that, likewise as much folly is uttered with painted polished speache, so many, boystyous and rude in language, see deepe indeed, and give right substanciall councell."[25]

In 1576, long after Sir Thomas More had been executed for his refusal to take the oath of loyalty to the new English church, freedom of speech again became a central concern of Parliament when Peter Wentworth of Cornwall, a member of the House of Commons, was arrested on orders from Elizabeth for having defended freedom of speech as his right. Addressing himself to the speaker, Wentworth said, "I find written in a little Volume these words in effect: Sweet is the name of Liberty, but the thing it self a value beyond all inestimable Treasure. So much the more it behoveth us to take care lest we contenting our selves with the sweetness of the name, lose and forgo the thing, being of the greatest value that can come unto this noble realm." Wentworth then claimed that "the inestimable Treasure" is the use of liberty in the House of Commons. He continued by developing a seven-point defense of freedom of speech in Parliament, which contained the explicit assertion that there must be open and fearless discussion of all questions of public concern, even those that may be considered "hurtful or perilous to the Prince or State": "What incommodity doth grow thereby? Verily I think none, nay will you have me to say my simple opinion therein, much good cometh thereof; how forsooth, for by the darkness of the Night the brightness of the Sun sheweth more excellent and clear, and how can truth appear and conquer until falsehood and all subtilties that should shadow and darken it be found out? For it is offered in this place a piece of fine Needle-work unto them that are most skilful therein, for there cannot be a false stitch (God aiding us) but will be found out." Wentworth went on to note that "sometimes a Message is brought into the House (from the Queen's Majesty) either of Commanding or Inhibiting, very injurious to the freedom of Speech and consultation."[26] What he was in effect advocating was the possibility of parliamentary debate and decisions taking place freely without interference from the crown. Elizabeth was not amused. Some years later, in 1593, she instructed her official spokesman, when representing her in Parliament for that year, to broach directly the question of free speech. Her message was, "It shalbe meete therefore that each man of yow conteyne his speech within the boundes of loyaltie and good discrecion, being assured, that as the contrary is punishable in all men, so most of all in them, that take upon them to be Counsellors and procurators of the commonwealth."[27]

The sixteenth-century English Parliament, then, saw a radical right of freedom of speech being powerfully declared; but it also saw that right being limited by princely power. By and large it seems fair to say that the sixteenth-century European parliaments made important progress toward a full-scale defense of freedom of thought and speech. They were, however, still too fragile and subject to royal control to act as a bulwark in defense of the individual citizen. Laws passed in favor of the freedom of the press, for example, would only start to be systematically considered in the centuries to come. The philosophers, scientists, and writers of the sixteenth and early seventeenth centuries remained frighteningly exposed to the prevailing atmosphere of violent polemic and institutional oppression. Patronage in high places, among the most liberal of the nobles and those in power, remained their best guarantee of a relative freedom of thought and expression, though always subject to the fickle changes of fortune's uncertain ways and whims.

The New Drama: William Shakespeare

Freedom of thought and speech is not only a political or a religious problem, but clearly also an artistic or more generally cultural one as well. The writers of the early modern world—whether poets, philosophers, or cultured men of letters such as Erasmus of Rotterdam or Michel de Montaigne—were caught up from the beginning in an almost insoluble dilemma, for the humanist movement of the early years of the Renaissance had revived much of the literature of ancient Greece and Rome, initiating a modern inquiry into both nature and the world of human affairs that defied the limits to human endeavor imposed by the medieval Christian society and its still universal church. Yet the freedom of inquiry and expression that the new humanists thought of as an essential prerogative for the fulfilling of their task was by no means always allowed them by the power structures of their time and was, as we have seen, almost nowhere guaranteed by law. Indeed, the religious struggles of their violent times created new and powerful obstacles to the free development of philosophical thought as well as the creative arts. This gave rise, in almost all the major writers of the early modern world, to a complex series of tensions between the author and authority—tensions that became an integral part of their world and of their works. Here attention will be directed toward one playwright in particular, William Shakespeare, considered not so much for the singularity of his remarkable poetic and dramatic achievement as in his relationships with other figures of his time who were deeply involved in a discourse on liberty and the toleration of new and unorthodox forms of thought.

On February 17, 1600, Giordano Bruno was burned at the stake in the Campo dei Fiori in Rome, accused of being a heretic who had refused to repent. Bruno had claimed that his views about God were those of a philosopher, arrived at through a long process of thought, and that there was nothing that he needed to repent. He added that he saw himself as a martyr, although without specifically indicating for what cause. These words have been interpreted variously by commentators as signifying martyrdom for the rights of the philosopher to proceed in his inquiry without interference from the theologians, or for a more general right for the liberty of thought itself.[28] Whatever meaning Bruno intended to have attached to these last words, news of his death arrived surprisingly quickly in England. According to a contemporary document that has recently been at the center of some attention, the Earl of Essex was informed of Bruno's execution only a few weeks after the event by an agent employed to send him news from Europe.[29] The message reminded Essex of Bruno's stay in England in the 1580s, where it is known that he had connections with aristocratic circles, in particular with the Italianate circle of the Earl of Leicester, uncle of Sir Philip Sidney, to whom Bruno had dedicated two of his philosophical works.[30]

At the time of Bruno's visit Essex was one of Elizabeth's great favorites, but by 1600 he was already in disgrace after disobeying orders from the queen during a mission in Ireland. The next year—having failed to attend to the words of Machiavelli—he attempted an abortive plot against the throne and was immediately beheaded. Essex's fall was a major blow for many Elizabethan intellectuals at the turn of the century, for he was widely admired for his courage and culture, and some hoped that he could become the childless Elizabeth's successor to the throne. Essex is thought to have had connections with the theater of the time: he was certainly much admired by Ben Jonson, who may have been part of the secretariat—which is thought to have included promising young intellectuals—that Essex attempted to put together in the 1590s. However that may be, Jonson would later write of him as the "noble and high" earl.[31]

Jonson's early plays were being performed in just these years by the major company of actors of the moment, the Lord Chamberlain's Men. The principal playwright for this company was William Shakespeare, who in 1595 had written a historical drama on the figure of the unfortunate and inept English king Richard II. Richard had been forced to cede his crown to one of history's most successful plotters, Henry Bolingbroke (or Bullingbrooke), who thus became Henry IV. On the evening before their abortive coup in 1601, Essex's followers are known—in what remains in many respects a still obscure episode—to have requested the Lord Chamberlain's Men to play a drama about Richard II in a special performance—which, with some reluctance, they agreed to do. Although the known documents relating to this episode offer no proof of the case, it is commonly assumed by his editors that the play concerned was Shakespeare's *Richard II*.[32] When Essex came up for the trial that eventually led to his execution, this episode was raised for discussion, and one

CHAPTER 3

of Shakespeare's fellow actors and a shareholder of the Lord Chamberlain's Men was required to give evidence. He seems to have been successful in convincing the judges that the company had nothing directly to do with the Essex uprising, for they remained unscathed, though the intermediary from Essex's faction who had requested them to put on the play was condemned and executed. The judicial authorities thus seem to have made a distinction between the intentions of the dramatist and of the actors who actually staged the text, and of those who made political use of it by commanding it to be staged on that particular evening. However, such a distinction should not be overemphasized, for Shakespeare's play had already been the subject of an official order censoring the scene showing the king actually ceding the crown to a usurper. This is known to be the case, because the first printed edition of the play, published in 1597, does not include this scene, which was only added in a fourth printing in 1608, after Elizabeth's death and with James I safely on the English throne.

It is not known whether the play commanded by the Essex faction—always assuming that it was Shakespeare's text rather than a production of some other contemporary version of Richard II's story—included the deposition scene or not. The fact that the earliest texts of Shakespeare's play, published in 1597 and 1598, did not include the deposition scene in any case reveals that the Elizabethan authorities were well aware of the political dangers that such a scene could represent. The aging and childless Elizabeth survived Essex's plot, continuing to reign until her natural death in 1603 when she was succeeded, according to her own wish, by the far less popular James VI of Scotland, the Protestant son of the Catholic Mary, Queen of Scots—another unsuccessful plotter, who had been beheaded on an order from her cousin Elizabeth I. It is generally recognized that the last years of Elizabeth's reign were tense and troubled times in England, with the problem of the succession looming large on the horizon and with religious oppression, at times including torture and death, much increased due to the mounting hostility to the Anglican Church both from the Roman Catholics and the radical reformers. It seems unlikely to have been a coincidence that in just those years Shakespeare's dramatic art assumed a tragic mood. His first full-fledged tragedy was *The Tragedie of Hamlet, Prince of Denmarke*, probably written in 1600; and there has long been speculation concerning a date that coincides so neatly not only with the downfall of Essex but also with the death of Bruno at the stake.[33]

It is unlikely that Essex himself would have acted as any kind of mediator between Bruno and a mere playwright such as Shakespeare. There were, however, other possible mediators on the London scene. It may be considered almost certain that the dramatist, concerned as he was in so many of his plays with all things Italian, would have known John Florio, a major cultural figure in London at that time and the son of Michelangelo Florio, one of the most prominent of the Italian exiles who had fled the inquisition to establish himself in England.[34] In just these years his son John was translating into English the essays of Montaigne, to produce a volume that Shakespeare was known to have read. John Florio could have told Shakespeare much about Bruno and his philosophy, for he was Bruno's closest friend during the philosopher's London years, and he mentioned this friendship in his introduction to Montaigne's essays.[35] Florio also included Bruno's Italian dialogues, written and published in London between 1584 and 1585, in the list of works he consulted when compiling his English–Italian dictionary, first published in 1598 under Elizabeth, and then again with the title *The New Worlde of Words* in 1608, when it was dedicated to James I's queen, Anne of Denmark.

The Florio connection is certain with respect to Bruno, for they both mentioned each other in their works, but it is uncertain, as is so much else, with respect to Shakespeare himself. The Essex connection is certain at the level of the document informing him of Bruno's death, and again at the level of his imprudent use of the actors of the company where Shakespeare worked. It is uncertain what kind of link, if any, may be established via this route between Bruno and Shakespeare himself. A complex web of intriguing relationships thus appears only partially defined through the moving mists of historical time. Nevertheless it can be held to link loosely together men, ideas, books, power structures, rebellions, and executions in ways that should not be forgotten when reading the tragedies written by Shakespeare in these years. In many of his major tragedies, and particularly in *Hamlet*, oppressive forms of monarchical power and the criminal excesses of absolutism are subjected to relentless scrutiny by dramatic heroes who claim the right to express their own most deeply held thoughts and sentiments, undaunted by those in power who attempt to tell them what they ought to do and say.

Hamlet's representation of courtly values takes place in two stages.[36] In the first scene of the play the ghost of his dead father appears repeatedly to the guards as well as to Hamlet's trusted friend Horatio at night on the castle ramparts. His figure is later conjured up by Hamlet himself in his first dramatic monologue, when he is still unaware of the presence of the ghost in the castle precincts. From these various appearances it becomes clear that the old Hamlet stands, in the mind of his mourning son, for courtly values in their most idealized form. These continued to be present to many of the humanists of the Renaissance who used the medieval courtly idea, permeated with Arthurian myth, to satirize and repudiate the modern courts and princes of their own more decadent world. The old Hamlet of Shakespeare's play, in his ghostly shining armor, belongs to a distant world founded on medieval memories and ideals. According to the words of one of the guards, he "is as the ayre, invulnerable."[37] Hamlet himself sees his father in his monologue as an "excellent king" with qualities of courtesy and wisdom that make him like a god: he is

CHAPTER 3

Hyperion, the light of the sun. In contrast to these images of divine light, which surround the memory of his father, a latter-day Elsinore appears in Hamlet's meditation through images of rank-smelling weeds, corrupt and going to seed.[38] It is ruled over by Hamlet's paternal uncle, Claudius, who has had no time for mourning before celebrating his suspiciously rapid takeover of power. Beside him stands Hamlet's mother who, already united in a new marriage to the present prince and wondering to see her son dressed in solemn black, is unfeeling enough to ask Hamlet why the death of his own father "seemes so perticuler with thee." Hamlet's rebuke of her scandalous question pointedly answers it by placing the value of truth (the *is*) against the value of dissimulation (that which *seems*) evidently considered by Shakespeare as the pervading evil of the modern court: "Seemes Maddam, nay it is, I know not seemes."[39]

Shakespeare's meditation on the cognitive value of words becomes more complex as the drama of Hamlet's search for the terrible truth about his father's sudden death takes him deeper and deeper into the labyrinth of falsehood and criminal deceit. In this context, one of the key moments of the play is the scintillating exchange of only apparent pleasantries that Hamlet indulges in with his ex-friends and comrades of his student days in Wittenberg, Rosencranz and Guildenstern. Hamlet rightly suspects them of spying on him in the service of the new king:

HAMLET. . . . What news?

ROSENCRANZ. None my lord, but the world's grown honest.

HAMLET. Then is doomsday near. But your news is not true. Let me question more in particular. What have you my good friends deserved at the hands of Fortune, that she sends you to prison hither?

GUILDENSTERN. Prison, my lord?

HAMLET. Denmark's a prison.

ROSENCRANZ. Then is the world one.

HAMLET. A goodly one, in which there are many confines, wards and dungeons; Denmark being one o' th' worst.

ROSENCRANZ. We thinke not so, my lord.

HAMLET. Why then 'tis none to you; for there is nothing either good or bad, but thinking makes it so. To me it is a prison.

ROSENCRANZ. Why, then your Ambition makes it one: 'tis too narrow for your minde.

HAMLET. O God, I could be bounded in a nutshell, and count myself king of infinite space—were it not that I have bad dreams.[40]

In the discussions of a possible presence of the infinite cosmology and accompanying relativistic epistemology of Giordano Bruno in Shakespeare's tragedy (a relevant aspect of late nineteenth- and early twentieth-century criticism of *Hamlet* that seems to have disappeared from memory today), this passage was treated as almost akin to proof of the relationship. At the turn of the century the Bible was still considered the major authority on questions of cosmology, as well as of salvation and of faith. Few were talking about Copernicanism at that time and, with Bruno long imprisoned and just burned at the stake as a particularly obstinate heretic, discussion of an infinite universe had been suppressed almost everywhere. There were reasons enough for Hamlet to have bad dreams, and a cosmology clearly similar to Bruno's own appears to have been one of them, for Bruno had declared that when the universe itself assumes the dimensions of infinite space there is no longer any single center but an infinite number of centers from which points can be measured only one against another. None of these centers has precedence, except within the specific system being considered.[41] In terms of values, as Shakespeare has Hamlet put it, "there is nothing either good or bad, but thinking makes it so."

The conclusion of such a logic can only be a philosophy increasingly centered on the individual conscience, for what Shakespeare is saying (as Bruno had before him) is that only good thinking makes for good ethics. Authority no longer lies primarily outside the mind, in a power structure, a theology, or a dogmatic philosophy such as the Scholastic one; it lies increasingly in the responsible thinking person in negotiation with other thinking persons. Such freedom and autonomy, however, require much courage, fortitude, and constancy. Shakespeare thus underlines a point that had continually been made by Machiavelli before him: that the caprices of fortune can only be successfully negotiated by societies whose citizens' ethical fiber allows them to stand firm in the face of temptation and corruption. Hamlet praises in precisely such terms the only character in his drama he can count on as his friend: the character who, with the court of Elsinore lying in ruins around him, Hamlet will eventually ask to tell his story:

HAMLET. Horatio, thou art e'en as just a man
As e'er my conversation cop'd withal.
         . . . blest are those
Whose blood and judgement are so well commeddled,
That they are not a pipe for Fortune's finger
To sound what stop she please. Give me that man
That is not passion's slave, and I will wear him
In my heart's core, ay, in my heart of heart,
As I do thee.[42]

CHAPTER 3

When later on in 1606 Shakespeare wrote *King Lear*, Elizabeth was already dead and the throne had passed to the Stuart dynasty of James VI of Scotland, who became James I of England. From the beginning the Stuarts showed evident tendencies toward an absolutism that the Tudors had managed to avoid. Shakespeare's tragedy *King Lear* was played at court in the presence of the new king, so that if the dramatist wanted to develop his criticism of courtly power and oppression, he could only do it in devious and subtle ways. His answer was to take a then well-known story, repeated in the chronicles and dramas of the time, that was set in Britain's distant and barbaric past. King Lear's violent and barbarous world is presented as alien to modern times so that the play could inspire satisfied sentiments of superiority on the part of a supposedly more refined and Christian monarch. The first version of the drama, published in 1608, was titled *The Historie of King Lear*. It is said on the frontispiece to correspond to the text presented at court in the presence of the king. Only the significantly revised version published much later on, in the first folio of 1623, would call the play a tragedy.[43]

Of all Shakespeare's tragedies, this is the one that assumes epic dimensions, creating from the first moments of the drama a violent and desperate world dominated by the sound and fury of an angry but fragile king. The clear, pure notes of truth in the words of Cordelia, who refuses to recite the lines expected of her in the love test her father subjects her to, followed by the ringing words of deliberate defiance of the Earl of Kent who takes her side, can only end in exile, separation, bloodshed, and war. This is a drama that pits truth against falsehood, liberty of speech and expression against those who claim to have the right to dictate to all the world what words should be publicly said and endorsed. The subplot repeats the story in the tragic failure of the Duke of Gloucester to rightly judge which of his sons is filled with love for him and which is devoured with hate. False words are at the origins of these errors as surely as they were in *Hamlet*: these are worlds of blind and absolute authority in which only dissimulation wins power and respect. The tragic consequences are revealed in the horrors and desperation awaiting those who attempt to speak the words of truth. And what if, after their failure to distinguish true words from the false, the two old men themselves are finally destroyed by the falsity they themselves have created? Shakespeare shows them to us, helped on their suffering way by an extraordinary medley of grotesque characters, from the court fool to their exiled friends who have returned to comfort them in loving if bizarre disguise. Thus escorted, he takes them to the edge of the abyss and beyond.

That way madness lies. Shakespeare's refusal to draw back from the ultimate sufferings of his dramatic heroes in this play—the tortures, the sudden and accidental deaths, the bewilderment and agonies, the suicides and madness real and feigned—was considered excessive by audiences of the Enlightenment. Between 1681 and 1843 the theaters were only prepared to stage

Nathum Tate's adaptation, which gave the play a happy ending. At the beginning of the seventeenth century, however, there were few happy endings in sight. Shakespeare thought that it would be possible to glimpse them on the horizon only if words were given back their value as true expressions of those who uttered them. His storm-laden drama proceeds to its exhausted ending on precisely this note of passage from heroic despair to qualified optimism. He seems not even to have been sure to whom he should give the celebrated last words of this play to pronounce. In the first quarto edition of 1608 they are recited by the Duke of Albany, the repentant husband of one of Lear's two cruel daughters, Goneril; the duke accepts the crown as he pronounces them. Albany, however, had previously married Goneril, and although he repudiates her for her violent punishment of Gloucester, Albany himself can at best be considered a late adherent to the ranks of honesty and truth. On the other hand Edgar, the loving son of Gloucester, reveals himself throughout the drama as the most balanced and ethically valid character of the play, a kind of extension of Hamlet's friend Horatio. Edgar is stoically vigilant and caring for all those in distress, and for him maturity in suffering is the key to wisdom in a world where tragedy is always close at hand: "ripeness is all." Shakespeare himself clearly came to judge him as the most appropriate character to round off his epic drama when in his final revision of the text, published only in 1623 after he had died, he gives to Edgar and not to Albany the concluding comment on his most powerful and moving play:

> The weight of this sad time we must obey;
> Speake what we feele, not what we ought to say.
> The oldest hath borne most, we that are young,
>   Shall never see so much, nor live so long.[44]

The New Science: From Giordano Bruno to Francis Bacon

John Pocock, writing in the 1970s on what he called the "Machiavellian moment" and its impact on the modern world, found it necessary to take into consideration, in a page of great interest, the thesis being put forward in those years by Eugenio Garin in Italy and by Frances Yates in the English-speaking world. These and other scholars of that time were claiming that the European Renaissance had been dominated to a previously unsuspected extent by magical and Hermetic doctrines of thought. Considering what might be the political implications of this thesis, Pocock comments,

> Hermetic and magic ideas permit it to be said that knowledge and language, articulating into consciousness the correspondences and principles by which all things are held together, make man in his intellectuality (not his *fantasia*) the governor and creator (under God) of all things in creation. Particular natures are universalised in being known by him,

and he himself partakes in universality through knowing them. But hermetics are no substitute for politics, if they cannot set up a scheme of relationships between men as equal individuals. The universe of Pico della Mirandola's *Oration on the Dignity of Man* is in the last analysis composed of intelligible objects and the intellect that knows them, and although knowledge for Pico has become an Adamic passion of identification and creation, self-identification and self-creation, the relation between citizens cannot really be reduced to the relation between the knower and the known.[45]

One of the aspects of the concept of a Hermetic renaissance, which was the subject of a lively discussion in those years, was the thesis that the new science came onto the intellectual scene of the sixteenth century deeply imbued with Hermetic and magical influences. In the work of Yates, in particular, this claim was accompanied by the conviction that the new science had to be viewed as having developed at a considerable distance from the nineteenth-century vision of it as, from the beginning, a purely rational conquest of an objective natural world that gave rise to a knowledge considered as universally true. The ensuing nineteenth-century claim that the new science was accompanied by a rational defense of liberty of thought—itself considered as a value of universal significance—was also taken by Yates to be off the mark: an "old" idea.[46] If that is true, a new science imbued with magic, insofar as it is primarily a relationship between an individual knower and the known, will, as Pocock notes in the quotation above, lie well outside the sphere of politics, which deals rather with "the relationships between men as equal individuals."

Looking back at such arguments over nearly three decades of discussion of the origins of modern science, it appears that things have moved on in rather different directions from the one previously suggested.[47] More recent fields of inquiry and debate have been concerned with other kinds of nonrational inferences that partly constituted the Scientific Revolution, such as the continuing theological and religious preoccupations of the early scientists, at least up to and including Sir Isaac Newton, as well as their complex relationships with the sociological and economic realities of their times. Early scientists, according to these more recent theses, were far from being isolated from concerns regarding the citizens and the society in which their inquiry was developing. Indeed, a number of works have emerged at the center of discussion that would seem to suggest quite the contrary. For many, science has become above all a social construction determined more by economical and pragmatic than by purely epistemological considerations. The consequences of such a development have included a radical rereading of the early years of the Scientific Revolution that attempts to show how, from its original formulation in the late Renaissance, modern science was closely interwoven with the interests and aims of both the religious and the political power structures of the times.[48]

LIBERTY OF THOUGHT

Some of the issues raised in this discussion of the origins of modern science can be illustrated by a reading of Giordano Bruno's remarkable last work titled *A Theory of Links*, probably written in 1591. Bruno's work is founded on his intuition of what Pocock calls "the correspondences and principles by which all things are held together": the principle linking all things in the universe being identified by Bruno in a world soul of Neoplatonic derivation. However, Bruno is specifically concerned in this work with how these correspondences, through the power of rhetoric, the passions, and reason working together translate into "relationships between men"—and indeed between men and women. Bruno however denies that such relationships will ever be between equals, for one of the theses he advances is that every human relationship within the universal network of correspondences is couched in terms of a desire for dominion, or the predominating influence of mind on mind.[49] Bruno also sees the mind in its relation to the natural world as the search for a new dominion over natural things. His work suggests that the science of the sixteenth century was sometimes closer to modern physics than to the classical mechanical science of the seventeenth and eighteenth centuries, for it considers the natural world as essentially undetermined. This is coherent with Bruno's portrayal of the contemporary post-Copernican cosmological debate as matter for a dialogue, which precedes Galileo Galilei's use of dialogue by many years. Important recognition of Bruno's contribution to the post-Copernican debate has been expressed by Robert Westman in his monumental study *The Copernican Question*, which attempts to achieve "a rigorous historicism, ruthlessly attentive to the pastness of the agents' own categories but also balanced by a judicious cultivation of modern epistemic resources."[50]

Bruno's concern in *The Ash Wednesday Supper* (1584), which proposes an extension to infinity of Copernican astronomy, may be defined precisely as that of placing the scientific discussion within a specific social as well as intellectual context. It is generally recognized that his portrayal of an aristocratic supper held in London—in the rooms of Fulke Greville, and possibly with the participation of Sir Philip Sidney—offers a brilliant, if often bitingly satirical, portrait of the English aristocratic and academic life of the time. To Bruno this is clearly quite in line with the fact that he was also attempting, during that supper, to put forward one of the earliest realist readings of Copernicus's new heliocentric astronomy. The Copernican astronomy was not yet accepted in the academic capitals of Europe, and Bruno found himself talking in the face of strong and scandalized opposition from two neo-Aristotelian academics from Oxford, who were among Fulke Greville's distinguished guests. Bruno's remarkable blend of scathing social critique and cosmological argument may create difficulties for the reader today, but it nevertheless suggests that the new ideas about the universe did not appear isolated from concepts of citizenship and social tensions dramatically present within the culture of the early modern world.[51] Shakespeare's *Hamlet*, as we have seen, may be taken as a case in point.

It can indeed be argued that it is precisely because the new science emerged so closely embedded within the social and political tensions of the time that it not only contained its own appeal for liberty of thought, but that such an appeal inevitably took place within the ecclesiastical and political contexts that have already been discussed earlier in this book. If we take the example of Francis Bacon, it becomes immediately clear how, after achieving high political office as well as becoming an expert student of law, he was claiming liberty for the instauration of his scientific project in terms that were in line both with his official position and with his legal occupations. In the first book of his *Advancement of Learning*, dedicated in 1605 to the English king James I, Bacon addresses the common complaint of the theologians that too much attention devoted to a fallen and sinful natural world turns the mind away from God: "And as for the conceite that too much knowledge should encline a man to Atheisme, and that the ignorance of second causes should make a more devoute dependance uppon God, which is the first cause; First, it is good to ask the question which Job asked of his friends, *Will you lye for God, as one man will do for another, to gratifie him?*" Bacon goes on to reach the conclusion that there must be unimpeded free inquiry both into questions concerning religion and into natural philosophy: "Let no man, upon a weake conceite of sobrietie or an ill applyed moderation thinke or maintaine, that a man can search too farre or bee too well studied in the Booke of God's word or in the Booke of God's workes; Divinitie or Philosophie; but rather let men endeavour an endlesse progress or proficience in both; only let men beware that they apply both to Charitie, and not to swelling; to use, and not to ostentation; and againe, that they do not unwisely mingle or confound these learnings together."[52]

In an interesting study of Bacon's scientific project with relation to his legal duties within the state, Julian Martin has claimed that Bacon always framed his proposal for a natural science in a vocabulary similar to the one that he used in his political life. This, according to Martin's analysis, was because Bacon saw his new natural philosophy as the learning of "administrators of knowledge" rather than that of men learned in a purely theoretical sense. Bacon, according to this reading of him, was not only interested in the epistemology of the new science—or the new forms of knowledge to which it was giving rise—but also in the way in which the new science would, and in his opinion *should*, become a new civil institution. Citing from book 2 of *The Advancement of Learning*, Martin demonstrates how for Bacon the new natural philosophy was in this respect analogous to a more traditional natural magic: "Is not the ground, which Machiavel wisely and largely discourseth concerning governments, that the way to establish and preserve them is to reduce them *ad principia*, a rule in physics and nature as well as in civil administration? Was not Persian magic a reduction or correspondence of the principles and architectures of nature to the rules and policy of governments?"[53]

Bacon's utopian society, described in his *New Atlantis*, which he wrote after a dramatic fall from favor with the king, makes it quite clear that the society that Bacon envisaged as the ideal one, in which advanced inquiry into the world of nature could take place, was of a very traditional kind in many important ways. It was based on a patriarchal system of family relationships conceived of in extremely hierarchical terms and was dedicated to stability and social harmony through a profound respect for those in positions of both civil and ecclesiastical power. Nevertheless, there are fundamental elements of novelty on this utopian island. To begin, its cosmopolitan character is underlined. Geographically it is situated in some oriental region of the world, albeit blessed by a miraculous moment of Christian revelation, suggesting that Bacon was interested in traditions of knowledge lying outside the framework of European thought. It is also inhabited by a significant Jewish community, which Bacon sees as an integral part of his ideal society as a whole. This was an important inclusion in a moment when the Jews were still officially banned from England, and it may have helped to achieve their eventual readmission later in the century. It is only within this well-defined social, political, and religious context that Bacon goes on to consider the dedication of his enquirers into the truths of nature to their common inquiries in his celebrated institute for research, the House of Salamon. Because it is situated at some distance from the city, in the House of Salamon social, political, and religious questions are finally left behind. For Bacon the new inquiries into natural truths require that—within parameters established by the enquirers themselves—freedom of investigation into natural phenomena be unlimited by external considerations of any kind. Once their new discoveries have been made, however, Bacon sees these exceptional men as returning to the city to make it into a place that becomes the locus of a new empire of the mind: "The end of our foundation is the knowledge of causes and secret motions of things, and the enlarging of the bounds of human empire, to the effecting of all things possible."[54]

The New Science: Galileo Galilei

In the same years in which Bacon was formulating his proposal for the instauration of a scientific project as an essential part of the modern state, Galileo Galilei was getting into increasingly serious difficulties in Italy for his refusal to abandon the Copernican cosmology. The extraordinary amount of attention dedicated in recent years to Galileo's long battle with the Roman Catholic Inquisition, the inquiry into the relevant documents and the close analyses of his trial on the part of both secular and religious commentators, and the rethinking of its inquisitorial past on the part of the Catholic Church itself have all lead to the accumulation of a formidable recent bibliography. An important moment of this rethinking of the "Galileo affair" was the official rehabili-

CHAPTER 3

tation of Galileo on the part of the Catholic Church after a twelve-year period of study and meditation that led to a major pronouncement on his case by Pope John Paul II in 1992: a significant statement of reconciliation, even if all commentators have not been entirely satisfied with it.[55]

Galileo has become undoubtedly one of the major subjects of the present-day intellectual debate concerning the early modern world, and once again, as in the case of Machiavelli, in terms that seem to reach well beyond the dimensions of a purely historical academic study. Galileo has turned into the principal historical pivot around which one of the most heated discussions of our own times is developing—that is, how far religious doctrine can, if at all, determine the inquiries of the scientists and the ways in which they are accepted by society and taught in its academies and schools.

It is not necessary for the purposes of this book to enter into the details of Galileo's ordeal at the hands of the Inquisition, or of the reasons that led him to abjure, thus avoiding death but suffering condemnation to house imprisonment until he died.[56] It is of more interest here to consider some of the major moments leading up to that ordeal, as well as the terms in which they are being discussed on the part of some of the most recent commentators on his case today. Above all, what appears from the present-day discussion is a realization that the sentence condemning Galileo cannot be seen as definitive in the sense of a historical closing of his case. Rather, it is increasingly being read as a beginning moment that has reverberated down through history, giving rise to retrials, reconsiderations, rehabilitations, new accusations, and new arguments in his defense. This remarkable and continuing historical repetition of the "Galileo affair" has now been studied systematically by Maurice Finocchiaro, who had previously made available in English the documents relating to the Galileo trial itself;[57] his book follows an intense discussion and exchange of views that, in a number of studies of great interest, raise the perennial problem of the relationship between biblical doctrine and scientific truth.

The result of this discussion has been to shift the principal locus of inquiry from the trial documents themselves to the correspondence of Galileo with a number of high-ranking figures of his time. The subject of discussion in this correspondence is precisely biblical doctrine and the problem of how to reconcile it with Galileo's discoveries with the telescope of unknown bodies in the skies. Above all the document that emerges as the central text over which this argument takes place is Galileo's much discussed letter of 1615 to the Grand Duchess of Tuscany, Christina of Lorena, when he was the official court astronomer in the service of her son, Cosimo II.[58]

This letter had a long and complex buildup behind it, of which it is only necessary here to recall the most salient moments. In 1610 Galileo had published his universally acclaimed *Starry Messenger*, giving an account of his discovery of the moons of Jupiter with the new instrument he had just made for himself: one of the first telescopes powerful enough to discover such previously unknown bodies in the skies.[59] In that work Galileo discusses the astronomical significance of his discovery in terms of the Copernican hypothesis of a central sun, with the known planets, including the earth and Jupiter itself, rotating around it. It is known that Galileo was a convinced Copernican before this date, but he had no need to expose himself with respect to a cosmological doctrine that was still frowned upon both in Catholic and Protestant Europe because of its apparent contradiction of a number of passages in the Bible. After the publication of his book—which took Europe by surprise and made Galileo overnight into one of its most illustrious citizens—the Catholic Church became divided in its reactions. There were those in high places who shared the general admiration of a man who was known to be in any case a devout Catholic, as well as those who started murmuring that his astronomical doctrines were dangerous and must be denounced as untrue because they denied the geocentric cosmology to be found in the Bible.

The intense, and at times violent, discussion soon raging in Italy over the respective claims of biblical and scientific truth has come to be known as "the first Galileo trial." It ended in 1616 when a committee of consultants reported to the Congregation of the Index in Rome that the heliocentric thesis was philosophically absurd and formally heretical because it was in contrast to biblical doctrine, which clearly posits a central earth. It was decided at once to put Copernicus's *On Heavenly Revolutions* on the Index of Prohibited Books, pending corrections that would eliminate any mention of a "real" heliocentricity, though it was considered acceptable on both sides of the religious divide to use Copernicus's cosmological findings as the bases of purely mathematical calculations.

Galileo went to Rome, where he was summoned by the leading inquisitor of the time, cardinal Roberto Bellarmino. Galileo was warned by Bellarmino that he must no longer propose Copernicus's doctrine in a realist sense. Because reports were circulating that Galileo had been tried in Rome, and condemned by the Inquisition, Bellarmino wrote a declaration that he gave to Galileo denying these rumors. The next day, however, Galileo received an official warning not to propagate or teach the Copernican astronomy, a warning that he was bound by the church to obey. It was because he failed to obey this warning later, after Bellarmino's death, by writing his famous pro-Copernican *Dialogue on the Two Chief World Systems*, that Galileo was brought to trial by the inquisition in 1633, soon after the publication of his book.[60] The trial itself is nowadays considered to have been more about the authority of the church, and the challenge to that authority on the part of Galileo when he disobeyed Bellarmino's warning, than about the conceptual question of the relative merits of scientific and religious truth. This was the theme of the discussion that had already taken place between 1610 and 1616, and the major text involved is generally recognized to have been a famous letter written by Galileo to Madama Christina Lorena.

CHAPTER 3

The letter was written sometime after a breakfast held at the Medici palace in Pisa in December 1613, at which Galileo himself was not present. The breakfast was attended, among others, by the young Grand Duke of Tuscany, Cosimo II; his mother Christina, the Grand Duchess of Lorraine; and Galileo's former student, the Benedictine friar Benedetto Castelli. During that breakfast, Christina asked Castelli to explain Galileo's new astronomical discoveries. In particular Castelli was asked to comment on the apparent contradictions between the Copernican astronomy and biblical passages that show how the sun moves round a central earth rather than the earth around a central sun. Particular attention was dedicated to a passage in the book of Joshua in which God commands the sun and moon to stand still in order to extend the daylight and let the Israelites wreak vengeance on their foes (Josh. 10:12–13). This passage had recently been emphasized, sometimes in public sermons, by a number of ecclesiastics hostile to Galileo, for—it was argued—if the Lord ordered the sun to stand still then it must have been moving and therefore could not have been still at the center of the universe, as the Copernican astronomy required. This biblical passage would become one of the cruxes around which the post-Copernican astronomical discussion was to revolve.

Castelli immediately wrote a letter to Galileo telling him about this conversation, and on December 21, 1613, Galileo wrote back to Castelli outlining his own opinions, and especially refuting the possibility that in astronomical terms it was possible to make sense of the Joshua passage within the context of an Aristotelian-Ptolemaic cosmology. A copy of Galileo's letter to Castelli is known to have reached Rome and to have been considered by the Holy Office of the Inquisition, where it was not thought necessary to intervene. Given that the debate between the new cosmology and the Bible continued to increase both in complexity and in intensity, in 1615 Galileo wrote another, much longer, letter on the subject, this time addressing himself directly to Grand Duchess Christina herself. This justly celebrated letter considerably enlarges on the opinions previously expressed to Castelli, as well as containing a vibrant plea for the liberty of the natural philosopher to inquire into the movements of the heavens without interference from the churchmen.[61]

Galileo enters into his subject at once, without preliminaries, referring to his discovery of many particular things in the sky that were not only previously invisible to the eye but also deny some natural propositions commonly received in the schools by the philosophers. Traditionalists criticize him because they prefer their own vain discourses to what Galileo considers the newly discovered truths. Committing an even more grave error, they try to justify their position by citing from the Scriptures passages they fail to understand. Such people continue in their attempt to "bring him down to earth" because they dislike the way in which he, Galileo, describes "the constitution of the parts of the world" (which here means the universe). Galileo then gives a brief outline of the new astronomical theory he endorses: the sun remains stationary in the center of the world while the earth revolves around it while also rotating on its own axis. Copernicus's name is not mentioned at first; rather, Galileo concentrates his attention on Aristotle and Ptolemy, if only to refute them as the classical authors of a conventional astronomy that agrees with the earth-centered astronomy to be found in the Bible. Galileo considers that his own celestial observations with the telescope "clearly deny" the Aristotelian-Ptolemaic system of the world. He stops short of talking about an actual proof of Copernism, which was not definitively established by his own discoveries. The new discoveries only made the Copernican hypothesis considerably more probable than it had been before.

At this point Copernicus is introduced as the original proponent of this new heliocentric astronomy, and his religious credentials as a Catholic priest and canon are underlined. Galileo makes much of Copernicus's high reputation with the Roman Curia of his time, and with the work on the new calendar that he was commissioned to do by the church authorities themselves. Copernicus's reputation as a heretic, Galileo points out, is very recent, and promoted by people who manipulate his name for their own obscure ends, often without even reading his *On Heavenly Revolutions*; if they were to read it, they would realize that it has nothing to do with religion or the Scriptures but only with "physical conclusions pertaining to celestial motions, and he treats of them with astronomical and geometrical demonstrations based above all on sensory experience and accurate observations."[62] Galileo quotes here from the end of Copernicus's dedication of *On Heavenly Revolutions* to Pope Paul III, a passage that seems to him to confirm this as the clear intention of Copernicus himself.

Galileo then starts to consider the question of biblical authority, which as a good Catholic he declares must never be denied. So what is to be done with those frequent biblical passages that undoubtedly do refer to a sun that revolves around a central earth? Galileo's first argument is that there is no need to take the words of the Bible in their "naked and literal sense." If we were to do this we would finish up by believing that God has hands and a face, or behaves in a human way—for example, by getting angry. According to Galileo, the Holy Spirit has only used words such as these to "accommodate the Scriptures to the understanding of the uncouth and barbaric multitude"; the educated reader will be wise enough to look for the hidden meaning lying underneath the biblical words. On its own, however, Galileo considers this a very trite argument with which all the theologians are familiar. He therefore goes on to add something relatively new (though Bruno had said it before[63]). The question of a biblical hermeneutics, Galileo insists, should not be limited to one of reading the Bible metaphorically or simply looking for an oblique meaning underlying the surface of the words. The vital question is to distinguish which biblical passages are dealing not with transcendental questions or issues involving the spiritual life but with considerations concerning the natural world.

In Galileo's opinion, when reading those passages in the Bible that deal with natural things it is essential to start from the truths demonstrated by the natural philosophers and not from the apparent truth of the biblical word itself. Nature's laws are immutable and necessary, and cannot be bent to accommodate the doctrines of the theologians; scriptural words, on the other hand, are not subject to the restrictions that define the laws of nature. Rather, they should be seen as guided by the dictates of the Holy Spirit as creator of the world. So, when faced by problems of natural philosophy as found in the Bible, the rule must be to start from the truths of nature as they have been established by an inquiry into natural things, and to pass from there to a religious reading of the passage in the light of these already established natural truths. Galileo insists that this rule for reading the passages of natural philosophy discovered in the Scriptures should not be interpreted as a lack of consideration for their holy meaning. It is simply based on the understanding that the Scriptures are not primarily concerned with teaching natural philosophy but instead with persuading the believer to attend to the salvation of his soul. This distinction can be used to reinterpret those biblical passages that seem to contradict the truths of nature as understood at present. The theologian's task is to penetrate into their hidden meaning as it touches the dimension that is really his—that is, the life of the spirit or the soul.

At this point Galileo produces a series of quotations from ecclesiastical authorities—mostly St. Augustine, but also the biblical book of Ecclesiastes—to demonstrate that it can never be justifiable to "block the way of freedom of philosophizing about things of the world and of nature."[64] These things cannot be established according to what happens to please this or that theologian; they can only be established by the logic of reasoning about natural things, as well as by a long tradition. Introducing here the subject of the history of the heliocentric theory, Galileo starts with Pythagoras, the first philosopher, and then shows how heliocentricity passes through Heraclitus, Philolaus, Plato, Aristarchus (as referred by Archimedes), Seleucus, Nicetas (as referred by Cicero), and only then to Copernicus himself. According to Galileo, none of this represents any substantial danger for the biblical word. The real danger for the interpretation of the Bible comes from the theologians themselves, and especially from those who claim to have understood it when they are really only expressing vain and fanciful thoughts. Galileo cites as examples here those theologians who attacked him after his discovery of the moons of Jupiter, claiming that he must be wrong because the Scriptures do not confirm their existence, as well as others who insisted that the moon is resplendent with its own light and not (as Galileo claimed) with the reflected light of the sun because the Bible speaks of a shining moon.

Galileo explicitly recognizes that he is faced by the problem that his own church considered theology to be the queen of the sciences, which cannot on any account lower itself to accommodate its doctrines to any other science. On this point, however, he feels the need to make some distinctions. On no account would he want to dethrone theology from its rightful place in those fields that are its own—that is, from the fields of faith. But it cannot claim to make measurements or solve problems of Euclidean geometry better than those who are experts in these lesser fields; if it were to do so, all buildings would be in danger of falling down. In the same way, the theologians should not claim to command the conclusions reached by the astronomers. This bold statement in favor of the natural philosophers allows Galileo to follow it up with a minor concession. He points out that those who study the ways of nature propose two different kinds of truth. On the one hand they propose doctrines that can be demonstrated to be true, and in that case it is the duty of the theologians to see how the words of the Bible can be reinterpreted to coincide with those truths; on the other hand they teach doctrines that derive from tradition, and if these turn out to be in contrast with the Scriptures, then traditional scientific thought must be questioned and its conclusions possibly modified.

Galileo is clearly writing with extreme caution here because he sees the danger of Copernicus's book being put on the Index of Prohibited Books—something that actually happened the following year. At this point in his letter Galileo attempts to prevent this outcome in a passage of remarkable rhetorical eloquence. Forbidding Copernicus's book, he insists, would solve no problems at all, for in order to uproot the heliocentric theory the church would have to forbid all books of astronomy, as well as forbidding the astronomers themselves to observe the movements of the bodies in the skies. It would have to clamp down on people's imagination and memory—indeed, on the faculty of thought itself. It is impossible to forbid people to use their eyes and their sight in order to look at the wonders of nature, which are the greatest treasures we possess.

Reining in at this point his remarkable rhetorical powers, Galileo continues by chiding at some length the ecclesiastical authorities he was concerned with correcting: a risky move, as he ends up by giving the impression of wishing to lay down the ecclesiastical law. He could not, obviously, think of doing such a thing except through reference to the highest ecclesiastical authorities of the past, and he chooses in particular St. Augustine's *On the Literal Interpretation of Genesis*, a work from which he quotes extensively throughout this letter. In particular he underlines the importance of a passage in which Augustine considers problems analogous to those being discussed in Galileo's own time. These concerned the shape of the skies, which had been shown by the astronomers of Augustine's time to be curved rather than flat; the Bible, however, talks about the sky being stretched out like the skin or hide of an animal. St. Augustine is not of the opinion that the theologians should therefore decree that the universe is flat when it has been shown by the natural philosophers to be curved. In St. Augustine's opinion, the theologians must find a way of showing how the words of the Scriptures can be reconciled with what the astronomers have demonstrated—by teaching, for example, that the Bible is not primarily concerned with natural truths, which are of no use for the salvation of the soul.

Galileo continues by noting that just as the doctrines of the theologians cannot determine what the astronomers demonstrate about the natural world, so the opinions of the common people cannot be taken as anything but frivolous in this respect. Sometimes it is necessary to talk as if the common doctrine were the true one, as most people find it easier to understand things that way. This, however, should not be confused with anything to do with natural truth. Galileo thinks that it is equally necessary to be skeptical concerning some of the things concluded and said both in the Bible and by the fathers of the church. What they have to say is mostly extremely remote from the world of nature and concerned with questions of religious faith; in that field their authority is evident and should never be denied. This means that in the field of natural philosophy, which they were not concerned with in the way of serious dispute or demonstration, their word should be taken as representing nothing other than the common doctrine held at their time. If one looks carefully, it is even possible to find passages in the Bible confirming the Copernican hypothesis. Here Galileo quotes a famous verse in the book of Job (a book much praised also by Giordano Bruno) saying that the earth moved from its usual place.[65]

At this point Galileo refers to the fourth session of the Council of Trent, or what he calls the "collective consensus of the fathers," where on all questions concerning faith it was laid down that the word of the church, based on the authority of the Bible and the patristic texts, could not be questioned or denied. Galileo, however, insists that this rule must be strictly applied *only* to questions concerning faith, which do not include the problem of the movement or stability of the earth. In this context he quotes from St. Jerome, who only gets two mentions in the whole letter, as well as from St. Thomas Aquinas, who is quoted only this once. They had both noted that facts of nature are sometimes reported in false terms in biblical texts but had concluded that this was because such words adhered to the beliefs common at that time, which could be more readily understood by the common people. Galileo, however, is clearly more at ease with St. Augustine, most particularly in his comments in *On the Literal Interpretation of Genesis*; this is made evident by the multiple quotations he gives from it. In one passage Galileo is concerned with a page in which Augustine advises his brethren on how to consider the question—also being discussed in the schools of Galileo's time—of whether the whole universe moves or stands still. Augustine is of the opinion that such questions require subtle and laborious study and dispute, which he has not the time to participate in and which, in any case, he does not consider necessary or useful—for either the well-being of believers or that of the church.

Continuing to make ample use of St. Augustine, Galileo proceeds by moving into a bitter attack on the theologians of his own time—not something that was likely to help him in furthering his own cause. Like Augustine, he claims, the theologians of his day also refuse to join in the astronomical debate, which Galileo considers too complicated for them to understand anyway. Unlike Augustine, however, they claim to reach epistemological conclusions concerning the natural world based on an evident manipulation of a small number of biblical texts. In the final pages of his letter, Galileo pauses to consider the principal biblical text being used in his day against the heliocentric theory: the words in the book of Joshua that say that the sun obeyed God's command to stand still in the sky in order to prolong the length of the day so that the Israelites could have vengeance on their foes (Josh. 10:12–13). This was the passage already discussed at the breakfast in Pisa, the occasion that gave rise to Galileo's letter to Grand Duchess Christina in the first place.

The theologians were taking the verses from Joshua as their principal biblical text, claiming that it clearly denies the Copernican heliocentric theory. Only if the sun were already moving in the sky, the theologians insisted, could the Lord have given it a command to stand still. For his part, Galileo cleverly argues (as he already done in his letter to Benedetto Castelli) that this text makes no sense if it is read in terms of the traditional Aristotelian-Ptolemaic cosmology. The traditional astronomy claims that the sun circles around the ecliptic, or its annual path on a celestial sphere around a central earth, from west to east—that is, in a movement contrary to that of the whole system of spheres, or prime mobile, which moves from east to west, giving rise to day and night. In the traditional astronomy, it is this movement of the whole universal system around a central earth that gives rise to the alternation of the day with the night. The contrary movement of the sun around the earth is annual, and gives rise to the changing seasons of the year. This means that if, in the terms of the traditional astronomy, the sun were to stop in its own particular orbit around the earth, the day would get shorter, not longer. If the Lord had wanted the day to be longer, he should have commanded the sun to move more quickly around the earth, not to stop in its tracks. Galileo points out that, according to the terms of the traditional astronomy, the sun would have to move approximately 360 times its usual speed in order for the day to be prolonged. The biblical arguments being used by the theologians of his time to refute the Copernican theory are therefore evidently absurd when considered from a scientific point of view.

Galileo then argues that a number of important biblical commentators, such as Dionysius the Areopagite as well as St. Augustine himself, were already aware that these words in the book of Joshua, if they are to make any sense,

CHAPTER 3

should really be taken to mean that the whole system of universal spheres was commanded to stop and not just the sun and moon in their journey around a central earth. From here Galileo goes on to make a claim that it is actually easier to interpret Joshua's words in terms of Copernicus's heliocentric theory, particularly if it is adapted to the discovery—which Galileo himself had just demonstrated in his work on sunspots—that the sun at the center of the world rotates on its own axis on a monthly basis. At this point, Galileo can conclude his letter by pointing out that a large number of other religious hymns and biblical texts are perfectly reconcilable with the Copernican idea of a universe that is in itself immobile but within which—around a central sun—the celestial bodies, including the earth, move in orderly revolutions. The problem has been solved. With the application of a proper attention to a correct biblical hermeneutics, Copernicus and the biblical word can be made to coincide.

The problem, however, not only remained unsolved but would continue to be at the center of heated discussion for centuries to come: indeed, up to our own day. A number of recent studies have emphasized, for example, the multiple and at times contradictory hermeneutical principles adopted by Galileo in this letter. It is not necessary here to enter into the detailed discussion developed by these commentators; it is enough to refer to some of the most important conclusions they reach—for example, that Galileo should have limited his argument to the principle that says that in the face of a scientific demonstration of the truth, biblical texts must be reinterpreted. By also considering in detail other hermeneutical principles that were adopted by the church itself—that is, by attempting to show how certain biblical passages should be read—he invades the ground traditionally considered by the theologians to be theirs. It was inevitable that this would raise angry reactions on the part of the ecclesiastical authorities. Ernan McMullin, however, points out that Galileo found himself in an impossible intellectual predicament because, according to his own hermeneutic precepts defined in the letter to Grand Duchess Christina, he could only expect to obtain a radical modification of the official church doctrine on cosmology if he had in hand a secure demonstration of the scientific truth of the Copernican theory. Not only did he not have one (and none would be discovered until much later on, in the work of James Bradley in 1729 and Léon Foucault in 1851), but he was put in a position after 1616 in which it was impossible for him to pursue one. In this context, the composition of the *Dialogue Concerning the Two Chief World Systems* becomes, in McMullin's opinion, an imprudent but understandable rebellious act against the forceful constriction of Galileo's intellectual faculties within an ideological framework imposed on him by the authority of the Roman Catholic Church.[66]

Marcello Pera, on the other hand, concludes that Cardinal Bellarmino (approved of centuries later by Pope Pius XII) used his authority to constrain Galileo on the basis of a biblical hermeneutics founded on the principle that

112

"there are factual questions essential to the salvation message of the Scriptures that cannot be revised." The Vatican would modify this position in succeeding years—especially during the twentieth century, when Pope John Paul II initiated the events that led up to the readmission of Galileo within the community of the Catholic Church. This is, however, a modification seen by Pera as a purely practical and ultimately political move intended to defuse the perennial danger of a conflict between science and religion; in Pera's opinion, it does nothing to solve the ongoing problem of a fundamental epistemological tension between scientific and religious truths—a problem that, in Pera's opinion, is destined to remain intact, ensuring that "the risk of conflict, like a fire smoldering under the ashes, is still there."[67]

Richard Blackwell's essay "Could There Be Another Galileo Case?" examines the problem in relation to what Blackwell claims to be the silent and officially accepted adulteration on the part of the Jesuit Edmond Lamalle of a book by Pio Paschini titled *The Life and Works of Galileo Galilei*. Paschini's book ran into severe trouble with the ecclesiastical authorities, and was eventually "silently" rewritten by Lamalle and published by the pontifical Academia delle scienze in 1964, as if authored purely by Paschini, with no acknowledgment of the "corrections" to which it had been subjected.[68] This obscure episode—which has subsequently been more fully researched—already constitutes, in Blackwell's opinion, "another Galileo case," and he is of the opinion that more such episodes may well continue to occur in the future.[69] Blackwell concludes that what he calls "intellectual honesty and freedom of thought" are not yet strong enough in the Catholic Church to prevent a new Galileo case from occurring again, though he concedes that they could become so in the future. A leading question these discussions raise is whether freedom of thought is to be considered the primary value that any church pursues, or whether what Pera considers the primary importance to religion of "the salvation message of the Scriptures" means that the conceptual conflict between religion and science will never be solved but will always remain a danger of which future generations should beware.

Revisionist historiography concerning the Galileo case has been increasing in the last few decades. Some historians and philosophers of science such as Rivka Feldhay claim that no real conflict ever occurred, or at least none that could not have been avoided with a minimum of tact and flexibility on the part of Galileo.[70] Her case is put from the point of view of the church, and particularly the Jesuits, who are seen as attempting, in good faith, to accommodate a particularly obstinate heretic who wanted to dictate to them how they should think and act. In the process of putting forward this interpretation of events, Galileo's scientific achievement tends to diminish, finishing up as little more than a few tiny specks of light in the sky glimpsed through a still imperfect instrument, and in need of further clarification in the decades to come.[71] Such clarification, it is suggested, often came from the Jesuits them-

CHAPTER 3

selves, who are nowadays recognized as having developed a prestigious scientific tradition of their own.[72] Against this revisionist point of view, prestigious historians of science such as Noel Swerdlow continue unperturbed to make the claim that "Galileo's researches in astronomy were more than original, they were unprecedented.... His discoveries with the telescope, as interesting as they are in themselves—and it is hard to think of more surprising discoveries in the entire history of science—are of still greater interest for the conclusions that he drew from them, for nearly all of them could be turned to the criticism of Aristotle and the defense of Copernicus, and in his *Dialogue on the Two Great Systems of the World*, that is just what Galileo did."[73]

From these few examples taken from the lively and complex discussion that continues to develop around the name of Galileo, it should be clear to what an extent his story continues to arouse interest and debate. For the purposes of this study, however, the core of Galileo's letter to Madama Christina Lorena lies not so much in the claims it makes for science or for religion as in those it makes for the freedom of thought and expression. A celebrated passage of intense rhetorical pleading for the liberty of the astronomer to continue unimpeded in his inquiry deserves to be quoted here in full:

> [W]hat the eyes see when they look at the external appearance of a human body is very insignificant in comparison to the admirable contrivances found in it by a competent and diligent philosopher-anatomist when he investigates how so many muscles, tendons, nerves, and bones are used; when he examines the function of the heart and the other principal organs; when he searches for the seat of the vital faculties; when he observes the wonderful structure of the senses; and, with no end to his astonishment and curiosity, when he studies the location of the imagination, memory and reason. Likewise, what the unaided sense of sight shows is almost nothing in comparison to the sublime marvels which the mind of intelligent investigators reveals in the heavens through long and accurate observation.[74]

"To the effecting of all things possible" (Bacon); "searching for the seat of the vital faculties" (Galileo): there was truly something Faustian about the new science, well captured by Christopher Marlowe in the intense verse of his hero's opening monologue in *Dr. Faustus*: "now tire my brains to gain a deity." Although Bacon's fall from power was due to a question of fraud, to which he pleaded guilty, there seems something inevitable about the disgrace and isolation in which these extraordinary men—Bacon and Galileo, like Bruno before them—passed their final years. They had all traveled mentally far beyond what the authorities of their time could either understand or permit. Nor even in our own time does it remain entirely clear how a more tame and domesticated science, well contained within public institutions, will fare with the jealous guardians of religious and political power as the inquiring scientific minds of today—building on the shoulders of giants—get progressively nearer to those ultimate truths that lie close to the origins of life and the universe.

Galileo, ignorant like all of us of what future lay in store, already saw many problems, which he attempted to outline in his letter to Grand Duchess Christina Lorena. It was a text that would become an important element in the gradual, historical rehabilitation of Galileo from his humiliation and disgrace in 1633. This would find a major starting point among a group of Italian Protestant refugees in the free city of Strasbourg where, in 1636, Elio Diodati was responsible for the publication of a Latin translation of Galileo's *Dialogue*, including a number of important appendices of other relevant documents concerning Galileo's trial. In the same year Diodati personally translated and published the "Letter to Madama Christina Lorena" in a facing Latin-Italian text. Diodati was a friend and correspondent of Galileo's and consulted him directly about his publications of these works. More important, as Maurice Finocchiaro has underlined, these publications contain an explicit plea for freedom of philosophical inquiry. Finocchiaro stresses that Diodati and his collaborators were careful not to implicate Galileo personally in their activities. However, "it was clear that they knew what they were doing and what they wanted to accomplish. Their aim began to emerge on the title page which exhibited two quotations. One was from Alcinous, in Greek, and means: 'One must be mentally free if one wants to become a philosopher.' The other was a Latin sentence from Seneca that means: 'It is especially among philosophers that one must have equal liberty.' "[75]

Galileo's words, both in the "Letter to Madama Christina Lorena" and in the *Dialogue on the Two Major World Systems*, would continue to resound in coming years in other texts that, as we will see, were at times not concerned with philosophy or science at all. His words carried beyond the bounds of science to become a part of a more general struggle for freedom of thought and responsible intellectual inquiry. It was a principle that would only gradually become defined, more and more clearly, as a fundamental right of every thinking person in whatever place or age.

CHAPTER 4

The Freedom of the Press

The Problems of Writing History:
From Jacques Auguste de Thou to Paolo Sarpi

Consideration of the complex personality and story of Galileo Galilei has to some extent taken us around in a circle. In Giordano Bruno's plea for the freedom of the natural philosopher, expressed in the letter of dedication of one of his works to the emperor Rudolf II, we saw the humanist tactic of rhetorical advice addressed to a prince. Francis Bacon, on the other hand, can more easily be linked to Niccolò Machiavelli and to those intellectuals who in the first years of the seventeenth century understood that the essential question not only for political and religious freedom but also for intellectual liberty was that of providing legal guarantees. It is evident that the high political office occupied by Bacon—as opposed to other, more isolated natural philosophers such as Bruno or Galileo—allowed him to more easily place his intellectual project ideally within a legal framework, even if the Stuart king he served never gave him any satisfaction in his desire to implement it. Galileo to some extent represents a step backward to the more traditional humanist stance; his letter is an exact parallel to Bruno's in its use of a courtly tradition of rhetorical appeal to those in power who it appears are being asked to concede the gift of liberty graciously as a concession rather than a right. In the cases of both Bruno and Galileo, it would be a mistake to interpret the unhappy outcomes of their stories to personal characteristics alone (such as their obstinacy or inflexibility, which are so often invoked by hostile critics). What their dramas of condemnation and disgrace really show are the fragility and inconstancy of the protection that the rulers of the time were disposed to extend to a natural philosophy that was becoming ever more subject to increasing ecclesiastical suspicion and severe control.

Rudolf II rewarded Bruno a sum of money for his dedication, but gave him no position either in his court or at the university. The Medici, for their part, took Galileo under their protection, but only for as long as he succeeded in

CHAPTER 4

containing his revolutionary scientific discoveries within the framework of the traditional court dispute. That Galileo himself understood how fragile the protection of the Medici was is well illustrated by an early version of his *Discourse on Bodies in Water*, quoted by Mario Biagioli in his book-length study *Galileo Courtier*. Anticipating that after the publication of his book he might need the protection of his Medici prince even more than before, Galileo addressed himself to his "Most Serene Lord," writing, "Now I, who am no Roland, possess nothing impenetrable but the shield of truth; for the rest naked and unarmed, I take refuge in the protection of Your Highness."[1] The metaphor of the knight with only the shield of reason to protect him, taken from the poem *Orlando furioso* by another much celebrated courtier, Ludovico Ariosto, is surely an eloquent testimony of Galileo's feeling of exposure within a world whose courtly mechanisms were oiled by favoritism and patronage. He knew that in the world of the Renaissance courts the fall to disgrace was always imminent, and that scientific reason was not high on the court's list of priorities. Galileo clearly thought that he could hope for protection from his old friend Maffeo Barbarini when Barbarini was elected Pope Urban VIII in 1623, but papal patronage turned out to be more complicated than he had supposed. The Medici court in Florence did little to protect Galileo once his trial and condemnation were seen to be a part of the papal agenda in Rome.

Biagioli himself is led to conclude that court patronage could never provide a prolonged or satisfactory answer to the needs of the new science. In the final pages of his book he proposes the private academies as more appropriate havens for the rebellious intellectuals of those times.[2] It can, however, be argued that the mosaic made up of the many private academies operative at that time, at least in Italy, was too mobile and fragile to act as a satisfactory substitute for the political power of a court, particularly as the academies were also constantly being observed, and often suppressed, by the church. Galileo's own Accademia dei Lincei, founded by the young prince Federico Cesi, gave him important protection and prestige for as long as it was able. Then the situation with respect to the Copernican astronomy became more tense and complex, and hostility to the academy, not least from other members of Cesi's own family, led to a gradual weakening of its ties with Galileo. In 1630, the academy entered a deep crisis with Cesi's premature death.[3]

Ultimately the path leads inexorably back to the solution put forward by Machiavelli early in the sixteenth century: the necessity to protect the liberty of the citizen through the law. Machiavelli himself does not appear to have been thinking specifically in terms of individual liberties such as those of speech and expression or freedom of the press. At the beginning of the seventeenth century, however, these issues assumed a new urgency, above all in the Catholic parts of Europe where the Congregation of the Index was severely limiting the publication of books only to those approved by the ecclesiastical authorities in Rome. One of the most dramatic cases of conflict in this context concerned a major figure in the Catholic culture of France, Jacques Auguste de Thou, whose way of writing history brought him into conflict with his own church in terms that presaged future events such as the story of Paolo Sarpi or the ordeal of Galileo. History was at this time also undergoing a profound change, from the medieval chronicle to a more modern study based on a humanist philology applied to the historical document. This raised a problem of documentary proof in the sphere of historical writing some years before Galileo's research with the telescope raised the problem of empirical proof in the sphere of natural philosophy, for if a document, carefully studied and decoded according to the latest philological standards, established a truth that the church was loath to recognize, who was to back down—the church, or the historian who failed to underwrite the narrative approved of by the ecclesiastical authorities?

Jacques Auguste de Thou came from a distinguished family in Orleans. He was born in Paris in 1553, son of Christophe de Thou, for many years a president of the Parlement de Paris, the most important national assembly of the Estates-General. Jacques Auguste was educated as a lawyer, but became acquainted with many influential figures also in the cultural sphere, such as Joseph Justus Scaliger and Michel de Montaigne. De Thou was already an important presence in the court of Henry III, but became a figure of particular prestige and influence during the reign of Henry IV, the formerly Protestant Henry of Navarre who converted to Catholicism after assuming the French crown in 1589.[4] Under this monarch de Thou—who had all his life been a Catholic—became, like his father, president of the Parlement de Paris, where he was particularly active in promoting the ratification of the king's Edict of Nantes conceding freedom of worship to the French Protestants. During these years of intense political activity, de Thou wrote in Latin his vast *History of His Own Time* narrating and deploring the French wars of religion, starting from 1545. When he died in 1616, the *History* had reached the year 1607, although he had intended to take it up to the tragic assassination of Henry IV in 1610. Publication of the *History* started in 1604–8 with an edition that took the history from 1545 to 1584; the remaining books were published only after de Thou's death. Right through the Enlightenment, and even into the nineteenth century, de Thou's history was considered essential reading, above all by those wishing to gain a detailed knowledge of the religious wars in sixteenth-century Europe, a considerable part of which de Thou had witnessed personally.[5]

De Thou accompanied his *History* with a lengthy and eloquent preface in the form of a letter to Henry IV. This famous preface was largely responsible for the immediate action taken in Rome, where de Thou's history was officially condemned and its suppression at once requested by the papal nuncio in France. De Thou was deeply distressed, and responded by making many changes, giving rise to a second edition of his *History* that started to appear later in 1604. In a letter to one of his nephews, however, he claimed that he

CHAPTER 4

was only toning down some particularly polemical passages, and not making radical changes, as "to portray things differently from how they are, or passively to dissimulate the truth, would offend my conscience."[6] The ecclesiastical authorities in Rome replied in 1609 by placing on the Index of Prohibited Books both editions of the entire first part of de Thou's *History*.

The French king, Henry IV, supported de Thou's work, however, refusing to suppress it in France and showing his particular admiration of the preface by personally ordering that it be translated into French by the Protestant Jean Hotman de Villiers, son of François Hotman, whom we have already met as one of the most revolutionary of the French Huguenots. François, who had lived in Bourges and taught at the university there, had narrowly escaped with his life in the St. Bartholomew Massacres of August 1572: "dressed in his professorial robes and doctor's bonnet, he went for a walk and kept walking past the guards posted at the gate by the catholics."[7] François's long walk took him first to Lyons and then on to Geneva.

Jean Hotman de Villiers's French translation of de Thou's Latin preface was published at once in Paris in 1604, separately from the *History* itself, with the title *L'excellente preface de M. de Thou*.[8] It was widely read and admired by discerning intellectuals throughout early modern Europe. De Thou never made changes to it, and the preface continued to be published, sometimes separately from the history it introduces. It was rightly considered an appeal of major importance for guaranteed forms of liberty not only of religion but also of the historian and of the press. Not surprisingly, it was much admired also in Protestant Europe, where de Thou's condemnation by the Roman Catholic authorities was strongly disliked. A partial anonymous English translation of the preface was published by Brewster in London in 1660. In 1729–30, Bernard Wilson translated the entire preface, together with an incomplete version of the *History*, that was published by E. Say in London. In 1733–34, Samuel Buckley published in London Thomas Carte's important translation of the *History* that included the preface. The most precise English translation, however, was made by John Collinson and published in his *Life of Thuanus* in 1807; this translation was reproduced without recognition of its true author by J. H. Walker in *A Brief Sketch of the Life of Thuanus* (1819), where the preface appears with a series of lengthy and often inaccurate notes, heavily slanted toward a Protestant stance.

The preface, which takes the form of a dedication to Henry IV, shows that de Thou was well aware of the risks he was taking: "When the design of writing a history of these times first engaged my thoughts, it did not escape me that such a work, however executed, would be exposed to various censures."[9] De Thou nevertheless carried out his project "amongst the oppressive labours of the law, foreign journeys and other avocations," convinced of finding protection under Henry IV who at the same time unites "liberty and regal power, two things usually thought incompatible." Behind de Thou's determination lies a precise idea of what writing history involves: "It is the first law of history to fear to record what is false, and, in the next place, not to want courage in relating the truth." Directly addressing Henry IV, he adds, "I should have been ashamed to prevaricate in a cause so honourable, and, through an absurd affectation of prudence, do injustice to the singular happiness of your majesty's times, in which every one is allowed to think what he pleases, and to speak what he thinks."[10]

The times are nevertheless full of calamities, and de Thou addresses the religious dissentions which, in addition to other evils, have infested what he thinks of as a corrupt age. The only way to avoid future calamities is to seek seasonable remedies, which must evidently be different from those that have so far been uselessly applied. At this point de Thou launches into a long description of the tortures, affliction, and pain that the various forms of inquisition were imposing throughout Europe on those whose religion was different from their own. All this appears to de Thou absurd as well as criminally violent and inhuman; affliction and pain have no power over those whose religion makes them glory in their strength. He gives numerous examples, from both history and his contemporary world, of those who have accepted willingly the most terrible forms of martyrdom, often causing their heresies to gain strength and spread more widely by their public example of fortitude. Religious persecution, therefore, must be considered not only cruel but also of no good effect. Against this form of scandalous ineptitude de Thou points to the example of wise princes such as Ferdinand I, Archduke of Austria (brother and later successor to the Holy Roman Emperor Charles V), who understood that "the interests of religion were most advanced by friendly discussions, of which method he had made frequent trials."[11] After the closing of the Council of Trent, which licensed a new age of the Inquisition and the new Index of Prohibited Books, Ferdinand attempted to institute a further council that would include the Protestants in an attempt to allow them and the Catholics to settle their differences in peace. Unfortunately his untimely death deprived Germany of any of the advantages that might have been expected from these plans.

Coming closer to his own times, de Thou admits that he is about "to handle a sore, barely to touch which, I fear, will be to my prejudice." He follows the French wars of religion in some detail, concentrating on those brief periods, such as the years 1563–67, in which "excellent laws of which France will never have reason to repent" diffused a serene calm throughout the land. De Thou refers here to the period of religious peace and toleration largely brought about—in the reign of Charles IX, supported by his mother, Maria dei Medici—by the efforts of Michel de l'Hospital, a councilor of the French parliament. Those years of peace, however, soon came to an end when France "inclined to a war which proved fatal not only to us." The reference here is to the decision supported by the most extreme Catholics to send the Duke of Alva into the Netherlands, where "he carried fire and sword with him; built citadels in all places; gave a death-blow to liberty." De Thou exclaims with shame, "Away therefore with those impertinent boasts in which some persons have indulged themselves to the scandal of the French name, because they have admitted no peace with heretics."[12]

Coming to the massacre of St. Bartholomew's Night, which represented a dramatic change in the royal policy, de Thou seems at a loss to find words to deprecate it, exclaiming only "may it be buried in eternal oblivion!" while at the same time celebrating the happy escape of Henry IV himself (at that time the still Protestant Henry of Navarre) destined to become "the restorer of France."[13] De Thou's reticence in the preface about the massacre is not repeated in his detailed treatment of it in book 52 of the *History* itself, widely considered as among his most celebrated pages. This may have been an effort to atone for the performance of his father Christophe who, as president of the Parlement de Paris found himself having officially to accept Charles IX's explanation of his reasons for ordering the massacres while they were still being perpetrated in the provinces. His son claims for him at least the courage of having asked the king why, if he thought (as he had claimed in the parliament) that there was a Protestant plot against him, he had not pursued the matter according to the laws of the land. Beyond this, however, Christophe—as his son reluctantly admits—felt obliged to resign himself to the customs of his place and age. De Thou nevertheless assures his readers that his father always hated that fatal day and referred to it by quoting some verses from the *Sylvae* (5.88) of the ancient Roman poet Statius which express a wish that some fatal crimes committed by his countrymen perish for ever from the memory of humankind.[14]

Referring to the events that occurred in France during the reign of Henry IV's predecessor, Henry III, de Thou notices this king's habit of accepting bad advice, which caused him to begin his reign by waging war against the Protestants, who "humbly deprecated it at his hands." Only in 1576 did he think better and publish an edict registered in the Parlement de Paris, the Edict of Beaulieu, that secured civil and religious privileges for the Protestants with legal guarantees. There were, however, "certain persons, impatient of rest" who at once started "provoking the country from its flourishing state." The result was once again violence and unrest, culminating in the assassination of Henry III by an extremist Dominican monk in 1589. This gives de Thou the opportunity of presenting the new king Henry IV as the man whose virtue "stopped the precipitate course of public calamity, which bore all before it like a wheel rolling down a steep descent." The new king understood what de Thou had always believed—that is, that "though all other things are subject to human laws, religion cannot be commanded." Moderation and lenity at once took the place of war and oppression, and de Thou, who describes himself as a modest man educated in liberty, can rejoice to see the Protestants "reinstated in their estates and good name." De Thou gives historical examples designed to demonstrate that all the most celebrated Christians have thought of those who differed from them as their "brethren" and have attempted to further a state of peace: "For the sake of the church's peace, they will bear patiently injuries and insults, and give an example with what affection and sincerity of charity God ought to be served." Although de Thou's Catholicism leads him to refer to "the error of dissenters," he claims that he always makes honorable mention of them, while deploring the "malice and intrigues" of many of his fellow Catholics.[15]

At this point, Thou's preface assumes a more specifically political slant, reminding the reader that he (like his father) had been for many years a public official of note. A good state, he claims, will not ask whether a man is Catholic or Protestant but will rather search for men of "tried integrity, who fear God and detest covetousness, and come recommended by merit alone." Henry IV's Edict of Nantes of 1598 has brought in an era that is dedicating itself to composing religious dissention, and "[g]ood morals will flourish with chastity and modesty, which have been hitherto exposed to ridicule; in fine, merit being restored to its due honour, the value, lustre, and influence of money will be seen to decrease."[16] These words are an interesting sign of de Thou's awareness that the religious wars had a definite economic dimension to them, being concerned with economic and political power just as much as with Christian dogma and doctrine. This was particularly so in France, where many of the Reformed Huguenots came from the wealthy and influential upper classes.

The final pages of de Thou's preface are dedicated to a celebration of "the laws of our country," and this is why it is so important to make "an exact numeration of particulars relating to our liberties, immunities, laws and rights." Recognizing that the Edict of Nantes had in fact become the law of the country, de Thou warns Henry IV that laws can change. In a prophetic passage he writes, "These rights, these laws, are the foundation upon which France has raised herself to her present extent of dominion, and eminence of grandeur. If there be any (and I wish there were not,) who would by degrees subvert these by mines and secret engines, aware that open force would not avail, we should be unworthy of the name of Frenchmen, if we did not make resistance unto death." De Thou follows this eloquent passage with a long panegyric on Henry IV, who is urged not to give way to France's secret enemies. Above all he is seen as the restorer of culture to a country devastated by war: "All the muses, driven from their ancient seats by the rage of war, congratulate you as their restorer. Under your auspices, the university of Paris has revived; and by the accession of Isaac Casaubon, that luminary of the age, to the custody of your majesty's truly royal library, it has lately acquired a splendid ornament." These words of praise for Casaubon are all the more impressive if it is remembered that he was a prestigious Protestant scholar and intellectual from Geneva. Upon the death of Henry IV Casaubon left France and went to England. For de Thou, however, writing at the turn of the century, Henry's death was still in the future.

CHAPTER 4

He clearly hoped that the authority of the law would protect the Edict of Nantes from those who preferred "the hazard of battle" to the security and prosperity of peace. It is with a panegyric of the law that de Thou ends his prefatory letter to Henry IV: "Assure yourself that the life and soul, and judgement, and understanding of the country, centre in the laws; and that a state without law, like a body deprived of its animating principle, is defunct and lifeless in its blood and members. Magistrates and judges are ministers and interpreters of the laws; and in fine, WE ARE ALL SERVANTS OF THE LAWS, THAT WE MAY BE FREE."[17]

Another important case of the writing of history coming into conflict with the official doctrines of the Catholic Church in this period concerns the complex train of events that surrounded the writing and publication of Paolo Sarpi's *History of the Council of Trent*, one of the great historical texts to emerge from the culture of early modern Europe. It is generally recognized that de Thou's *History* was one of Sarpi's sources for his own *History*, especially when de Thou was writing about the French wars of religion.[18] Indeed, on receiving a copy of volume 1 of de Thou's *History* through the good offices of Philippe Canaye de Fresne (a Protestant close to Henri IV who had converted to Catholicism in 1601, and had subsequently been appointed French ambassador to Venice), Sarpi wrote a letter of thanks to de Thou dated March 23, 1604. His letter, written in Italian, contained the following passage:

> Ho sino al presente avidamente letto li 10 primi libri portato dall'ardore d'intendere particolari, de quali nelle tenebre di queste reggioni non ci è cognitione alcuna. Veggo molto chiaro che se bene ella s'ha proposto per scopo principale la verita et la libertà di esprimerla senza odio o timore, che sono li più contrarii affetti a chi professa historia, nello stile ancora et nelle alter conditioni di buon'historico ha pareggiato li scrittori latini. . . . facia Dio che l'Italia vogli esser degna di goderne li frutti.
>
> Up to now, I have avidly read the first ten books, ardently desiring to learn many particulars that in this region of shadows are quite unknown to us. I see very clearly that you have proposed truth and liberty as your principal purpose, setting aside hate and fear, which are the deadly enemies of historical writing, and that in your style and other gifts as a historian you can be compared with the great Latin writers. . . . I pray to God that Italy will be worthy of enjoying such fruits.[19]

Sarpi's prayers were not to be answered, however; as we have seen, the ecclesiastical authorities in Rome were immediately hostile to these first books of de Thou's *History* and, in spite of his willingness to partially rewrite them, the Congregation of the Index finished up by placing the entire text on the Index of Prohibited Books in 1609.

Paolo Sarpi was a renowned Servite friar who, after holding high office in the ecclesiastical sphere, became a consultant of the Venetian Senate on January 28, 1606, when he was assumed in their service as a theologian and expert of canon law. At the time he attained this prestigious position Sarpi was already fifty-four years old. His early life had been dedicated not only to his ecclesiastical duties, but also to scientific interests and natural philosophy; his studies of magnetism, for example, are considered by some to have been a source for William Gilbert's *On the Magnet* (1600).[20] Sarpi's early scientific interests were much enhanced by the arrival of Galileo at the University of Padua in 1592. The two become close friends, and often met in Venice to discuss scientific matters until Galileo left the city for the Medici court in Florence in 1610.

Sarpi's fundamental concern, in spite of his distinguished ecclesiastical position, was the well-being of the Venetian state. His desire to serve Venice was so deeply felt that he thanked the senate in moving terms for the trust it was placing in his capacities: "There is nothing I have more ardently desired," claimed Sarpi, "than to be able to serve my Prince and Serene Highness, under whose sway I was born in this wonderful city."[21] Sarpi's religious calling clearly did not prevent him from considering his role as a citizen of Venice of the greatest importance—a stand that was gratefully recognized by the Venetian Republic in those very years. In April 1606 the Roman Church cast out Venice from its midst on account of the Venetian Senate's refusal to recognize the church's right to control directly its priests and its considerable properties within the Venetian state, irrespective of Venetian law. In this period of crisis in the relations between Venice and Rome, known as the Venetian Interdict, Sarpi acted as a major consultant to the Venetian Senate on matters concerning conflicts between church and state, between canon and civil law. Tensions ran high, with war threatening as Spain supported the church, while France under Henry IV was inclined toward Venice. Many Protestant countries, including the England of James I, waited impatiently for Venice to break with Rome altogether and move into the Protestant camp.[22] This never happened, however, as the Venetians were opposing the political (and financial) power of the church rather than its spiritual dominion. For its part, the church realized in a relatively short time that Venice required special treatment if it was to remain within a Catholic sphere of influence. The specific questions that were causing the conflict gradually came to be solved, and in April 1607 the interdict was lifted, although tensions between Venice and Rome would remain more or less intense for many years to come.

Throughout this period of particularly bitter conflict between the Venetian republic and the Roman Church, Sarpi undoubtedly played a major role in supporting and advising the Venetian Senate, and particularly its new doge, Leonardo Donà, who was openly hostile to papal influence in affairs concerning the Venetian state. Sarpi was able to play this role because he himself felt that ecclesiastical and political affairs should be considered as two distinct spheres of influence and kept rigorously apart. At times, his statements to this effect assume an emphatically secular tone, giving rise to the conviction of some commentators that his primary concerns were really political and not religious at all.[23] In 1983 David Wooton published a book on Sarpi that caused a considerable stir among the community of Sarpi scholars by claiming that far from being religious, Sarpi was certainly a freethinker and probably an atheist. This meant, as Wooton explicitly admitted, that Sarpi's entire religious life and activity must have been based on a sustained policy of hypocrisy. Wooton was only able to argue for this thesis by basing the main thrust of his argument on a group of texts known as Sarpi's *Pensieri*, or private thoughts, on various subjects that Sarpi noted down throughout his life but never published. Among the many issues raised by Wooton's thesis, which has had a considerable influence on Sarpi scholarship, is the question of the relative importance of private versus public statements—an issue of great interest, though not one that it is possible to pursue in detail here. Rather, it needs to be emphasized that in more recent years attention has once again become directed toward Sarpi's public statements, and especially the reports he presented to the Venetian Senate in the period during and after the interdict. These are now readily available, published in 2001 in two substantial volumes with the title *Consulti*, or *Consultant Reports*.

The editor of these volumes, Corrado Pin, emphasizes the importance of the second of the *Reports*, notable for the themes of "the sovereignty of the state, the critique of the Roman Curia, the unfavorable comparison between the ancient and the modern church, the freedom of the individual conscience."[24] This early report to the Venetian Senate was handed in sometime previous to the church's pronouncement of the interdict, when the tensions were already high and mounting—probably a few days before Sarpi's engagement as consultant to the senate on January 28, 1606. It may have been responsible for the appointment he was so happy to receive. The lengthy and substantial *Report No. 2* is titled *A Treatise on the Power and Value of Just and Unjust Excommunication; and on the* de Jure *and* de Facto *Strategies to Be Used against Unjust Censures*. The rigorously argued terms in which Sarpi uses his remarkable historical knowledge to oppose the concept of papal infallibility, and claim the right of the state to repudiate an excommunication caused only by its determination to pursue its own legitimate policies of government, placed him on the international stage, while Europe watched with bated breath the outcome of this initially epic struggle between Venice and Rome.

Sarpi's initial argument in *Report No. 2* is that excommunication from the Christian community was started by Christ himself and accepted by St. Paul, but limited to exceptionally grave cases of individual guilt.[25] It was only in 1150 that excommunication started to be meted out by the church to a civil society: a city, a kingdom, or a state. This, in Sarpi's opinion, was an error because such forms of excommunication punish the innocent together with the guilty. Furthermore, in some places such interdicts have been applied for futile and venial motives, such as the failure of a community to pay the tributes levied by the church. Excommunications in these terms are a form of injustice unfavorable to true religion, and discredit the church that applies them. At this point Sarpi has justified the Venetian Senate in its opposition to the interdict with which it was threatened: not only does Venice have a right to repudiate its excommunication, but it actively helps to restore the dignity of the church's government by doing so. Sarpi then goes on to consider the two principal ways in which the Venetian Senate should proceed in its opposition to the interdict.

The first possibility, which should take a legal form, is to put in a formal request for a church council to be called to debate the question; this is a traditionally recognized way of solving important issues of dissent within the Catholic Church. Sarpi, however, strongly advises the Venetian Senate against taking such a decision. He points out that in those very years the question of a new Christian council was being energetically put forward by the Protestants, who had been refused an adequate hearing at the Council of Trent. Furthermore, the Protestants were claiming that a properly convened council would have the authority to oppose the word of the pope, whereas the Council of Trent had only recently sanctioned the absolute authority of the pope and the ecclesiastical authorities in Rome. The church would inevitably be irritated by such a request from Venice at just that time, and Sarpi advises the doge and the senate to avoid attempting such an unpromising solution to their problem. The proper way to proceed is through a practical strategy of refusal to accept, or even to recognize, the church's authority in affairs relating to Venetian law or government. Here Sarpi brings in as witnesses a number of prestigious Catholic theologians of the past who had recognized the possibility of a pope acting "tyrannically," and the consequent possibility of a community opposing resistance to papal authority with a clear conscience and without committing any sin. The senate should therefore pass its laws without any reference to the authority of Rome. Sarpi will advise this line of intransigent autonomy of the state with respect to the church throughout the year in which the church attempted, unsuccessfully, to enforce its interdict in Venice. The later *Reports* energetically oppose the signs of compromise and accommodation on the part of the Venetian Senate that eventually lead to the interdict being raised. Sarpi's position of head-on resistance to what he calls the "totalizing" authority of the Counter-Reformation church can therefore be seen as being defeated by the final turn of events, so much so that the following year he would write to a Protestant friend in France, "Io vado dubitando

CHAPTER 4

che a poco a poco perderemo quell principio di libertà che Dio ci aveva aperta" (I am afraid that we are gradually losing that principle of liberty that God had given us).[26]

During these years of the Venetian Interdict, Sarpi became associated with the Croatian-born Marco Antonio de Dominis who, after theological training with the Jesuits, became the Catholic archbishop of Split (Spalato) in Croatia from 1602 to 1616. In this period de Dominis attended assiduously to his pastoral duties but often came into bitter contrast with the authoritarian attitudes of the Roman Curia. During the Venetian Interdict, he sided with his then friend Sarpi, supporting the right of Venice to govern autonomously its secular affairs without interference from the Catholic Church. In 1616, exasperated by the rigid severity of the post-Tridentine ecclesiastical authorities in Rome, he left Croatia for Venice, where he applied for permission to resign as the archbishop of Spalato. The papal consistory accepted his resignation on August 22, and his writings were immediately placed on the Index of Prohibited Books. De Dominis left Venice prudently for England.

During his journey, de Dominis was given an imposing welcome at Heidelberg, then under the rule of the Elector Palatine, Frederick V, later to become the king of Bohemia as well. De Dominis was the guest of Elizabeth, daughter of the English king, James I. Elizabeth had been married to Frederick V in 1613, and de Dominis caught them in 1616, before their brief "winter monarchy" as king and queen of Bohemia from 1619 to 1620 was interrupted on November 8, 1620, by their defeat at the hands of Catholic forces at the battle of the White Mountain, close to Prague. Before this defeat—which decreed the consequent fall of the palatinate also into the hands of Catholic forces—Heidelberg had constituted an important stage in the Protestant corridor linking the north of Italy to England. It was in this still Protestant Heidelberg that de Dominis published a manifesto of his religious views, intended as a prelude to his arrival in London as a much desired guest of the English king and his archbishop, George Abbott. The defection from the Catholic Church of a major ecclesiastic such as de Dominis was seen by them as an important moment in their affirmation of the Anglican Church as the true inheritor of the church of the early fathers. As Noel Malcolm puts it, James was "keen to fish for disaffected Catholics whose presence in his kingdom would add weight to his claims that the Church of England was an embodiment of the true, ancient, apostolic and universal church."[27] So there was good reason for James I's daughter Elizabeth to extend to de Dominis a welcome he described as "extremely favorable" and which was soon to be repeated in London itself.[28]

During his years in Split, de Dominis had developed a theory of the church that was decidedly antipapal in character. This had its foundation in a series of works written before and during the Venetian Interdict of 1606–7. These works attack papal claims of power over temporal rulers, emphasizing that the jurisdiction of the church should be spiritual only. A similar argument had been put forward by Martin Luther, and in some of the works of this period de Dominis praises those Protestants—even if for him they are still "heretics"—who attack such abuses by the Catholic clergy. For de Dominis (as Sarpi had also argued during the interdict in Venice) the spiritual and the temporal spheres are separate and must remain mutually independent. To one of his principal Catholic adversaries, the powerful cardinal Roberto Bellarmino, who observed that you cannot have two heads on one body, de Dominis replied that the church and the state are two separate bodies.[29] In England, de Dominis published in 1617, with the king's printer John Bill, the first part of his major work *On the Ecclesiastic Republic*, in which he defended the establishment of national churches. The major activity of de Dominis in England, however, was his involvement in the publication of Sarpi's great work, *The History of the Council of Trent*.[30]

During the years following the Venetian Interdict, Sarpi had become one of the most influential Catholic critics of the Council of Trent (1545–63), which had sanctioned a major reorganization of the system of church government, giving rise to what is commonly known as the Counter-Reformation. Sarpi considered the Council of Trent responsible for the violent religious tensions of the period. This was an unusual and unorthodox stand in Catholic Italy, where the blame for the religious violence of the times was officially placed on Luther, and then the entire Protestant movement, for their decision to create a schism within the Christian community rather than trying to resolve their differences from the inside. Sarpi, however, insisted that the schism was due to the Catholic Church's choice to exclude the Protestants from their religious discussions. His overtly critical *History of the Council of Trent* also condemned the Catholic Church's tendency to invade the sphere of civil power and rights, which Sarpi thought should be kept strictly separate from ecclesiastical concerns. Furthermore, he was deeply critical of what he considered the excessive influence of the bishops, and even more so of what he called the "totality," or the absolutism, of the power of the pope, both of which had been strongly reaffirmed in the Council of Trent.

This complex critical stance with respect to the major contemporary event within his own church has long given rise to speculation as to the true nature of Sarpi's religious beliefs.[31] These were already being doubted in his own times by the Inquisition, which pursued Sarpi on a number of accounts, though frustrated to the end by the protection that continued to be afforded him by the Venetian authorities. Tensions between Venice and Rome had again become intense when on October 5, 1607, six months after the lifting of the interdict, Sarpi was attacked late one evening on a dark Venetian bridge by a group of men armed with daggers, who succeeded in wounding him severely though not killing him, as was clearly their intent. This chilling episode is narrated in detail by Sarpi's monastic colleague and biographer, Fulgenzio Micanzio, who not only gives the names of the would-be assassins but also tells the story of how they were eventually discarded by the ecclesiastical authorities in Rome for having failed in their mission. Of particular interest, however, in Micanzio's account, are the references by Sarpi himself to this brutal attack during and after his recovery. While still in his sickbed, as the doctors started getting to work on the deepest of his wounds, he is reported to have said, "E pure il mondo vuole che sia data stile Romanae Curiae." He must have had great presence of mind to joke under such circumstances, for the exclamation is a play on the word *stile*, which can mean either "style" or "dagger." So, according to Sarpi, the world is saying that the attack was carried out in the "style" of the Roman Curia, or that it was made with the "dagger" of the Roman Curia (the Latin word *curia* was used originally by the ancient Romans in reference to their senate, and then adopted by the medieval church to refer to their ecclesiastical system of government). Later on, after his recovery and in a more serious vein, Sarpi is reported by Micanzio to have remarked frequently that nothing is more damaging to the Catholic religion than when the church interprets its religious liberty to mean religious license.[32]

Sarpi would continue to be harassed by the Inquisition, on which he wrote a report delivered to the Venetian Senate on November 18, 1613. Modern editors include this text among Sarpi's juridical papers, as he was primarily concerned with laying out for the senators' convenience the major legal documents governing the courts of the Inquisition in Venice.[33] These were permitted to operate according to a legal agreement between the Republic of Venice and the ecclesiastical authorities in Rome, dated August 28, 1289, going back to the pontificate of Niccolò IV. There it was clearly laid down that the Inquisition in Venice was far from being allowed to operate with a free hand. On the contrary, three secular officers were required to attend all inquisitorial trials in Venice to ensure that the proceedings, and especially the sentences meted out to the condemned, were contained within the laws of the republic—where, for example, it was forbidden to burn heretics alive in public places. Sarpi, who cites the authority of St. Augustine, appears to accept the necessity for inquisitorial proceedings, especially where God has been offended and the public peace disturbed. But he warns the Venetian senate that Rome is constantly inclined to overstep the bounds of the jurisdiction allowed by their mutual agreement, and must be monitored with attention in that sense. For example, there must be no trials where the secular observers take an oath at the hands of the ecclesiastical judges, as this would weaken their position as neutral observers of the doctrinal discussions taking place, their specific task being to contain all stages of the proceedings within Venetian law.

Sarpi's little treatise on the Inquisition contains a substantial section dedicated to the problem of the new Indexes of Prohibited Books.[34] This subject had recently been negotiated with Counter-Reformation Rome in 1596, and it is one that worries Sarpi because the Roman authorities had established that their indexes should be enforced throughout Catholic Europe, and therefore in Venice as well, even if the Venetian authorities had played no part in drawing them up. So Sarpi's very critical *History of the Council of Trent* had no chance of being published in a Catholic country at that time, not even in the relatively tolerant Venice. The manuscript was eventually smuggled out of Venice and taken to London, where it was published in Italian in 1619 in an edition that Sarpi himself refused to recognize. Soon translated into both English and Latin, it was immediately taken up and read avidly by Protestant cultures that considered it the official history of what had happened at Trent for many years—indeed, for centuries to come.

Exactly how far Sarpi himself contributed to the publication of his *History* in London in 1619 remains something of a mystery. What has been established as certain is that, over a series of months, the sheets of his text were hidden in the luggage of an English agent in Venice of the archbishop of Canterbury, George Abbott. The agent, Nathaniel Brent, smuggled Sarpi's text to London with the knowledge of de Dominis, who claimed most of the merit for this successful subterfuge. De Dominis himself then wrote a bitterly anti-Catholic letter of dedication of the text to King James I, only to find himself criticized in Venice by Sarpi for doing so.[35] Sarpi claimed publicly to disapprove of the London publication altogether, and some years later edited himself a revised version of the *History* that was published in Geneva. Not only did neither Sarpi nor Venice pass over to the Anglican Church, as James I had hoped, but de Dominis himself soon became impatient of the constant pressure exerted on him in London to criticize Catholicism in all its forms. In 1621 he left once more for Italy, drawn back to Rome by his close personal ties with the newly elected pope, Gregory XV. Gregory, however, died in 1623, leaving de Dominis open to the recriminations for his inconstancy of the new pope, Urban VIII, who would later supervise the condemnation of Galileo. De Dominis was imprisoned by the Inquisition but was lucky enough to escape burning at the stake by dying in prison beforehand. Unrelentingly, the church authorities decreed that his dead body be publicly burned in the Campo dei Fiori, where Giordano Bruno had been burned alive at the beginning of the century.

In London de Dominis had played a major role in overseeing the publication of Sarpi's *History*, which came out in the original Italian in 1619, with John Bill's name as the king's printer. The author's name was given as Pietro Soave Polano, a near anagram of Paolo Sarpi Veneto. Shortly afterward, in 1620, it appeared in an English translation said on the title page to be by Nathaniel Brent (who was probably helped by others). This edition carried the names of both John Bill and Robert Barker as the king's printers, and contained an English version of the dedicatory letter by de Dominis. In the same year a Latin translation appeared containing no information concerning printer or translator, though it too has been proven to be the work of John Bill as printer. The introductory letter by de Dominis to the Italian edition was not included, but he was probably involved in the Latin translation of Sarpi's text, together with other people close to the government and to Venetian affairs. The rapid appearances of these three editions show how important Sarpi's text was considered in English government circles, where—as Graham Rees and Maria Wakeley point out—it was thought that he had "delivered into the hands of the reformers a devastating propaganda weapon which appeared to strike at the very roots of Counter-Reformation doctrine."[36]

The religious conflict de Dominis clearly wished to emphasize in his dedicatory letter is visibly expressed to the reader as soon as the Italian edition of Sarpi's *History* of 1619 is opened at the title page, where on the left is printed a portrait of Pope Paul III, the pope who first convened the Council of Trent in 1545, while opposite it we see the royal arms of the British monarch and written underneath the monarch's motto "Dieu e mon droit" (God and my lawful right). The full title of the volume was *Historia del Concilio tridentino nella quale si scoprono tutti gli artifici della Corte di Roma, per impedire che né la verità di dogmi si palesasse, né la riforma del Papato, & della Chiesa si trattasse*; this would be translated in the English edition as *The Historie of the Councel of Trent. Conteining eight bookes. In which (besides the ordinarie Actes of the Councel) are declared many notable occurences which happened in Christendome, during the space of fourtie yeeres and more. And, particularly, the practises of the Court of Rome, to hinder the reformation of their errors, and to maintaine their greatnesse*. With this council, in the opinion of de Dominis, the Catholics had only managed to entrench the recent religious schisms "in order to maintain the temporal power of the Court of Rome by oppressing the true Christian doctrines." De Dominis, warming to his subject, goes on to denounce "the diabolic inventions and stratagems that have exiled and extinguished true Councils, ruining and corrupting as well as oppressing those that managed to meet with great difficulty."[37] The meetings held at Trent, according to de Dominis, demonstrate how fraud and violence ensured that the council was unable to reach the truth; to the contrary, they served only to increase the power of those in control of it and to restrict the liberty of the true church.

What Sarpi—not without reason—considered the overly violent polemical tone of the dedicatory letter written by de Dominis is not reflected in the far more balanced and nuanced discourse of his own opening pages. For his part, Sarpi himself opens his *Historie* by insisting on the value of the long search for documentary material that underlies his account of what happened at Trent and his sincere desire to understand the causes of what he considered the council's failure to respond to a true desire for religious peace and reform, for the council, writes Sarpi, "continually met and then broke up, always pursuing different ends, until finally it assumed a form and outcome utterly different from those which had originally inspired it." Sarpi considers the interferences of the various princes of the period, both religious and temporal, one of the principal causes of this failure. The council, he writes, "was desired and procured by pious men with the intent of reuniting the church, which had begun to be divided. But the interference of princes with the processes of reform of the ecclesiastical order led to the greatest muddle to be seen since the beginning of Christendom, with the result that the Council finished up by entrenching the schism and hardening the opposing sides into irreconcilable discord."[38]

These strong criticisms of the sixteenth-century Roman Church were among the reasons that induced the English in the reign of James I to hope, unavailingly, for a conversion of Venice, or at least of Sarpi himself, to the Protestant cause. More important for the purposes of this study, however, is to notice that a young Protestant in London, already proficient in the Italian language, was soon reading Sarpi's book in the first edition published by John Bill in 1619. John Milton would include both Galileo and Sarpi among his principal points of reference when, in 1644, he came to write and publish the first systematic plea for the liberty of the press to appear in early modern Europe. We may also add here that Milton's *Commonplace Book*, in which he wrote out extracts from the authors he was reading, contains a substantial number of quotations from the *History* of Jacques Auguste de Thou. Milton's own pamphlet, titled *Areopagitica*, was addressed to the English Parliament.

The Search for New Liberties: John Milton

Both as a poet and as a political and theological polemicist, John Milton's reputation has long been a subject of at times violent controversy. Throughout most of his life and up to the end of the seventeenth century, he was closely identified with the English parliamentary struggles and civil war: an apologist for the regicide of Charles I, an active collaborator in the republican commonwealth of Oliver Cromwell, and at the same time an independent religious thinker who defied the very idea of churches and priestly power. On the restoration of Charles II in 1660, he was condemned to a brief period of imprisonment. Later on Milton became a cultural hero for radical intellectuals such as John Toland who, after Milton's death, refused to abandon "the Good Old Cause" of English republicanism, contributing to the formation of what has recently become known as the Radical Enlightenment. At the end of the seventeenth century, Toland wrote a strongly apologetic biography of Milton as well as republishing in Amsterdam all his prorepublican political tracts. Official Enlightenment critics, on the other hand, gradually managed to absorb Milton's epic poetry into increasingly orthodox parameters, preparing the ground for the more comfortable nineteenth-century image of him as the officially endorsed epic poet of an English parliamentary-libertarian tradition. The most illuminated expressions of this image of Milton are to be found in a famous essay by Thomas Babington Macaulay, which inspired the monumental and still essential biography by David Masson.[39]

CHAPTER 4

It was not until the polarization of ideologies in the early twentieth century, with the buildup of the opposing fronts of communism and fascism, that this image was challenged by T. S. Eliot in two famous essays that denounced Milton as a dangerously radical poet infected by an outmoded form of poetic diction added to an embittered and unrestrained polemical style in prose.[40] The later of these two essays to some extent mitigated the earlier criticisms, which nevertheless did much damage to Milton's reputation. It is easy enough today to recognize Eliot's powerful anti-Miltonic stand as deriving from his conviction that only a disciplined form of highly orthodox Anglicanism could withstand the destructive pressures of modern political ideology. Its effect at the time, however, was to oust Milton from his privileged place on the English Parnassus, and consequently from the scholastic and academic curricula of Britain and America in the mid-twentieth century. The restoration of Milton to academic respectability can be dated to the volume edited by Frank Kermode titled *The Living Milton*, published in 1960. In its wake came major studies such as *Milton's Grand Style* by Christopher Ricks, which reestablished Milton on the highest slopes of Mount Parnassus, where, as an epic poet, he appears still safely positioned today.[41] His reputation as a prose writer, on the other hand, continues to be the subject of ebb and flux, with revisionist and antirevisionist claims in multiple versions subjecting his reputation to sometimes alarming variations, which at times invest the text being taken into consideration here, Milton's famous *Areopagitica, a Speech of Mr. John Milton for the Liberty of Unlicenc'd Printing to the Parliament of England*, published in 1644.[42]

Another of Milton's texts, the Latin *On the Christian Doctrine*, has recently been the subject of a strong revisionist critique, even including a claim that it was not written by Milton himself. *De doctrina Christiana* was traditionally considered to contain Milton's own very personal version of Christianity, including numerous heterodox ideas such as his anti-Trinitarianism, his Arminian-based refutation of John Calvin's doctrine of predestination, and a strong antiecclesiastical stand based on his radically Protestant conviction that all religious truths are available to the individual believer through the Bible. Thought to have been elaborated by Milton over a considerable number of years, and considered by him "my best and most precious possession," *On the Christian Doctrine* amounts to a richly documented and intense expression of heterodox religious thinking.[43] It remained in manuscript form upon Milton's death and was only published for the first time in 1823. An attempt was made in 1992 to discredit this text as Milton's on the basis of the name of the author, which was clearly added to the only remaining manuscript at a later date. This highly polemical claim led to a flurry of polemics in the review *Studies in English Literature*.[44] The result appears to have been a clear victory for those who reclaimed the text for Milton on the basis of a number of convincing internal arguments that related it to the evolution of his religious thought as it developed both in his prose tracts during the years of his political activity as well as in his later epic poems. The leading figure among the opponents of this dramatically revisionist thesis was undoubtedly Barbara K. Lewalski, who went on to offer a detailed and extended reading of this text in her influential biography *The Life of John Milton*.[45]

An essential aspect of this most recent form of revisionism, which Lewalski opposes, is the attempt on which it is evidently based to reestablish Milton once again as an orthodox reformation Christian thinker whose works represent nothing remarkable in the sphere of religious thought. However, as Lewalski points out in the opening pages of her impressive biography, these forms of revisionism, which characterized the Milton discussion in the last decades of the twentieth century, are now themselves being revised. Her own work as well as that of many others has in more recent years tended once again to emphasize the heterodox, often very personal, and surprisingly radical aspects of Milton's thought both in the political and the religious spheres, fashioning him once again into Milton the Heretic.[46] This important development in recent Milton studies can be linked up with the work done by Blair Worden on the republican aspects of Milton's political tracts, which has been carried out in the wake of Quentin Skinner's work on the political republicanism of early modern Europe deriving from the *Discourses* of Niccolò Machiavelli. Worden's attention to Milton's prose works in a republican context has had the effect of endorsing them as a valid moment of modern political philosophy rather than as mere subtexts of a great epic poet, although they are clearly that as well.[47]

John Milton was acutely aware that what he, as a Reformed Christian, thought of as divine providence, or what Machiavelli thought of as *fortuna*, had destined Milton to live his life in a period and in a country characterized by profound and dramatic political events. Milton was born in 1605, when Shakespeare was still alive and writing his great tragedies, with James I firmly established on the British throne. Milton's education, initially directed toward the Anglican priesthood and then deviated toward an exalted conception of poetry as prophecy, contained from the beginning an unusually pronounced humanistic slant. This was originally due to his education at St. Paul's School in London, founded in the early years of the sixteenth century by John Colet, who consulted Erasmus when establishing its curriculum. There Milton met and became firm friends with the young Charles Diodati, of a distinguished family of Italian Protestant exiles from Lucca, in Tuscany, who established themselves partly in Geneva and partly in London. The Genevan branch of the Diodati family, in the person of Elio Diodati, has already been referred to in chapter 3 as involved in the Latin translation of Galileo's great *Dialogue of the Two Major World Systems*.

As a young man Milton had acquired exceptional skills in the reading of classical Latin and Greek, and he learned to both read and speak Italian. After his years at the University of Cambridge, which he found frustratingly orthodox in its dogmatic Aristotelianism, he dedicated himself to several years of rustic retreat during which he subjected himself to a rigorous cultural preparation in ecclesiastical and secular history. These years of unremitting study undoubtedly made of him one of the most cultured young poets of his generation. Such cultural intensity contrasted dramatically with the political doldrums of the 1630s, with Charles I governing according to his idea of a royal prerogative that denied the rights of Parliament, which Charles subjected to a long recession. In the religious sphere, Archbishop William Laud was threatening with violent forms of oppression the radical reformation theology with which Milton was already beginning to sympathize. Milton nevertheless managed to find a space for his poetry within the genres permitted by the times, writing and publishing his first major works such as his masque *Comus* or his pastoral elegy *Lycidas* in remembrance of Edward King, a young Cambridge poet who had died by drowning. These poems skillfully made use of traditional and highly respected literary forms such as the court masque or the classical genre of the pastoral to develop an idea of poetry as a cultural and religious calling based on a deep sense of moral and personal independence and dedication. Yet Milton clearly yearned for a different and more stimulating society in which to express himself: a yearning that projected his mind toward what, at the end of *Lycidas*, he called "pastures new." Uncertain of exactly what arena to choose for the expression of his already exceptional cultural and literary gifts, in the spring of 1638 Milton left England for a journey to Italy and Greece.

Much work has been done on the year Milton spent in Italy, and the details of his journey are well known.[48] They included two lengthy stays in Florence, where he was admired for his readings of his poems (many of them in Latin) in the private academies, and where he made many long-lasting friendships with cultured Florentines, among them Jacopo Gaddi, Carlo Dati, and Benedetto Buonmattei, who was a professor at the University of Pisa. According to the account given by Milton's nephew Edward Phillips, these men "caress'd him with all the Honours and Civilities imaginable." (Phillips was one of the nephews educated by Milton in his house in London after his return from Italy, and one of his earliest biographers; he was clearly repeating words he had heard from Milton himself.[49])

At some time during his Florentine stay Milton was taken to visit the aging Galileo, subjected to house imprisonment at his villa in Arcetri. Farther south, in Naples, he met and befriended Giovanni Battista Manso, then an old man but previously a patron and protector of Torquato Tasso and Giambattista Marino, both poets known to and admired by Milton. Milton would later dedicate a verse letter in hexameters to Manso. In Rome Milton was well received by cardinal Francesco Barberini at an elegant musical evening that Milton seems to have much enjoyed. These well-established moments of one of the most significant literary journeys to Italy by an English writer and poet interest us here for the surprising capacity, even eagerness, they show on Milton's part not only to meet and converse with but also to make friends with Italian Catholics whose Christian beliefs were diametrically opposed to his own. Clearly his own reading was also by no means limited to writers of his own faith or creed. These are aspects of Milton's personality and culture that suggest that it may be necessary to reconsider the image of him as a rabid and uncompromising anti-Catholic or an intransigent radical Protestant, an image of him that is widespread among many of his commentators.

There can be no question of any weakness in attitude on Milton's part with respect to the decidedly Protestant aspects of his own religious beliefs. The rule of conduct that Milton forged for himself in Italy was based rather on the open acceptance of radical differences in doctrine as necessary aspects of a society based on libertarian principles. When Henry Wotton, a former ambassador in Venice and a friend of Milton's father, wrote to him before his departure for Italy advising a discreet silence about religion and related political issues, Milton replied by adopting an alternative stance: "I would not indeed begin a conversation about religion, but if questioned about my faith would hide nothing, whatever the consequences." These words are Milton's own, written in a number of revealing autobiographical pages of his *Second Defense of the People of England* (1654), in which he addresses critics of his Italian journey and his morals by claiming, "I knew beforehand that Italy was not, as you think, a refuge or asylum for criminals, but instead the lodging place of *humanitas* and of all the arts of civilization, and so I found it."[50] Milton's journey to Italy is of major importance because it brought him face to face with a practical issue on which he would elaborate from a more conceptual viewpoint in his *Areopagitica*—that is, how to negotiate human relationships in society when the differences in doctrine or ideology are not marginal or points of differing nuance but deeply rooted and extreme. It was not all plain sailing; in Naples particularly, still under Spanish dominion, there must have been some tensions. Manso sent him a witty Latin epigram, applying to Milton a distich already to be found in Bede: "If your mind, form, grace, features, and manners were equaled by your religion, then by Hercules, you would be no 'Angle' but a very angel." Milton was sensible enough to reply with a Latin verse epistle gratefully acknowledging Manso's friendship. Milton's remarkable and surprising success in negotiating long-lasting friendships with his Italian contemporaries is too often forgotten by commentators wishing to underline what they consider his intransigent Protestant faith.

Milton probably received in Naples news of the sudden death of his Italian friend from his schooldays in London, Charles Diodati, celebrated by him in what many commentators consider his finest poem in Latin, *Epitaphium Damonis* (An Epitaph for Damon). It is significant that in this poem Milton's long-standing affection for the Protestant Diodati is remembered together with that for his new Italian friends. In Naples, Milton also received news of the First Bishops' War on Scotland, which had ended with a defeat of the bishops and the establishment in Scotland of a national Presbyterian Church of Calvinist inspiration. Milton seems at once to have understood that major events were in the making; he decided that it was time to return home, and take a hand, renouncing his intention of reaching Greece. Remembering the dramatic years 1639–40 in the autobiographical passage of his later *Second Defense*, Milton wrote that then were taken the first steps on "the true path to liberty" and registered his decision "to devote to this conflict all my talents and all my active powers."[51]

The years 1639–42 witnessed all the major parliamentary events that laid the foundation for the eventual instauration of Cromwell's commonwealth. After eleven years of total disregard for his parliament, the king convened the so-called Short Parliament on April 13, 1640, and almost immediately suspended it because members insisted on discussing the redress of their numerous grievances rather than voting the taxes needed by the king to wage war on the rebellious Scots. The Second Bishops' War was nevertheless fought against the Scottish army, and lost, in August of that year; in October the king was obliged to convene a new parliament—soon known as the Long Parliament—that, for the first time in England, effectively established legislation under parliamentary rule. A triennial act assured that parliaments must be convened every three years, while a further act prohibited the dissolution of any parliament without the members' consent. The king's two nearest advisers, William Laud and Thomas Wentworth, Earl of Strafford, were impeached for subversion of laws of government and religion, sent to the tower, and executed. In January 1642 the king, still formerly head of state but in effect powerless to resist the Long Parliament's decisions, unwisely attempted to reassert himself by sending officers to the House of Commons to arrest five widely respected parliamentary leaders. The five escaped into the city, where they were protected by an angry populace. In February, Charles I moved north to York, and the country prepared for civil war.

Some recent scholars of the brief period of the English republic have been arguing that the king was executed in 1649, while a republican government was instituted by Oliver Cromwell and his supporters, more by the pressure of events than according to any preconceived plan. We are told that there was little clearly antimonarchical sentiment in the early 1640s and that Milton, along with his contemporaries, was still thinking of a figure of a just king rather than of no king at all.[52] Undoubtedly Milton took time to decide how to intervene in the events of these early years, and when he did so it was initially in terms of the religious dispute rather than at the political level of events. Nevertheless, the religious issues of the time were closely linked to the political ones. When Milton took up arms on the question of church government, placing all his historical knowledge and rhetorical skills at the service of a widespread campaign against the bishops that would eventually lead to a Presbyterian victory in both England and Scotland, as well as to the official dismantling of the Anglican Church, he was implicitly rebelling against monarchical power.

There is no need here to follow up in detail the development of Milton's intense activity as an anti-Episcopal pamphleteer in these years.[53] What needs to be underlined is instead the way in which he uses the question of the power of the bishops to raise major questions concerning the political agenda at hand. The Presbyterian idea of a church appeals to Milton in this first phase of his foray into the public field because he is convinced that biblical authority stands behind the idea of what he calls "full and free Election" by God's people of those ministers who are charged with the instructing and disciplining of their spiritual lives: "And why should not the Piety, and Conscience of *Englishmen* as members of the church be trusted in the election of Pastors . . . as well as their worldly wisedoms are priviledg'd as members of the State in suffraging their Knights, and Burgesses?" Here we see Milton expounding favorably on the question of parliamentary voting and electoral procedure while participating in the controversy over the Episcopal hierarchy of the Anglican Church. In the same way, we see Milton in another passage of the same tract, *On Reformation*, raising the question of the tyranny of absolutist monarchs while claiming that prelacy and high-church Laudian liturgy are nowhere contemplated by either the Bible or the church fathers: "The soure levin of humane Traditions mixt in one putrifi'd Masse with the poisonous dregs of hypocrasie in the hearts of *Prelates* that lye basking in the Sunny warmth of Wealth, and Promotion, is the Serpent's Egge that will hatch an Antichrist wheresoever, and ingender the same Monstrer as big, or little as the Lump is which breeds him."[54]

This passage already presages Milton's imminent parting of company from the Presbyterians, for here it is the abolition of ministers of God of any kind—elected by the congregation or not—that he is advocating. Ultimately Milton saw no need for intermediaries other than the Bible between the believer and his god, as his admirer William Blake would emphasize later during the years of the French Revolution. In this passage Milton is saying what would become music to Blake's ears, that it is the introduction of priesthood itself that has turned religion into a "soure levin" producing monstrous births that "keep up the floting carcass of a crazie and diseased Monarchy." Surely Milton is remembering here that the image of the "Serpents Egge" had been used by Shakespeare in his historical Roman play *Julius Caesar*. In the monologue spoken by Brutus, just before taking his momentous decision to join the conspiracy against Caesar's life, Brutus recognizes that Caesar is not a tyrant yet; but, like a serpent's egg, he may hatch the brood of tyranny if left unrestrained:

CHAPTER 4

> And since the Quarrel
> Will beare no colour, for the thing he is,
> Fashion it thus; that what he is, augmented,
> Would runne to these, and these extremities:
> And therefore thinke him as a Serpents egge,
> Which hatch'd, would as his kinde grow mischievous;
> And kill him in the shell.[55]

In spite of what recent commentators say about there being no thoughts of regicide in England in these early years of the 1640s, Milton, it seems—in his tract *On Reformation Touching Church-Discipline in England: And the Causes that hitherto have hindred it*, published in 1641—was already thinking along the same lines as Shakespeare's Brutus. It is true that he conceals his thoughts under the cover of metaphorical expression and literary allusion. Nevertheless, it becomes difficult in the face of passages of ominous but vigorous prose like these to endorse the revisionist claim of an orthodox and docile Milton in the years immediately following his return from Italy.

John Milton: Areopagitica

In the years of the civil war, which led up to the regicide of 1649, Milton's attention turned to subjects of a rather different nature from the public concerns, ecclesiastical and political, that had occupied his time during the controversy over the power of the bishops. With the withdrawal of Charles I from London, the entire monarchical structure of legislation collapsed, leading to years of fervent discussion and debate as well as to deeply conflicting ideas as to how to proceed with the construction of alternative forms of church and state. Before the regicide, the two houses of Parliament remained intact, though the bishops were gradually excluded from the House of Lords. In this period all acts of Parliament were referred to as ordinances, given that even when they had received the approval of both houses they could not become official acts because of the absence of the king as head of state to ratify them. They began nevertheless to be treated as fully legislative measures, so that gradually a new legislature evolved.[56] One of the most important ordinances of these years concerned the institution of what became known as the Westminster Assembly of Divines. The collapse of monarchical legislation virtually meant the corresponding collapse of the Anglican Church, of which the reigning monarch was the temporal head; and the task allotted to the Westminster Assembly of largely Presbyterian representatives, which started sitting in 1644, was that of advising Parliament as to what alternative form of ecclesiastical structure to introduce in England.[57] Watching this happen as a private citizen in London, Milton—as a fervent supporter of the new parliamentary order of things—found himself wondering at times how new the new legislation really was. Were not some of the old forms of monarchical legislation simply being reintroduced in a new form? Was the Westminster Assembly, dominated by a clearly Presbyterian majority eager to install its own form of church government in England and in Scotland, really that seat of liberty that he had dreamed of while returning home from Italy? Or were not new forms of tyranny of a parliamentary nature—what Alexis de Tocqueville in the nineteenth century, looking to the more recent American form of parliamentary democracy, would call the "tyranny of the majority"—already beginning to rear their ugly heads?[58] The vigilant Milton was not going to see this happen without making his voice eloquently heard.

The context in which the fervently parliamentary Milton found himself unexpectedly cast in the role of opposition to the new parliamentary legislation was, paradoxically, one of an exquisitely private nature. In 1642 Milton had married. His choice was wildly mistaken; for, after a short journey outside London, he brought back from the provinces the daughter of a family with royalist leanings, totally out of sympathy with his intellectual pursuits. The marriage broke up after a few weeks, and was only reluctantly patched up by Milton later on, after the end of the civil war. In the meantime, Milton wanted to divorce, only to find that the survival of canon law in England did not allow it. Convinced that there was no biblical justification for keeping legally yoked together two people unable to communicate or converse, Milton sat down to write a series of pamphlets arguing the case for introducing legal divorce.[59] In this same period, when Milton was educating in his house two of his nephews, he received a request from Samuel Hartlib to write a pamphlet outlining his ideas on the subject, giving rise to the brief pamphlet *On Education*; this was a theme on which Milton had much of interest to say, and the text was well received. The divorce tracts, on the other hand, were bitterly opposed by the Presbyterians, previously supported by Milton in their war against the bishops. Their opposition sanctioned a final rupture between them, which was deep and something more than a war of words, for in 1643, the Long Parliament, afraid of the sudden outpouring of printed material of all kinds stimulated by the collapse of all previous legislation, reintroduced a law sanctioning censorship of all printed texts.

The new law reintroduced many of the measures contained in the decree on the same subject passed by the Star Chamber of Charles I in 1637. It was immediately used to order the burning of books such as Roger Williams's *The Bloudy Tenant*, accused of promoting the toleration of all sorts of religion. At the same time, the Presbyterians began openly to denounce Milton's divorce tracts, outraged at what they considered a particularly pernicious and dangerous heresy threatening to destroy that bastion of Christian society, the family itself. Milton, wounded by those he had formerly considered his allies and his friends, responded by writing in a few weeks and immediately publishing, without permission, his *Areopagitica: A Speech of Mr. John Milton for the Lib-*

erty of Unlicens'd Printing. The pamphlet appeared with the name of the author for all to see, but without the name of the publisher, and no sign of a license. In 1645, Milton was summoned to respond to Parliament for publishing without the permission required by the new law. It is not known what was said on that occasion, but it seems that it was wisely thought fit not to intervene.

Before considering the arguments developed by Milton in this much celebrated text in favor of freedom of the press, it is important to note that in his later years he would refer to these works of 1643–44 on divorce, education, and freedom from censorship as concerned with the "private or domestic liberties," distinguishing them from his works on subjects of a more public and political nature. The distinction is an important one, not commonly found in so explicit a form in works of this time, though the definition may contain some echo from Montaigne, whose "Note to the Reader" introducing his *Essays* claims them as pertaining to a purely "domestic and private" sphere.[60] The concept that Milton elaborates here corresponds already to what a later liberal tradition would come to know as "individual" liberties; it implies a locus for liberty in the idea of a person, in this case specifically an "author" rather than a community, city, or state. We have seen how, in the course of the sixteenth century, liberty became increasingly located within the individual mind, both as the locus of the religious "conscience" as it would develop in Luther himself, informing the ensuing Protestant struggle for religious recognition, and also as a philosophical idea of the enquiring mind as the ultimate locus of logic and reason. Milton's explicit sense of a clear distinction that needs to be made between the political liberties of the community and the "domestic" or private liberties of the individual reminds us that René Descartes's *Discourse on Method*, elaborating *cogito ergo sum* (I think, therefore I am) had been published in French in 1637 and translated into Latin for the first time in this same year, 1644. In Milton, too, a modern idea of subjectivity is already in the making.

It was an idea of subjectivity that required a distinct measure of free will, acting in Milton as a solvent of the certainties of the Reformed religion in its commitment to Lutheran, and then to Calvinist, predestination theology. Milton undoubtedly read Erasmus of Rotterdam, paradoxically more honored in Protestant culture—in spite of his defiance of Luther on the freedom of the will—than in the Catholic world, where his works long remained on the Index of Prohibited Books. Inspired by Erasmus, the Protestant world had gradually developed its own reaction to the pious despondency generated in many by a rigorously preordained universe. This was indeed a increasingly urgent necessity, for Luther's doctrine of predestination had been given a particularly severe interpretation by Calvin, while in some of Calvin's immediate successors, such as Theodore Beza, extreme developments had even given rise to a doctrine of double predestination. Beza taught supralapsarianism, or the doctrine that God had drawn up his complete list of the damned and the saved at the beginning of time—before Adam and Eve had even committed their original sin—to which Beza added the corollary that Christ had died on the cross only for those who were, from the beginning, elect. The ineluctable destination of the damned became dire indeed. We have already seen in chapter 3 of this book how during the developments that led in 1581 to the declaration of the Dutch republic the libertarian Dirck Volckertszoon Coornhert publicly questioned these doctrines at Leiden in the name of freedom of conscience, causing considerable dismay. As a result, an erstwhile Dutch pupil of Beza, the Calvinist pastor Jacob Arminius, was called on to defend the doctrines of Calvin, but in the doing of it ended up by endorsing the doctrine of free will he had been called on to confute. Arminius, as we have seen in chapter 2, was no freethinker such as Coornhert, and he limited himself to the cautious suggestion that damnation is limited to those who actively reject God's grace. This, however, was enough to reintroduce some measure of free will into the mechanism of the cosmic drama as it was lived out in the Protestant world, as a battle between evil and good.[61]

Arminianism, as we have seen, gave rise to a bitter debate within the Calvinist parts of Europe and was officially condemned in 1618 at the famous Dutch Synod of Dort. Arminianism nevertheless remained of lasting significance in modifying the rigors of Calvinist theology throughout the Protestant world. In England it was associated at first with the Anglicanism of the Stuart monarchy rather than with the Calvinist Protestantism of the Presbyterians or the radical sects. Milton, however, adopted a characteristically independent stance on this matter, using the ideas of Arminius to develop an increasingly critical attitude toward Calvinist doctrines of predestination.[62] His one brief mention of Arminius in the *Areopagitica* refers to him as "the acute and distinct" Arminius, suggesting that Milton himself is already clearly on the side of freedom of conscience and the will. For the complexity of Milton's text lies in the tension it immediately creates between the newly established person of the single citizen—increasingly aware of his own identity and autonomy, and therefore requiring freedom to express himself in thoughts that may be of criticism and dissent—and the newly established power of a Parliament that had just introduced a law of censorship that Milton thought pernicious and mistaken in the extreme. The first long, eloquent, and tortuous paragraph of the *Areopagitica* raises precisely this problem. It is still of vital importance today, and destined to remain so as long as, and wherever, parliaments exist, for the problem that Milton is raising, at a very early stage of modern parliamentary life, is that of establishing the correct and legal means by which the individual citizen can closely observe, and if necessary criticize, his elected representatives once the mandate for government has been assigned and power has passed out of the citizen's hands. In the centuries since Milton's time, nongovernmental organizations, local communities, and groups, as well as impressive and at times even overbearing mechanisms of mass media, have learned how to channel the private citizen's discontent into the public arena of extra-parliamentary discussion and debate. In Milton's time there were as yet no such forms of control available, and he was one of the first to become aware of the potential for parliamentary oppression and tyranny to which such a lack could give rise.

Milton's solution was to use his remarkable humanist culture to invent an answer to his problem by looking back to ancient times, and particularly to the example of ancient Greece. His title *Areopagitica* echoes that of the seventh oration, titled *Areopagiticus*, of the ancient Greek rhetorician Isocrates, who—in the Athens of his contemporary, Plato—founded a famous school of oratory. Within the Athenian society of the time, Isocrates represented an alternative cultural choice to that of Plato, who favored a political theory of absolute justice and authority founded on severe vigilance and censorship of the individual citizen on the part of the guardians of a republican city-state. Milton, in several passages of his text, voices sharp criticism of Plato's approval of official censorship. Isocrates, on the other hand, proposed rhetoric as a choice of practical reason, flexibility, and liberty of individual expression within the community.[63] In his *Areopagiticus* Isocrates writes from his house as a private citizen, creating a rhetorical fiction by imagining himself addressing the public meetings on the hill of the Areopagus, situated below the Parthenon in Athens, where he exhorts his fellow citizens to restore to their traditional meeting place its pristine function of ensuring just democratic government. Milton, praising "the old and elegant humanity of Greece," immediately identifies himself with "him who from his private house wrote that discourse to the Parlament of Athens, that perswades them, to change the form of *Democraty* which was then established."[64] Milton, too, is attempting to persuade the new parliament to change its attitude of censorial suppression of the freedom of the press.

What right has he, as a private citizen, to do that? On his frontispiece Milton has already attempted to establish that right, again looking back at the example of ancient Greece, by quoting a cogent passage from a drama by Euripides, *The Suppliant Women*:

> This is true Liberty when free born men
> Having to advise the public may speak free,
> Which he who can, and will, deserv's high praise,
> Who neither can nor will, may hold his peace;
>   What can be juster in a state then this?[65]

In the spirit of Isocrates and Euripides, after assuring the lords and commons of his appreciation of their "undaunted Wisdome" and "indefatigable virtues," Milton bluntly observes that "it would fare better with truth, learning, and the Commonwealth, if one of your publisht Orders which I should name, were call'd in."⁶⁶ The naming of the order is not long delayed. Milton's pamphlet is about to advise Parliament concerning "that Order which ye have ordain'd to regulate printing." There are parts of the new law of which Milton can approve of, such as the clause that "preserves every man's Copy to himself," or that which dedicates some of the revenue from a published book to the poor. The core of the Order, however, Milton cannot approve of: "*That no book, pamphlet or paper shall be henceforth Printed, unless the same be first approv'd and licens'd by such,* or at least one of such as shall be thereto appointed."⁶⁷

On this subject Milton intends to write what he calls a "homily," summoning all his considerable rhetorical powers to carrying out his task. Under the massive rhetorical construction that ensues, it is possible to follow a tightly organized logical design. Milton himself announces that he is going to divide his argument into three parts. First, he will illustrate the origins of censorship in a way designed to make Parliament realize that it is following the example of those it should not wish to imitate. Second, he will widen his subject to a general consideration of what it means to read a book so as to show that the new order will never succeed in suppressing undesirable books as it intends to do. Third, he will show that censorship, insofar as it does succeed, amounts to an effort to "stop the truth, not only by disexercising and blunting our abilities in what we know already, but by hindring and cropping the discovery that might bee yet further made both in religious and civill Wisdome."⁶⁸ Before starting out, however, Milton needs a definition of a book. He elaborates this definition in one of the most justly celebrated pages of English prose: "a good Booke is the pretious life-blood of a master spirit, imbalm'd and treasur'd up on purpose to a life beyond life." This definition allows Milton to consider censorship as "a kinde of homicide" that, if it extends to the whole impression, becomes a massacre. Thinking through this concept further, Milton arrives at the conclusion that censorship is even worse than a massacre, which only slays "an elementall life," whereas killing a book amounts to striking "at that ethereall and fift essence, the breath of reason it selfe." The Order passed by the new Parliament is worse than homicide: it "slaies an immortality rather than a life."⁶⁹

The first stage of Milton's plan, designed to show Parliament where and with whom its law on censorship originated, takes the form of a brief history of censorship from earliest times to the present day. Modern editors have satisfactorily established that this part of Milton's text is derived directly from the section on the history of censorship in Paolo Sarpi's *History of the Council of Trent*. Although failing openly to acknowledge the extent of his debt to Sarpi, Milton does praise him in these pages as "*Padre Paolo* the great unmasker of the *Trentine* Councel." Furthermore, he indicates that Sarpi had already underlined what he, Milton, also gleans from this history: that early forms of censorship, both in the ancient and medieval worlds at least up to the year 800, were occasional and sporadic rather than systematic and consistent.[70] Early Christian forms of censorship in particular tended only to "declare what books were not commendable," leaving it to the conscience of individual believers whether or not they should be read. It was only after the year 800 that an ever more organized system of censorship gradually began to take effect, leading to the suppression by the medieval church in the fifteenth century of the earliest proponents of a reformed theology such as John Wyclif and Jan Huss.

This historical theorem regarding censorship that Milton outlines, following in the footsteps of Sarpi, may be too neat to cover all the complex facts involved. It nevertheless allows Milton to reach his desired conclusion that it was the Council of Trent and the newly reestablished Roman Catholic Inquisition that introduced "expurging Indexes that rake through the entralls of many an old good Author, with a violation, wors then any could be offer'd to his tomb."[71] Milton was writing a polemical tract, and in order to make his point he at times develops his discourse at some distance from historical exactitude. It could certainly be objected that he makes no mention of a native English tradition of book censorship that had been amply used throughout the long reign of Elizabeth I as a means of protecting the newly founded Anglican Church. He also fails to mention that his own objections to censorship are not exactly identifiable with those of Sarpi himself, whose historical evidence Milton at times interprets freely in his own terms.[72] Sarpi's primary concern was to separate ecclesiastical from secular affairs rather than to attack the concept of censorship as such; he objected above all to the way in which the Catholic Church encroached on areas of culture that, in his opinion, should not come under its control. Milton, on the other hand, is against the idea of censorship by any authority and in any field, even if his critical position on the subject is limited to what is known today as "preventive censorship."[73] That is to say, Milton is against the idea that a book need obtain an official "license" or permission (technically, an *imprimatur*) in order to be published and appear before the world. That is why he never uses the word *censorship* in a technical sense, but always the word *licensing*. Milton feels that, once published with the name of its author and publisher for all too see, a book has to compete in the forum of the world and show itself capable of defying the criticism and censorship it might attract. If it goes against the natural or human law, then it can, in Milton's opinion, rightly be suppressed. A book, however, has a right to come into the world, with or without a license. On the basis of this firmly held conviction, Milton urges the Long Parliament not to pass oppressive or mistaken laws. The new law of licensing did little other than reintroduce the law already in force during the monarchy of Charles I, which Milton has little difficulty in characterizing as a pale imitation of the laws introduced by the Roman Catholic Inquisition. So what is the English Reformation Parliament doing "so apishly Romanizing," when it should have been keeping its distance from, "the Inventors and the originall of Book-licensing"?[74]

The central sections of Milton's pamphlet expand the subject being treated to become a more general series of considerations on the acts of reading and writing (called by Milton "learning") that is designed to reach the conclusion that the licensing of books, however systematic and organized, can never succeed in suffocating the creative act of human thought. This is a consideration that we have already found in Galileo's "Letter to Madama Christina Lorena" in the context of scientific investigation; it is thus perfectly consistent with Milton's argument if we find Galileo introduced at this point of the *Areopagitica* as the prime example of the damage done to a nation by licensing. Milton is again thinking of Italy here, and he is concerned with explaining to his English readers how the Inquisition and censorship have "dampt the glory of Italian wits." He goes on to remember that "there it was that I found and visited the famous *Galileo* grown old, a prisoner to the Inquisition, for thinking in Astronomy otherwise then the Franciscan and Dominican licensers thought."[75] Francis Bacon, as well as Galileo, becomes an essential point of reference for Milton in this central section of the *Areopagitica*, which contains numerous references to Bacon's work—and particularly to his dedicatory letter to James I in the *Advancement of Learning*. Furthermore, Milton wrote down in his *Commonplace Book* this comment, under the heading *Gentleness*: "Prohibition of books not the wisest cours. '*When ideas are punished, power blazes forth*, and indeed wee ever see that the forbidden writing is thought to be a certain spark of truth that flyeth up in the faces of them that seek to chok and tread it out, wheras a book autorized is thought to be but the language of the time.'"[76] The phrase given here in italics is from the ancient Roman historian Tacitus. The quotation in which it is embedded is from a 1589 work by Francis Bacon, published posthumously in 1641 with the title *A Wise and Moderate Discourse Concerning Church-Affaires*.

In the *Areopagitica* Milton identifies the new presbyters as the new enemies of tolerance in England. In this respect, bishops and presbyters are "the same to us both name and thing," and what they are now threatening in England is a tyranny over learning. But Milton is certain that "a State govern'd by the rules of justice and fortitude, or a Church built upon the rock of faith and true knowledge, cannot be so pusillanimous" as to try to protect itself with a law of censorship. It is interesting to see Milton chastising censorship here as a breeder of weakness. Censorship denies the capacity of the individual mind to make its own judgments when involved in a process of learning, which necessarily means coming face-to-face both with good and evil. These must both be known and experienced if meaningful moral and cultural choices are to be *made* rather than *made for* the reader by someone else. Milton's reasoning on this point is founded on his idea of truth not as static and stagnant dogma but as a streaming fountain in perpetual movement. Truth and knowledge are always in the process of coming into being, and "where there is much desire to learn, there of necessity will be much arguing, much writing, many opinions, for opinion in good men is but knowledge in the making." In a final, pointed thrust of his argument, Milton claims that if these ideas of truth and knowledge are followed through to their logical conclusion, then censorship betrays the values that lie behind the concept of Parliament itself. The very idea of a parliament introducing a law of censorship becomes for Milton a logical paradox: "Ye cannot make us now lesse capable, lesse knowing, lesse eagerly pursuing of the truth, unlesse ye first make your selves, that made us so, lesse the lovers, lesse the founders of our true liberty."77

Milton's concept of learning as a process continually in the making leads him on to the last section of his pamphlet, which is designed to show that where licensing does have an effect it can only lead to cultural as well as moral, religious, and political stagnation. Milton gives free rein here to all his extraordinary literary gifts in order to express his concept in a series of powerful metaphors. Truth, under the new licensing act, will become a "muddy pool of conformity and tradition," an "old wrinkled skin of corruption," an "old Proteus who spake oracles only when he was caught and bound," a "stark and dead congealment of *wood and hay and stubble* forc't and frozen together," a "triple ice clung about our hearts." It is against these multiple metaphors of stagnation and cultural paralysis that Milton develops his celebrated mixed metaphor of the ascension of Christ and his Apostles into heaven as the moment when "the virgin Truth," seen as the Egyptian figure of Osiris, was deceived by Typhon and his conspirators and cut into a thousand pieces, scattered by the wind to the farthest corners of the earth. This complex metaphor unites the ancient pre-Christian to the modern world in an idea of history as a continuous progression toward ever more complete and perfect forms of knowledge. The searcher after truth is like Isis, the lover of Osiris, who with her followers "went up and down gathering up limb by limb as they could find them." Transposing his classical metaphor into a Christian dimension, Milton states his belief that perfect truth will never be regained within this world, at least until "her Masters second coming." As a Reformed Christian, Milton believes that a new light has been discovered by Luther and his followers, but he insists that it has been far from revealing truth in its perfection. Milton refers to "this slow Reformation," clearly indicating to the English Parliament that its new law of licensing is to be seen as yet another grave impediment to the progress of religious, social, and intellectual reform. There is no point in always wearily repeating the same dogmas or religious truths, however inspiring they may seem to the newly reformed religious believer. Milton proposes another way of using the new light that through Luther's Reformation had, in his opinion, arisen over the horizon of the modern world: "The light which we have gain'd, was giv'n us, not to be ever staring on, but by it to discover onward things more remote from our knowledge."78

The Virtues of Schisms and Sects

In this last section concerning Milton's *Areopagitica* attention will be drawn above all to one of his major themes: his treatment throughout the work of the problem of schisms and sects. The importance of this theme is manifold. First, it constitutes one of Milton's major statements about his own historical period and the proliferation of sects and schisms that characterized it, particularly in England during the period of the so-called English Revolution. Second, it links this pamphlet up with Machiavelli's treatment of the turmoil and tensions between the different components of a city in his *Discourses*, illustrating the way in which thinking about liberty in this period develops a number of unifying concepts that will remain fundamental in the centuries to come. Third, it is through a consideration of Milton's thinking about this subject that it becomes necessary to take account of the limits that he places on the liberty he is prepared to contemplate. This subject has been at the center of a number of strongly polemical and critical studies of the *Areopagitica* in recent years, and a consideration of this problem can be useful in attempting to determine how far and to what an extent the early modern debate about liberty developed, and its significance for the modern world.[79]

The problem of sects and schisms had been a part of the Protestant experience since its earliest years. Luther had already been made to deviate from his early tolerant stance by the extremism of some of the radical groups that soon began protesting against his attempts to dominate the Protestant Reformation. Calvin, who himself operated a schism with respect to orthodox Lutheranism, had certainly been no less antagonistic toward radical opponents of his own version of Protestantism, often organized in small but militant confraternities. This fragmentation of the Protestant world was undoubtedly one of the exasperating factors in the years of unparalleled confusion and violence that characterized the Thirty Years' War in central Europe (1618–48), sparked off by a bitter struggle by the Catholics to limit the Protestant dominion of the continent.[80] The proliferation of sects and schisms had been contained to some extent in England by the departure for the New World of many of the most extreme Protestants during the reigns of James I and Charles I. It became again widespread once the monarchy started to lose its control over the religious life of the country and, after 1642, a free press offered a brief but vitally important space for their pubic expression in print. In a series of influential studies of what he called the radical underground, Christopher Hill drew attention to both the ideological and political importance of groups such as the Levellers and the Ranters, which had previously been considered as operating at the margins of the English experience of commonwealth.[81]

Milton's attitude regarding what appears to be an inbuilt Protestant tendency toward the formation of sects and schisms was articulate, complex, and deeply significant for his concept of political liberty and religious toleration.

He never himself identified with any of the sects of what Hill has since come to call the radical underground, which Milton clearly did not consider as presenting a credible political alternative within the power struggles of the time. This attitude leads Hill, in his full-length study *Milton and the English Revolution*, to consider with a note of irony Milton's obstinate support of Cromwell throughout the years of the protectorate in a religious position known as independency, for Cromwell and the independents were often critical, and even oppressive, with respect to the protests and at times the remarkably democratic ideas put forward by the radical sects. Hill considers Milton—the major cultural figure of the commonwealth years—to be as responsible as Cromwell for the ultimate failure of an experience that might have succeeded if only the more radical voices of the time had been heard rather than silenced.[82] On the other hand, it could well be claimed that Macaulay in the nineteenth century, in what remains the classic "liberal" study of Milton, judged the historical situation more correctly when he pointed out that the choice that Milton faced was not one between Cromwell and various radical groups requesting increasing liberty, but one between Cromwell and the Stuarts.[83] Milton remained loyal to Cromwell to the bitter end because he saw him as the only viable political alternative to an absolute monarchy. At the same time Milton attempted, by various modes and means, to voice what was clearly, in many respects, a deeply critical attitude toward the regime he faithfully served.

In 1644, when Milton wrote the *Areopagitica*, the Thirty Years' War was still raging in Europe while, in England, Cromwell had not yet achieved the military victories in the civil war that would later bring him, supported by his New Model Army, to undisputed political power. Milton is directing his discourse directly to Parliament, whose new licensing law at once appeared to him as an expression of the increasing ascendancy of the Presbyterians in both Parliament itself and in the newly installed Westminster Assembly; he saw their influence as being directed to a large extent toward the silencing of the schisms and the sects. Milton raises his voice decisively in their favor: "Under these fantastic terrors of sect and schism, we wrong the earnest and zealous thirst after knowledge and understanding which God hath stirr'd up in this City." It is necessary, Milton continues, "to forgoe this Prelaticall tradition of crowding free consciences and Christian liberties into canons and precepts of men." Milton's reasoning here culminates in a vision of the slow construction of what he calls the Temple of the Lord, in which reason itself is seen as standing on the side of variety and diversity of opinion and of faith, and the attack against diversity is criticized: "as if, while the temple of the Lord was building, some cutting, some squaring the marble, others hewing the cedars, there should be a sort of irrational men who could not consider there must be many schisms and many dissections made in the quarry and in the timber, ere the house of God can be built." Another image of unity in diversity immediately follows: the newly reformed society of a new era becomes a tree out of whose firm root all the many different branches grow. The adversary of diversity watches in the shadows, scheming: "when they have branched themselves out small enough into parties and partitions, then will be our time." Milton's reply is immediate and clear: "Fool! He sees not the firm root, out of which we all grow, though into branches: nor will beware until he see our small divided maniples cutting through at every angle of his ill united and unwieldy brigade. And that we are to hope better of all these supposed sects and schisms, and that we shall not need that solicitude honest perhaps though over timorous of them that vex in this behalf, but shall laugh in the end, at those malicious applauders of our differences, I have reasons to persuade me."[84]

Milton's reasons for believing in the fortifying power of difference represented by the radical sects is expressed in an image of the city of London "wholly tak'n up with the study of highest and most important matters to be reform'd . . . disputing, reasoning, reading, inventing, discoursing, ev'n to a rarity, and admiration, things not before discourst or writt'n of."[85] Here London has clearly become a latter-day version of Machiavelli's ideal vision of Florence, itself a reflection of the power and vitality of ancient republican Rome. Machiavelli is not openly mentioned in the *Areopagitica*, but significant passages from his *Discourses* were copied by Milton in this period into his *Commonplace Book*, including the passage from book 1, chapter 4 of the *Discourses*, where Machiavelli claims that the conflicts between the nobles and the common people "were the principal means of keeping Rome free."[86] Milton clearly agrees with Machiavelli that legally recognized forms of division, conflict, and dissent, contained within the *ordini* or constitution of the state, fortify and enrich the life of a republic rather than weakening it or causing it to disintegrate and fall.

The final question to be considered here, and perhaps the most important from our point of view today, is how, and in what ways, do these ideas on liberty of expression and toleration appear qualified in Milton's text? By extension, are there limits to his idea of liberty of thought and expression, and if so of what sort are they or should they be? Milton himself is quite aware of the importance of this problem. He clearly specifies his position on the subject while he is developing his image of the construction of the temple of the Lord, "whose perfection consists in this, that out of many moderat varieties and brotherly dissimilitudes that are not vastly disproportionall arises the goodly and graceful symmetry that commends the whole pile and structure." These words suggest a significant limitation on what in other pages of Milton's text appears as a decidedly generous and advanced concept of liberty, especially when considered against the violent and bloody backdrop of his time. The exact nature of the "dissimilitudes" that Milton is thinking of only gets spelled out in a later page of the *Areopagitica* where he starts out by making a general claim that it is difficult to deny: "Yet if all cannot be of one mind, as who looks they should be? this doubtless is more wholesome, more prudent, and more

Christian that many be tolerated, rather than all compell'd." Then come two more problematical limiting clauses: first, "I mean not tolerated Popery, and open superstition, which as it extirpats all religions and civil supremacies, so it self should be extirpat, provided first that all charitable and compassionate means be us'd to win and regain the weak and misled"; and second, "that also which is impious or evil absolutely either against faith or manners no law can possibly permit."[87]

The second statement quoted here is so generic that it is difficult to pin down: Milton probably means no more here than to say that there must be laws that curb criminal or "absolutely" evil behavior that defies the fundamental laws of nature if society is to remain civil at all. The first statement is more precise, and needs to be considered with great care, particularly as it has often been at the center of radical criticism of Milton as a thinker of a libertarian kind.[88]

Behind this phrase in *Areopagitica* lies Milton's important journey to Italy and his friendships with many of the most cultured Catholics of his time. It would be a mistake to think that the words used by Milton here in any way deny the significance of that experience, which he will return to in memory some years later, still in terms of gratitude and affection. What he calls "Popery" in this phrase of the *Areopagitica* does not invest the doctrinal beliefs of those who had been his friends: religious beliefs that Milton, as we have seen, had always declared to be very different from his own, but which he seems to have had no problem tolerating. What is being repudiated here is rather the Catholic Church in its inquisitorial, Counter-Reformation phase initiated by the Council of Trent—that is, a church engaged in an exercise which, as an openly declared policy at that very moment being executed in the course of the Thirty Years War, threatened to "extirpat" not only all other religions but also rebellious civil supremacies. Insofar as it was doing that—and *only* insofar as it was doing that—Milton is claiming that Roman Catholicism itself "should be extirpat," for it is threatening both the civil and religious foundations of all those parts of Europe that are different from itself.

The problem being raised here is one that will exercise many more modern writers on liberty, and which can still be found in John Stuart Mill and beyond—that is, how should a liberal society act with respect to a power structure which threatens the very idea of liberty itself? This problem is still exercising the commentators of the liberal political philosophy of John Rawls, who claims that justice requires that liberty be limited only "for the sake of liberty" itself.[89] As far as the Catholic Church is concerned, it is good to remember that John Locke's much celebrated *Letter on Toleration* of 1689 would fully endorse Milton's position, maintaining that the Catholics continued in his time to represent a danger to the civil supremacy of the British Crown. The problem for Locke presented itself with respect to the prospect of the accession to the throne of James II, the Catholic brother of Charles II. In the middle of the nineteenth century, Macaulay's essay on Milton, considering the ultimate exclusion of James II from the throne, would put the problem in the following terms: "Our ancestors . . . did not drive out a tyrant because he was a Catholic, but they excluded Catholics from the crown because they thought them likely to be tyrants."[90] Macaulay himself was writing in a century when such an attitude could and would finally change. The Inquisition had been formally abolished, and the British Parliament would at last introduce a law allowing Catholics to cover public positions from which they had formerly been excluded. In Milton's time, on the contrary, the danger to the civil as well as the religious life of all the Protestant parts of Europe due to the militant Catholicism of the post-Tridentine church in Rome was not something that it was possible to ignore.

Before leaving Milton and the Catholic question, it is necessary to consider briefly his written *Observations* on the situation in Ireland, which he was required to prepare in 1649 as the first task set him by the Cromwellian Council of State. After the regicide, which Milton had publicly supported, the council had engaged his services as its secretary for foreign languages. Earlier in 1649, before the regicide, the Catholic Confederacy in Ireland had begun an armed revolt against English domination, and had been vigorously wooed by Charles I as a potential invasion force to put down the English parliamentary rebellion against the Crown. Use of the always predominantly Catholic Ireland as a convenient starting point for Catholic entrance into England was no novelty; the church in Rome had at once seen Ireland's potential in this sense, and since the time of Queen Elizabeth I, the Jesuits had used it to come and go in their attempt to organize an anti-Elizabethan plot. When Jesuits engaged in such activities—such as the famous Edmund Campion—were captured, they were mercilessly tortured and killed. The paintings by Niccolò Circignani in the chapel of the English College of the Jesuits in Rome, which date from 1583, are an eloquent testimony of the way in which Roman Catholic priests were being brutally tortured on the rack.[91] The Elizabethan authorities used none of those "charitable and compassionate means" that Milton would advise in his *Areopagitica* when they saw themselves threatened by what the Anglican Settlement had officially established as a foreign power.

Cromwell's regime would be even more merciless in its systematic massacre of Irish Catholics, accompanied by the exile of Catholic landowners to the bleakest parts of the island. It may well be, as Diarmaid MacCulloch suggests, that some of Cromwell's violence was confessional spite, an answer to the unprecedented atrocities and massacres of Protestants so recently carried out by the Habsburg government in central Europe during the Thirty Years' War. Nevertheless, the question remains: How could Milton, after his plea for liberty and tolerance in *Areopagitica*, endorse the official commonwealth policy in Ireland without making a complaint? If Milton's moral and intellectual integrity are to remain intact, the answer must be that he was unable to do so. One attenuating factor is that he was writing the *Areopagitica* before Cromwell's army began its devastating massacres in Ireland. Furthermore, if, then or later on, he had publicly opposed the official government policy in Ireland, he would have had immediately to relinquish his position as a paid official of the newly republican commonwealth he had chosen to serve. The realization of how far Milton was obliged to dissimulate his own personal beliefs in order to serve Cromwell's parliaments and protectorate up to the bitter end is only now beginning to develop with some of the most recent studies of his political career. It has been argued, for example, that Milton's publication in 1658 of a work titled *The Cabinet Council*, which he thought was by Sir Walter Raleigh (but was actually an anonymous compilation of various materials) on the eve of the restoration of Charles II was not undertaken, as has traditionally been supposed, because he agreed with a text proposing the "art of policie" through a series of secondhand aphorisms put hurriedly together in the form of an advice book to a prince. Rather, the statecraft this little text embodied seemed to Milton, ironically, in line with the quasi-monarchical degeneration by that time of Cromwell's regime.[92] According to this reading, Milton published this text precisely because he disapproved of the ideology behind it, in much the same way as Machiavelli disapproved of the ideology that inspired his *Prince*. They were both saying (or so it can be argued): this is where we now stand—be prepared. Accordingly, Milton's *Observations* on the documents published by Parliament in 1649 concerning the Irish rebellion should be read as representing not all that he thought on the subject, but instead the extreme limit to which in his first public act as the new secretary of foreign languages he felt it possible to go. He was no longer a private citizen writing to Parliament to criticize it, as he had been in *Areopagitica*;. he was now, by his own free choice, a paid servant of the new republican state. Read in this light, the moments of heavy-handed abuse of the "Irish barbarians" become no more justifiable, and no less distasteful, to the reader today. It seems reasonable to follow Barbara Lewalski, however, in noting what a small part of Milton's text they occupy.[93] His principal aim in these pages is to restate, in his newly official position, some of the fundamental concepts and beliefs that had inspired his political choice.[94]

Milton's primary aim in his *Observations* is to yoke together the papist rebels of Ireland and the "Insolent and seditious Representation from the Scotch Presbytery at Belfast" that had joined in the rebellion instead of opposing it. This alliance represented a real danger to the Council of State in London, where in 1648 the Westminster Assembly had succeeded in establishing Presbyterianism as the new English church. In England too, however, a considerable number of Presbyterians had been strongly critical of the regicide, and were threatening opposition to the new republican regime. Nevertheless, there were still many independents, like Milton and Cromwell, who failed to recognize this position. Milton, who had already attacked the Presbyterian support for the law on censorship in *Areopagitica*, was not going to lose this opportunity of claiming that he had been right to see them as similar to the Catholics in their political use of religious dominion. Their open alliance with the Catholics in Ireland meant that he could develop "but one and the same Vindication against them both." Milton is particularly indignant at the accusation that the new Parliament is opposing Presbyterian government, which the Presbyters have claimed as "the hedg and bulwark of Religion." On the contrary, Milton replies, the Parliament has adopted Presbyterianism "with all freedom, wherever it hath been desir'd. Nevertheless as we perceive it aspiring to be a compulsive power upon all without exception . . . we hold it no more to be *the hedg and bulwark of Religion*, then the Popish and Prelaticall Courts, or the *Spanish Inquisition*." The position Milton is defending here, as he had always done, is one of opposition to any form of imposition of a state religion and the right to independent choice in the question of religious belief.

The second position Milton is concerned with restating in the clearest possible terms is his classical republicanism. His indignation is directed not so much toward the Irish rebellion as such as it is toward the king's remarkably generous concessions to "His Majesties Roman Catholique Subjects," specified in thirty-five articles of peace that were published before Milton's *Observations*, together with the correspondence that had passed between the king's representatives and the governor of Ireland, the Marquess of Ormond.[95] These concessions were far-reaching, and amounted to a virtual freedom of Ireland from its ties with England (except formally to the Crown) including the right to an independent Irish parliament and complete freedom of conscience in religious affairs. Whether the king would have honored this pact if his plan had been successful we shall never know. In any case, had the Parliament in London on this occasion copied the policy proposed by the king, much bloodshed might have been avoided both then and later. What made it difficult if not impossible for it to do so was that these concessions had been decided without consultation with—and, indeed, with the clear intent of humiliating—the Parliament in London. Milton notes indignantly that "a King in no case, though of extremist necessity, might alienate the Patrimony of his Crown, whereof he is but onely *Usu-fructuary*, as Civilians term it, the propriety remaining ever to the Kingdome, not the King." There can be no doubts as to Milton's republicanism. It is less clear to what extent he is to be considered an imperialist, particularly as far as Ireland is concerned. In his *Commonplace Book* he wrote, "It is not the duty of every state to enlarge the boundaries of its power to bring other nations under its rule. On the contrary, Machiavelli wisely shows that it is dangerous to do so unless that state is wisely ordered and unless the addition of that new realm is justly administered."[96] As time went on, Milton was to become less and less convinced that the newly republican England was as wisely ordered as he had initially hoped and wished.

The third position that Milton is concerned with clarifying in his *Observations* on Ireland is that what he considers the right of the English Parliament

CHAPTER 4

to defend itself in civilian terms against the Irish rebels does not include a right to oppress them in their private religious beliefs. The parliamentarians, he claims, "have been so prudent as never to imploy the Civill sword further then the edge of it could reach; that is, to Civill offences onely; proving always against objects that were spirituall a ridiculous weapon." Later on in his *Observations* he repeats several times that the Irish Catholics must not be offended in their "consciences." This is entirely in line with a quotation in Milton's *Commonplace Book*, where, after mentioning a page from Camden concerning the reign of Elizabeth I that claims "separation between religion and the state cannot be," Milton adds, "Hospital, the very wise chancellor of France, was of the opposite opinion. 'Many,' he says, 'can be citizens who are by no means Christians, and he who is far from the bosom of the church does not cease to be a loyal citizen, and we can live peacefully with those who do not reverence the same religious rites as we do.'" Milton himself supplies the reference for his quote here. It is from book 29 of Jacques Auguste de Thou's *History of His Own Time*.[97]

Cromwell and his army failed to heed Milton's distinction between self-defense by the civil sword and religious oppression of the Irish Catholics, with dire and terrible results. Milton went on serving Cromwell until the end, losing his eyesight in the process of writing defenses of the Commonwealth in front of the rest of the world. He had from the beginning cast his vote in favor of an experiment in civil government without a king, creating a vision of London in his mind as the modern equivalent of ancient republican Rome. Milton never wavered in his dedication to that idea—not when the course taken by events led to a dramatic falling off from his ideals, and not even when the restoration of Charles II in 1660 dashed all his political hopes. Milton's survival of the collapse of his political dream, old and blind as he was, and his emergence from it as a great epic poet, are among the most remarkable achievements of all time. What interests us here, however, is the way in which the greatest of his epics, *Paradise Lost*, characterizes the events to which Milton had dedicated the most active years of his adult life. His choice of placing the parliamentary experience in hell, with pandemonium as its palace and Satan as its hero, implies a devastating judgment on the Cromwellian leadership as well as formulating in resonating poetry a lesson for the modern world. Milton's epic poem teaches that parliaments of themselves, even if they bring together spirits of great vigor and rhetorical ability, are not necessarily or intrinsically good. Milton certainly remained a dedicated parliamentarian at a time when absolute monarchies still abounded, but he had learned that parliaments, too, can become corrupt. They, too, can become tyrannical, dominated by ambition for unlimited power, wealth, and prestige: "Satan with vast and haughty strides advanced, / Came towering, armed in adamant and gold."[98] Parliaments, too, can bring oppression and evil into the world—in Milton's poetic vision, via the gigantic bridge forged by Satan between hell and earth that allows the constant coming and going of sin and death. Milton's final judgment on the experience he had lived through so intensely brings the attention back, as it did for Machiavelli before him, to the ethical integrity of both the governors and the citizens as the necessary foundation of a good political life, of a successful republican and parliamentary regime, and of the liberty that, as they both had learned, it is so hard to come by in this world.

CHAPTER 5

Epilogue

Henry Neville, the Republic of Venice, and the "Glorious Revolution" of 1689

It has been noted in chapter 1 how much work has been done in recent decades on the influence of Niccolò Machiavelli on the development of parliamentary political systems in seventeenth- and eighteenth-century Britain and America. This line of inquiry has involved a radical change in Anglo-Saxon attitudes toward the Florentine Machiavelli, who is nowadays seldom read as the diabolical proponent of political violence and deceit, but instead as the proponent of virtuous republican rule in a state governed by constitutional laws, or *ordini*. This radical change in the reading of Machiavelli can also be summed up as a return to an original positive reading of the Florentine in Elizabethan England, where in 1584 John Wolfe published an Italian-language edition of Machiavelli's *Discourses* with an important introduction by someone who calls himself the "Stampatore" (printer). This introduction claims that its author had previously been influenced by the mistakenly negative attitudes toward Machiavelli that were already prevalent in his times but had since studied the works of the Florentine carefully, reaching an entirely different opinion: "in short, I learned more from them in one day about the governance of the world than I had previously grasped in all of the history I had ever read." The printer then goes on to specify exactly what those lessons were: "I learned to recognize the difference between a just prince and a tyrant, to tell the government of a majority of the greatest good from that of the least evil, and to distinguish between a well-regulated community and a confused and licentious mob."[1]

This printer is usually identified as Giacomo Castelvetro, a nephew of the more famous humanist Ludovico Castelvetro. Giacomo was one of the numerous Italian exiles in Elizabethan London; he collaborated closely with Wolfe in his production of Italian language texts, which also included, in the same year, an edition of Machiavelli's *The Prince*. This positive reading of Ma-

CHAPTER 5

chiavelli was to be short-lived in Elizabethan London, where only a few years later Wolfe himself would publish a pamphlet bitterly attacking "the great subtilitie" of Italians and suggesting that the state "shut up from them al accesse or entrance into our Countrey."[2] The publication of Machiavelli's *Discourses* in such a positive light has, nevertheless, to be recognized as an important moment in the Elizabethan political discussion, representing also an anticipation of many recent readings of Machiavelli, which are characterized by an ever more decisive movement away from *The Prince* as his principal statement of political philosophy and a growing appreciation of the underlying republicanism of his *Discourses on the First Ten Books of Titus Livy*. In the English-speaking world, two books lie at the origins of this contemporary line of development in Machiavelli studies: Felix Raab's *The English Face of Machiavelli: A Changing Interpretation 1500–1700* (1964) and John Pocock's *The Machiavellian Moment: Florentine Political Thought and the Atlantic Republican Tradition* (1974). As has already been noted in this book, this line of inquiry has more recently become associated with a number of other distinguished scholars such as Quentin Skinner, Blair Worden, and Maurizio Viroli, among many others.

Both Raab and Pocock, and indeed many other scholars mentioned in this volume, have stressed the importance of the reference to Machiavelli's republicanism in the years of the commonwealth governed by Oliver Cromwell in seventeenth-century Britain. Particular emphasis has been given in this sense, both by Raab and Pocock, to James Harrington's *The Commonwealth of Oceana*, first published in 1656, when Cromwell's brief period as lord protector was already showing signs of decline. Harrington criticized long-term personal power and proposed frequent ballots and changes of governing bodies, which not surprisingly angered Cromwell, to whom Harrington had dedicated his work. It was only published with difficulty, but nevertheless became an immediate point of reference for the dwindling numbers of British republicans, remaining so well after the restoration of the Stuart monarchy in 1660. Pocock considered Harrington's *Oceana* so important as a continuing sign of a positive historical reading of Machiavellian republicanism in Cromwell's England that in 1992 he edited a modern edition of the text. In the part of his introduction titled "*Oceana* and English Republicanism" he claimed that Harrington's text was not, as is often thought, about a utopia but instead outlines what he considered a realistic system of republican government: "Harrington's republicanism is more Machiavellian than Platonic—the Florentine was an author he deeply admired—because of its concern with the *de facto*. He wanted to know how the English parliamentary monarchy, the government of king, lords and commons, had come to collapse, and he wanted to know what should replace it."[3]

Only two years after the publication of Harrington's *Oceana* everything changed with the death of Cromwell in 1658; the evident incapacity of his son

EPILOGUE

Richard, whom he named as his successor, to continue to govern the rapidly disintegrating commonwealth; and, in 1660, the restoration of the Stuart monarchy in the person of Charles II, sanctioned by a vote in Parliament. Harrington immediately became part of a strictly watched and often persecuted republican minority. Like John Milton, he was imprisoned for a short time, but unlike the by then blind Milton he seems to have suffered a complete breakdown. Eventually he retired to private life until his death in 1677.

The restoration of the Stuart monarchy in 1660 far from eliminated all republican sympathies in Britain. One of those who continued to maintain a faith in what was to become known (in John Toland's phrase) as "the good old cause" was Harrington's friend Henry Neville, who, in the later years of Cromwell's commonwealth had been a close friend also to Milton. Harrington and Neville were also personally close, and had initially collaborated as members of Cromwell's parliaments, although they later reacted against his parliamentary purges; both collaborated with Richard Cromwell's brief parliaments in the hope of a restoration of a true republican system, only to be disappointed yet again. They seem to have reacted differently to the traumatic restoration of monarchical rule in 1660. Neville was briefly imprisoned in 1663 but subsequently released without punishment. He went abroad, having always been a great traveler, particularly to Italy where he established a close relationship with Cosimo III, Grand Duke of Tuscany.[4] However, he returned to London and continued to write, publishing his satire on gender and politics, *The Isle of Pines*, in 1667.[5] In 1680, three years after Harrington's death, he published anonymously his *Plato redivivus* (Plato reborn), a work that continued the discussion of republican rule under the influence of a reading of Machiavelli. Indeed, only some years earlier, Neville is thought to have been behind the publication of a volume of English translations of eleven of Machiavelli's best known works, and this was republished in 1680, the same year as *Plato redivivus*.[6] Both Raab and Pocock mention Neville only briefly, however; the latter considers his *Plato redivivus* as little more than a continuation of the discussion of commonwealths "in the neo-Harringtonian style."[7] The two works have traditionally been coupled together; in 1732, an edition of both *Oceana* and *Plato redivivus* edited by John Toland was published in Dublin by Thomas Birch and would later appear in London as well. Indeed, in a 1681 reedition of Neville's *Plato redivivus*, an introductory "Letter from the Publisher to the Reader," anticipates the possible accusation of plagiarism from Harrington's *Oceana*, defending Neville by claiming that both he and Harrington were inspired by the same classical authors, in particular Polybius and Titus Livy. Although he fails to mention Machiavelli's name at this point, the publisher must have known that these were precisely the authors who lay behind Machiavelli's republicanism.[8]

It can, furthermore, be plausibly argued that Neville's work was written in a fundamentally different political and historical context than Harrington's, a

CHAPTER 5

context closer to the Machiavelli of the *The Discourse on the Situation in Florence after the Death of Lorenzo dei Medici Junior* than to the Machiavelli of the *Discourses on the First Ten Books of Titus Livy*. Machiavelli's *Discourse on the Situation in Florence* was an occasional piece and does not appear among Neville's Machiavellian translations. That is hardly surprising given that the first printed edition came out only in 1760, in a volume titled *Unedited Works of Niccolò Machiavelli*, published in the Tuscan town of Lucca but with the place of publication given as London—a sign of the continuing aura of danger associated with the name of Machiavelli in eighteenth-century Italy.[9] Neville is thus unlikely to have read this text of Machiavelli's, but it is interesting to note that one of the two earliest manuscript copies of this work, now in the Biblioteca Nazionale in Florence, is thought to derive from a no longer extant original manuscript that in the seventeenth century was cataloged in the library of the Florentine humanist Jacopo Gaddi. It is known that this manuscript was bound together with the report by Alessandro Pazzi that had been critical of Machiavelli, and also that Gaddi reread both manuscripts in his library in 1647.[10] Neville stayed in Florence during his first Italian journey of 1643–44, and also later when he returned after his release from prison in 1663, but it is not known if he had contacts with Gaddi. Jacopo Gaddi was, however, one of the Florentine humanists who had met and admired John Milton during his visits to Florence in 1638 and 1639. Indeed, the meetings of the Accademia degli Svogliati, which Milton is known to have frequented, took place in Gaddi's Florentine house. The possibility that Milton studied in Gaddi's library and saw this rare manuscript is a remote one but cannot be completely ruled out; he could have done so, and referred its contents to Neville, a fellow republican and friend.

Whether Neville had heard of this text of Machiavelli's or not, the similarity of situation is suggestive and merits underlining. Machiavelli's *Discourse on the Situation in Florence* was written when Medici rule in Florence had already survived for a decade as a force that needed to be reckoned with. Neville was writing at a time when the restored Stuart monarchy had already survived for twenty years and appeared to be entrenching itself ever more securely. To be sure, it was now a constitutional monarchy, deriving its power not so much from the divine right of kings as from the parliamentary sanction that had authorized the return of Charles II from exile in 1660. Nevertheless, its powers were still extensive, and also had to be reckoned with in a sense that had not been the case when Harrington wrote his *Oceana*. Additionally the monarchy, and with it the entire country, were about to reach an inevitable crux with the approaching demise of the officially childless Charles II. The heir to the British throne—Charles's brother, who in 1685 would briefly become James II—was showing every sign of wishing to return the country to an absolutist Catholicism viewed with alarm even by many of those who had supported the restoration in earlier years. Only five years separate the first publication of

Neville's *Plato redivivus* from this future event, which means he was addressing a very different situation from that which had inspired Harrington's *Oceana*.

According to Raab's brief but perceptive pages on Neville in his chapter "Harrington, Hobbes, God and Machiavelli," Neville was, like Machiavelli, sufficiently realistic to realize that single rulers were political realities. As such he proposed that they be controlled (and perhaps influenced), and not merely bemoaned or adored. Neville, in other words—like Machiavelli—was a political pragmatist, though Raab thinks it would be more accurate to say that both men had pragmatism forced upon them by circumstances, for at heart Neville, as much as Machiavelli, remained a republican. Raab underlines how, in 1659, Neville and Harrington, with a group of republicans that included Cyriac Skinner, a scholar in John Milton's circle, would meet regularly in Miles's Coffee House to instill their republican principles into others. Harrington's *Oceana* had already been published in 1656, and Hobbes would say that Henry Neville had a finger in that pie. Raab, however, goes on to distinguish Neville's book from Harrington's. Neville's *Plato redivivus*, like Harrington's *Oceana*, is founded on a central political maxim: empire always follows the balance of property. However, *Oceana* is an imaginary and radically republican scheme, whereas *Plato redivivus* claims, more realistically, that it contains in its own pages the method of rendering a monarchy—and particularly the monarchy of Great Britain—both happy at home and powerful abroad, a method that consists in conjugating monarchy with republican virtues.[11]

In the following pages I shall be arguing that Neville's book is indeed different from Harrington's *Oceana* in both kind and content, and that it needs to be read carefully for its own sake and not just as an appendix to Harrington's text. To begin with, it is entirely different in its form. *Oceana* may allow an idealized Cromwellian political reality to be glimpsed quite clearly through the filigree of Harrington's utopian scheme, as Pocock argues, but it nevertheless follows quite closely the traditional form of a utopia as introduced by Thomas More at the beginning of the sixteenth century—that is, an introductory section, almost equivalent to a first book, outlines the underlying political concepts and historical situation involved, while the whole second part of the text is devoted to the construction of the perfect form of society envisaged by its author. On the contrary, Neville's *Plato redivivus* is written throughout in the form of a political dialogue, and according to the introductory "Letter from the Publisher to the Reader" it is above all the dialogue form, rather than any utopian characteristics, that justifies the reference to Plato in its title. In fact Neville, in contrast to Harrington, seldom makes any reference at all to a Platonic concept of a perfect society as representative of a sphere of transcendental ideas. His use of the dialogue form instead looks back to the Renaissance preference for dialogue over dogma, and forward to the importance of dialogue in the establishment of any system of parliamentary rule. Even the characters in Neville's dialogue are representative of his own contemporary world; they are presented in the "First Day" of the dialogue as if they were real people known to him personally. The central character is called The Stranger, or the Noble Venetian, and is a visiting nobleman from Venice. His host, called in the text The English Gentleman, can be identified as Neville himself. The Physician is explicitly said to be not only a friend but one of the most distinguished medical practitioners of the time, author of fundamental works in Latin; he is probably to be identified as Richard Lower, who in 1667 demonstrated to the Royal Society in London one of the first blood transfusions in Western history.

Neville's *Plato redivivus* begins with an account of the arrival in London of the Noble Venetian, who has been advised by Italian friends to contact the author of the dialogue, or Neville himself, thus underlining the Italian inspiration behind his political republicanism. As well as the Machiavellian influence, there is clearly a major reference here to Venetian republicanism as the most valid practical model to propose to a British public, for the more aristocratic character of Venetian republicanism allowed it to survive into the seventeenth century and beyond, while the more socially open character of Florentine republicanism led it to collapse under the assault of the Medici. Machiavelli himself in the *Discourse on the Situation in Florence* seems to be casting an eye on the more successful Venetian model while discarding previous Florentine republics as too fragile to survive into a world still to a large extent founded on princely forms of absolutism.[12] This means that Neville's text should be read not only in the light of Machiavellian republicanism (to which he makes numerous positive references) but also in the light of the classical studies of the success of the Venetian model, such as the *Dialogue on the Republic of Venice* published in 1540 by Donato Giannotti, a friend of Machiavelli's and a fervent republican, or more specifically *The Commonwealth and Government of Venice* published in 1543 by Gasparo Contarini and translated into English by Lewes Lewkenor in 1599.[13] These sixteenth-century works, which had also been an inspiration to Harrington, lay behind a number of seventeenth-century studies of Venetian policy and government that are explicitly cited by Neville himself as his sources—in particular *The Policy and Government of the Venetians* by the Sieur de la Haye, published in an English translation in 1671.[14] Neville, however, is not writing entirely in praise of the Venetian form of aristocratic republicanism, for which he clearly has some sympathy but which at times he criticizes in the light of Machiavelli's less aristocratic and more liberal version. Indeed, Machiavelli himself, as we shall see, was often sharply critical of the Republic of Venice, and it is clear that Neville was aware of the terms of his criticism.

The "First Day" describes how the discussion related in the text came about. The Noble Venetian travels into England via France, where he has been staying with a relative, an ambassador to the court. In London he stays with the English Gentleman. The Gentleman goes into the country but has to return suddenly on hearing that the Venetian is seriously ill; when he arrives he finds the Venetian almost restored to health, and in the company of the Doctor. They all discuss the Venetian's disease and compliment each other on his recovery. This clearly has a symbolic value, as the whole work is about political disease and its remedy. In the "Second Day" Machiavelli is first called upon in this context: "Machiavel says, that diseases in government are like marasmus in the body natural, which is very hard to be discovered, whilst it is curable; and after it comes to be easy to discern, difficult (if not impossible) to be remedy'd." Although Neville himself gives no specific reference, he is referring here to a famous passage in the *Discourses*, book 1, chapters 16–18, where Machiavelli starts out from the dramatic declaration that "un popolo dove in tutto è entrata la corruzione, non può, non che piccol tempo, ma punto vivere libero" (a people that has become completely corrupt is unable to live in freedom, not only for a short time, but for any time at all).[15]

The Noble Venetian's specific disease also seems to be considered by Neville in the light of further readings of Machiavelli, and particularly in the light of the Florentine's repeated insistence that a republic must be armed and capable of ensuring its own defense.[16] Venice, on the contrary, was loath to arm its own citizens and often relied on mercenary troops. As Contarini had put it in book 1 of *The Commonwealth and Government of Venice*, the Venetians have always been more concerned with governing their city in peace than with war, which they carry out through "mercenarie people and hired servants" rather than involving the noble Venetian citizens themselves.[17] Sieur de la Haye, for his part, devotes half of his entire book on Venice to their military policy, underlining that although their *generalissimo* is always appointed from the Venetian nobility itself, they nevertheless "on occasion have been necessitated to have recourse to Strangers, and to give them considerable commands."[18] This was not a policy of which Machiavelli approved. Indeed, his lifelong concern with the idea that a healthy republic must depend on its own arms has recently been at the center of attention of a number of commentators.[19]

It may be usefully asked at this point if the Venetian's serious (indeed, almost mortal) illness, followed by his unexpected return to health, may not also be an oblique reference on Neville's part to the dramatic sequence of historical events surrounding the famous city in the early decades of the previous century. For at the turn of the sixteenth century, the rapidly increasing power of Venice both on land and overseas, and its ever vaster imperial possessions, were alarming more than one of the European governments of the time. The year 1508 saw the signing of the so-called League of Cambrai, comprising the Holy Roman emperor Maximilian of Austria, Pope Julius II, and King Louis XII of France. These major European powers joined up together with the specific intent of conquering and dividing among themselves both the city of Venice and the wealthy territories under its command. The most violent battles took place when in 1509 King Louis XII led his army over the Adda River

CHAPTER 5

at Cassano, near Cremona, and went on to approach the Venetian city of Padua, beyond which lay the appetizing treasures of the ancient city of Venice itself. In book 5 of his text, Contarini describes the defeat of the Venetian army at Agnadello, near Cassano, as "humiliating," underlining how dire the situation of Venice had become, with both the Germans and Pope Julius surrounding the city from all sides. He may have had in mind Machiavelli's sharp criticism of the Venetian republic a few years later: writing to Francesco Vettori on August 26, 1513, with reference to the Venetian defeat at Agnadello, Machiavelli exclaimed, "What makes me criticize them [the Venetians] is their way of organizing their military without captains or soldiers of their own."[20] Yet, against all odds, Contarini claims proudly that the Venetian people refrained from rebelling against their governors; instead they all joined together, nobles and commons alike, to resist the siege of Padua, succeeding in fending off the hostile troops until winter set in and the attacking armies were forced to retreat.[21]

In 1510 the situation for Venice began to improve, for Pope Julius II started to become fearful that the belligerent presence of French armies in the Italian Peninsula could become a danger for the papal territories as well. He decided to withdraw papal support from the League of Cambrai, which quickly disintegrated, and entered into an anti-French alliance, the so-called Holy Alliance. This included Venice itself, and was supported from 1511 on by a number of other European countries, including briefly Henry VIII's England. The doge in Venice in this period was Leonardo Loredan, who succeeded in deftly handling this rapidly evolving situation, leading it toward an end of the threat to Venice in 1516. In 1517 the Treaties of Noyon and Brussels returned the Venetian territories to more or less the situation before Venice's troubles began, although obliging the Venetians to give up their hopes of expanding their territories further into the Italian Peninsula. For Contarini, however, this relative success is not to be attributed only to the undoubted ability of the doge. Rather, it derives from the wisdom of the ancient Venetians who had decided not to put political power directly into the hands of the people but instead to encourage their leaders to make laws to help and sustain those who had no property or riches of their own. The wisdom of this decision, according to Contarini, assured that in times of danger the people and their leaders would work together to defeat their enemies. Contarini ends his description of the institutions of Venetian government with the classical metaphor of the body politic as a human body, governed by all-seeing eyes, while each organ and limb carries out its specific functions according to the directions it receives.[22] In the course of his treatise, however, there had been moments when Contarini had felt obliged to admit that modern Venice had not always lived up to the intentions of the ancient citizens who had laid down its unique constitution. In book 4 he admits that in the course of time the ability of Venice to protect its republican liberties with just wars had declined, but he goes on to

166

claim that the city is seeking remedies for "this wearing and alwaies downe-declining course of nature." Modern Venice is no longer ill but instead seeking to make those provisions that are to be considered necessary for the good health of the commonwealth.[23]

The "First Day" of Neville's *Plato redivivus*, then, tells us about the illness of the Noble Venetian, though more through implicit historical suggestions than through explicit explanations of its causes. On the contrary, in the "Second Day" Neville has the Noble Venetian, now completely restored to health, questioning the English Gentleman about the illness of British society. Britain, he claims, is scarcely valued on the European continent; why is this? The English Gentleman replies with a brisk survey of contemporary England that refuses to place the blame for Britain's troubles, or present weakness, on any one class or sector of society. Rather, he indicates a deeper political malaise that he sums up as "playing handy-dandy" with the idea of a parliament. The English Gentleman insists on the importance of keeping alive a just and active parliament—an importance, in his opinion, that has not been respected sufficiently by either side in the turbulent events characterizing recent British history and its traumatic civil war. It is a passage that is clearly reminiscent of Machiavelli's insistence in the *Discourse on the Situation in Florence* on keeping open the doors of a senate, representative of the will of the people from all levels of society; so it is surely no coincidence that it is precisely in this context that the first explicit reference to Machiavelli, and the concept of political illness, is to be found. At this point, however, the English Gentleman feels that if he is to explain himself clearly to the Noble Venetian, he needs to look more closely at the origins of the idea of a parliament and, indeed, of political society itself. Neville thus goes on to offer his reader a brief history of the beginnings of government narrated by the English Gentleman.

Neville's discourse here is basically Hobbesian in seeing the primitive state as one of conflict and war. At some point the primitive peoples agree to lose their natural state of liberty to ensure their own safety and that of their property: "Whatsoever the frame or constitution was first, it was made by the persuasion and mediation of some wise and virtuous person, and consented to by the whole number." When the Noble Venetian asks the English Gentleman why he has not mentioned patriarchal government as the first form of government, the Englishman replies that government did not descend from patriarchal authority, which has a natural or rather divine origin, but from consent. The first forms of government from consent were probably monarchical in origin and despotic—that is, unlimited by any laws—though we know almost nothing about them. Later on we get aristocratic government, or government by the *ottimati*, which is to be contrasted to democratic government, or government by the people. Original government by the *ottomati*, the best leaders, must have been benign; otherwise the ancient peoples would never have handed over their liberties by consent. However, in some countries, aristocratic government has recently become so tyrannical that it will almost certainly lead with time to violent popular uprisings. Neville points to the France of Louis XIV as a case in point, foreseeing in the meantime the French Revolution of a century later: "the great power of the king of France may diminish much, when his enraged and oppressed subjects come to be commanded by a prince of less courage, wisdom, and military virtue; when it will be very hard for any such king to govern tyrannically a country which is not entirely his own." Neville adds that the Britain of his time is no longer in this situation because a decadent and declining aristocracy has allowed its estates to be gradually absorbed by an up-and-coming middle class that is unlikely to permit a return to the tyranny of an absolute monarch. Recent commentators have underlined how this conviction led Neville to be far less alarmed than many of his contemporaries by the probable succession to the throne of Charles II's Catholic brother James, for Neville was less interested in the personal characteristics of the monarch than in the constitutional limits he claimed as essential to containing the absolutist tendencies to which he considered all monarchy to be inclined.[24]

The English Gentleman continues his analysis of the history of governments by contrasting aristocratic systems of government with democratic republics. The former are of limited effect because they cannot arm the people for fear that they will overturn the government itself, while democratic government resides in the people. In a democratic government, the people consent to representation of their will in Parliament. It consists of three fundamental orders: the senate proposing, the people resolving, and the magistrates executing. This description of democratic government can be found in precisely the same words in Harrington, too, but as Harrington points out, it has a Machiavellian origin.[25] Moreover, it is Machiavelli himself who claims that the definition goes back to "the ancients." Democratic government, Neville continues (again paraphrasing Machiavelli), is more powerful than aristocratic government because it can arm the people, who will not take up arms against themselves. Its inability to arm the people fully, and therefore its dependence on mercenary armed forces, is what weakens the aristocratic Venetian republic (hence the cause of the Noble Venetian's illness) that otherwise, according to the "divine Machiavil," would mount up to heaven.

With his pride somewhat stung the Noble Venetian launches into a history of the development of government in Venice since its foundation on the lagoon as a defense against the barbaric invasions from north of the Alps. He describes how the city was originally governed somewhat informally by a council of those who were requested to participate in it because of their ability. This worked well, and the city started to acquire increasing wealth and foreign territories. These began to require a more formal system of government, and "we pitch upon an Aristocracy: by ordering that those who had been called to council for that present year and for four years before, should have the govern-

EPILOGUE

ment in their hands." The Venetian nobleman recognizes that such a system creates a clear divide between the governing classes and the governed—the people. In Venice, however, this divide has not led to strife or unrest because the people, who come from many nations to live there, seek nothing but their safety and ease. The Venetians have not sought to expand their territory except when necessary, and when they have done so they have always respected the property of the conquered peoples. Their foreign territories, however, are governed strictly by the Venetians themselves, which is why their empire has lasted for so long.

The word then returns to the English Gentleman, who continues his long history of governments, divided once again into the Aristotelian extremes of oligarchic and democratic. He starts with Sparta and Lycurgus, presented with explicitly Plutarchian echoes as prime examples of balanced democracy based on the governing powers of a senate, and arrives at Machiavelli and modern Florence, where a change from aristocratic government means *chiamar il popolo a parlamento, e ripigliar lo stato* (calling the people to a parliament and taking over the state). For the more moderate Neville, however—in contrast to Machiavelli—such excessive democracy is imperfect because it includes people without any property at all who are bound, in Neville's opinion, to be "less careful of the publick concerns." Generally speaking, for Neville as for the Noble Venetian, the question of property and its correct distribution is considered crucial to the success of any form of government. As the Noble Venetian puts it, all changes of government "have turned upon this hinge of property" so that the fixing of property "with good laws in the beginning or first institution of a state, and the holding to those laws afterward, is the only way to make a commonwealth immortal." It is as a demonstration of this principle that the English Gentleman continues with a long series of unoriginal historical narratives characterized by a tendency to see correct forms of government as based more on the principle of just and equal property distribution than on the power of the common people. Nevertheless, oligarchical or aristocratic models of government, where too much property is amassed in too few hands, are seen as ultimately doomed to failure due to the inevitable uprisings of an oppressed populace. During his speeches on this subject, the English Gentleman declares, "The Roman emperors I reckon among the tyrants." When the subject of religion is raised, the English Gentleman reveals himself to be a radical Puritan claiming that priests have exercised far too much power and that any person may perform sacred functions without being ordained. The Noble Venetian agrees with the first part of this proposition, but finds the second one "strange."

At this point the English Gentleman feels that he can return to the subject of the English Parliament, which resides in king, lords, and commons. He remarks that, as things stand, the king calls and dissolves parliaments, presides over them, and is their supreme magistrate. This induces the Doctor to ob-

CHAPTER 5

serve that such a king is "a very absolute prince," an objection of which the English Gentleman thoroughly approves. More history, from Anglo-Saxon times through the Magna Carta and beyond, shows that the present monarchy is incorrectly allowed not only command of the militia but also that of repealing acts of parliament. The Noble Venetian points out that the doge of Venice would not be able to do any of these things, and if he did the Venetians could not call themselves a free people. The English Gentleman explains to him that the ancient laws of the English constitution gave the people entire freedom in their lives, properties, and their persons that could not suffer except according to the law, but this excellent government of England came to decay when the lords and the king became the major holders of the land, and this gave them excessive power in parliament. The English Gentleman thinks that the parliament in power after the restoration suffers from exactly the same defects as those before the civil war, which has made no essential difference. When the Noble Venetian asks him to talk about the civil war, he notes that "our parliament never did, as they pretended, make war against the king: for he by law can do no wrong, and therefore cannot be quarrelled with. The war they declared was undertaken to rescue the king's person out of those mens hands who led him from his parliament, and made use of his name to levy a war against them." When that happens, as the Noble Venetian's "own countryman Machiavel" well knew, the two competing—instead of collaborating—powers will "fall together by the ears." There is a lot of hedging here about the execution of Charles I, which virtually goes unmentioned. Neville is certainly not Milton on this point, and England is once again a monarchy.

The "Third Day," in fact, shows the English Gentleman very hesitant to speak up openly about any contemporary questions of government: "How can any man, without hesitation, presume to be so confident as to deliver his private opinion in a point, upon which for almost two hundred year (for so long our government has been crazy) no man has ventured?" He goes on to claim that "as for making new laws, I hold it absolutely needless; those we have already against arbitrary power being abundantly sufficient." He then discreetly raises the fear of succumbing again to popery, which makes the Noble Venetian reply that he will not be offended by such fears. For, as to the government of the Venetian state: "the pope or his priests have as little influence upon it, as your clergy have here." The remedy for a situation that could only see Charles II's Catholic brother—then the Duke of Monmouth—assume the Crown would naturally be that of a popular revolt; but this is considered by all the participants in the dialogue as undesirable. Machiavelli is called on here to confirm Neville's peaceful intentions: "do you not know that Machiavel, the best and most honest of all the modern politicians, has suffered sufficiently by means of the priests, and other ignorant persons who do not understand his writings, and therefore impute to him the teaching subjects how they should rebel and conspire against their princes; which if he were in any kind guilty of, he would deserve all the reproaches that have been cast upon him, and ten times more ?"[26] The English Gentleman, who is a republican but clearly no revolutionary, insists again and again that "the less change the better." All that can be said—and this is Neville's crucial point, as it had been Machiavelli's in the *Discourse on the Situation in Florence*—is that "there is a necessity of a senate." The models are ancient Sparta and Rome, "which Machiavel so much extols."[27] If these models are forgotten there will once more be civil war; if they are remembered, "we shall be the happiest and greatest nation in the world in a little time."

Neville's pragmatic dialogue is very different from his friend Harrington's more utopian *Oceana*, even if it is inspired by the same political ideal. Neville's work is a cautious consideration of a specific, inevitable, historical event that would later arise with the death of Charles II in 1685. It is not a work of theory, but of practical advice to the nation. Neville already foresees the possibility of a silent or bloodless revolution aimed only at removing from the throne the absolutist brother of the king. However, what Neville himself is most interested in is the development of a new and more fully parliamentary phase of British history. The reference to Venice here is of primary importance. The whole of book 2 of Contarini's *The Commonwealth and Government of Venice* is concerned with defining and explaining the power of the Venetian doge, called a monarch by Contarini himself, who underlines that the doge ruled for life in spite of being subject to a complicated process of election described in detail in the text. Above all, however, Contarini is concerned with underlining that "nevertheless so is this authoritie of his by laws retracted, that alone he may not doe any thing." Precisely because of the doge's subjection to Venetian law, like all the other citizens, "the citie of Venice need stand less in feare, then that their prince should at any time be able to invade their liberty, or trouble their common quiet."[28] Furthermore, in book 3, in which he describes the mode of election and the powers of the various governing bodies of the city, Contarini underlines the central importance of the Council of Ten, a tribunal of magistrates established "to prevent factions or the attempts of any wicked citizen that shoulde conspire against the liberty of the commonwealth: of which sort of mischiefe if there should by evil destiny any creepe into the commonwealth, they then to have absolute authority to punish and chasten the same, least otherwise the commonwealth might thereby receive harm."[29]

Contarini makes of the aristocratic or mixed republicanism of Venice and its political system something of a utopia: a perfect system, unrivaled even by the ancients. He was clearly an important point of reference for Neville, even if Neville himself, as we have seen, had become in the course of the twenty years of the restored Stuart monarchy increasingly a pragmatist, accepting the resuscitated monarchical powers of his time as a reality that he may not have loved but that had to be reckoned with. In this acceptance, beyond or behind the Venetian reference, Neville's text is also surprisingly close to the more prag-

CHAPTER 5

matic Machiavelli of the *Discourse on the Situation in Florence*. Indeed, the whole of Neville's *Plato redivivus* is a testimony of a careful and intelligent study of the works of Machiavelli. The Florentine's "diabolic" reputation was already well established by this time in Protestant as well as Catholic countries, and in the latter his works had long been on the Index of Prohibited Books. Neville ignores it, absorbing from Machiavelli's works many lessons concerning the political wisdom of ordering governments not on the basis of absolute monarchical power but on principles of republican justice and liberty to be guaranteed by the *ordini*, or constitutional laws, of a state ruled primarily by its senate. Neville's book is an eloquent testimony that Machiavelli's conversations with the ancients in his study had not been held in vain.

Conclusion

The aim of this book has been to investigate a number of aspects of the historical foundation on which the modern discourse of liberty and toleration is based. It has taken as its specific moment of time the period frequently referred to as "the long sixteenth century," between 1500 and approximately 1650, specifically between the time of Niccolò Machiavelli and John Milton, for that was the period in which the principal concepts and themes concerning liberty in the modern world began to emerge against a background of unprecedented violence and oppression. Clearly there can be no question of denying the importance of earlier historical periods, which acted in their turn as the foundation on which the early modern idea of liberty developed. Classical antiquity was essential in offering an original series of historical perspectives and conceptual elaborations of the idea of liberty that the figures considered in this study were often eager to claim as their direct forbears and inspiration. The medieval experiences of the Scholastics and the neo-Thomists, in particular, offered an important basis for the formulation of ideas about civil jurisdiction and relations between church and state that were undoubtedly remembered in the early modern world; even if the strong anti-Scholastic bias of Renaissance culture as a whole led to them being present in more muted forms. It should not be forgotten, however, that the long sixteenth century witnessed a series of dramatic crises that altered the map of European society and culture, bringing about changes so radical and lasting that all the values that had guided the previous centuries had to be recast in entirely different and unfamiliar molds.

Two principal crises deeply affected the traditional thinking about liberty and toleration in this period. On the one hand there was a rapid and rigorous entrenchment of centralized forms of monarchical power, or the process seen by Machiavelli as the arrival of a new prince; on the other hand the long-established power of the Catholic Church as the unique guardian of the religious life of Europe was dramatically challenged by the Protestant Reformation. Religious conflict, fragmentation, and dissent, which for centuries had

CONCLUSION

occupied a place at the margins of European society, moved in the course of a few convulsed years to take center stage. These two forces moved in diametrically opposite directions, creating an antimony between the principles of authority and liberty that would act as a signpost toward the modern world. They also created a series of conflicts of unprecedented violence. On one side of the picture, the pressure was toward ever more centralized and systematic power structures on the part of the late Renaissance princes and their courts, including (especially after the Council of Trent) the papal court in Rome. These power structures did not consider liberty a desirable value and were often concerned above all with stamping it out. On the other side, new forces of religious dissent tended to break up old and new allegiances, fragmenting the religious map of Europe and powerfully affecting the political discourses of the time. From this situation an entirely different Europe emerged for which historical experiences were available only as distant models or conceptual instruments with which to forge new values and ideas. It was at this moment in time that thinking about liberty and toleration assumed an unusual intensity, forging a new discourse that would eventually establish them as the primary values of the modern Western world.

Other crises in the background of this story served to undermine even further the traditional certainties of the Christian, feudal Europe of the Middle Ages. The collapse of the eastern empire, the advance of Islam toward the boundaries of the Christian world, and the increasingly active process of colonization of the recently discovered New World all played their part in creating new and unfamiliar roles for the traditional European powers. Attention in the present study, however, has been largely limited to the central conflicts within the Christian world itself, seen as the locus in which the earliest modern discourses on liberty were principally being forged. The texts discussed here belong exclusively to the European culture of the period under consideration. Even within that limited context, they make no pretense of offering either the only possible picture or a picture that is in any way complete. They should rather be taken as a series of exemplary case studies, designed to illustrate the ways—or at least some of the principal ways—in which a discourse about liberty emerged in Europe in a century and a half that saw it convulsed in the throes of unprecedented conflict and war. As the study of these texts has shown, there was no linear movement forward as far as the values of liberty and toleration were concerned. Significant moments of progress often caused violent backlashes, in many cases overwhelming those very figures who had done most to promote new ideas of diversity, discussion, and dissent. More often than not those ideas themselves remained in the form of a utopian vision, to be implemented successfully only in the decades, if not centuries, to come.

The question of defining the most appropriate modes of implementation of the ideas of liberty and toleration that emerged in this period has nevertheless

CONCLUSION

been considered of primary importance throughout this book. It was not immediately obvious to those concerned what form of political or religious power structure would prove most successful in offering the necessary guarantees for a pluralistic and tolerant society to emerge. From the time of Machiavelli onward the political sphere, and in particular the republican ideal, appear as closely linked to discourses on liberty, though there was much discussion as to what form of republicanism was to be preferred. The most extreme form of republicanism, which envisaged modes of communal government without a hereditary prince, was not accepted by many at that time, and has been a point of particularly lively discussion among modern commentators of today. Often republicanism meant mixed forms of government in which a prince was more or less involved in the constitutional arrangements of the state. What does appear essential is instead the emergence of some kind of parliamentary forum, which Machiavelli called the council chamber, whose door needed to be kept open if liberty, tolerance, and diversity were to be secured for the community at large rather than flying off like sparks into the atmosphere as pure ideas or exhilarating but powerless words. That is why, throughout this book, attention has been continually paid not only to the libertarian ideas being discussed but also to the forms of institutional support they could or could not command. Ultimately, even in these early years, parliaments of some kind proved essential, even if experiences such as those of Machiavelli or Milton dramatically illustrate the necessity for parliaments themselves to develop forms of checks and balances designed to limit the ambition for an excess of power from which, as our story so eloquently demonstrates, they too are never entirely immune.

Another defining characteristic of this study has been the interdisciplinary impetus behind the choice of texts. The tendency of scholars concerned with defining the historical background to the modern discourse on toleration and liberty has often been to limit the field of vision to their own specific discipline, be it political philosophy, theology, natural philosophy, ethics, or at times the arts. These distinctions, however, were seldom present, let alone essential, to the figures discussed in this book. The discourse on liberty that emerged in the sixteenth century as a challenge to the increasingly absolutist tendencies of monarchical and ecclesiastical power pervaded every aspect of the culture of the time, from religion to politics, from the new science to the new drama. It united the public sphere to the domestic sphere, the formation of new confessional groups to the formation of new political experiences, and the investigation of the world of nature to the investigation of the human mind. It was without boundaries, either disciplinary or national, and it invested (and at times rocked to their foundations) all the religious confessions and political structures of a tempestuous and violent age.

A characteristic of much of the Anglo-American study of this subject has been a perception of the new "liberty speech" as belonging primarily to the

CONCLUSION

Protestant world. This is not an approach this study has adopted nor its results have confirmed. Just as Protestant dogmatism and oppression were often in the period studied here as merciless and unrelenting as those of the post-Tridentine Catholic Church, so the rich texture of Catholic culture produced voices raised in the name of liberty as eloquent and forward-looking as those of Protestant derivation. On both sides there were those who moved away from a Christian viewpoint altogether; and often their formulation of the problems with which this study has been concerned were particularly radical and profound. To limit the discourse on liberty to its most radical voices, however, has not been an objective of this book. More moderate positions were often able to reach and influence, at times more directly, the public of the time; and men like Erasmus of Rotterdam or Jacques Auguste de Thou on the Catholic side, or Richard Hooker or Jacobus Arminius on the Protestant side—who never renounced their Christian beliefs while still vigorously protesting the ways in which they were being enforced—gave powerful expression to ideas of liberty and tolerance within the early modern world.

It has to be emphasized that the discourse on liberty that emerged in the period considered here remains in many respects fragmentary and at times still unrefined. On the other hand, it seldom lacks in dramatic intensity, often related to direct experiences of oppression and personal suffering or affliction. Inevitably these tended to limit the power and depth of attempts to elaborate a theoretical concept of liberty. The development of a more rigorously philosophical libertarian discourse would be one of the major achievements, at a later date, of the European and American Enlightenments. This study limits itself to the claim that the long sixteenth century began to elaborate the fundamental, conceptual building blocks with which a more refined discourse on liberty, justice, and democracy could then be developed. It did so in a world in which many were still unable to understand, let alone to appreciate, the idea of difference as a source of variety and progress rather than of evil and confusion. That was not an ideal setting for formulating an articulate theory of liberty; but what the principal actors of our drama lacked in theoretical refinement, they gained in vigor, intensity, and at times in wit.

This study has advanced the claim that the sixteenth- and early seventeenth-century discourses on liberty deserve closer attention than they often receive. It was a century and a half of appalling destruction and violence, but also of remarkable creativity and change. Its fortunes have recently sagged with respect to the attention paid to the medieval world and the seventeenth-century Enlightenment. This study has attempted to demonstrate that any modern discourse on liberty, justice, and democracy that ignores the convulsions of the long sixteenth century, and the first, often bright, glimmerings of a modern concept of liberty and tolerance which emerged from them risks denying the importance of the very moment in which modernity began to take shape.

Notes

INTRODUCTION

1. See Berlin (1970), 121.
2. See, in particular, Skinner (1998).
3. The French libertine movement was originally studied in Pintard (1943); see also the important contribution by Gregory (1998).
4. See "Two Concepts of Liberty" in Berlin (1970), 118–72.
5. See "John Stuart Mill and the Ends of Life" in Berlin (1970), 173–206.
6. For a critical reading of Berlin's idea of liberty, see, in particular, Taylor (1979).
7. See Skinner (1984).
8. Hobbes's two chapters on "Of the Liberty of Subjects" and "Of Systems Subject, Political and Private" are in the section *Of Commonwealth* in Hobbes (2008), 111–246.
9. See Descartes (1996), 37–44.
10. See Rubenstein (1966), 149, and Rubenstein (1986).
11. See Hill (1940) and, in particular, Hill (1972).
12. See Van Gelderen and Skinner (2002), and Skinner (2002).
13. See Pocock (1976), often cited by Skinner himself as a key work for the formulation of his own studies. For republicanism as a theory of freedom and government, see Petit (1997).
14. See Pocock (1976).
15. See Viroli (2004), (2005), and (2013).
16. See Kahn (1994), 4.
17. See, for example, Murphy (2001). A more broad European picture can be found in Nederman and Laursen (1996) and Laursen and Nederman (1998).
18. See the by now classic study by Cantimori ([1939] 2002).
19. See Rotondò ([1974] 2008) and the two substantial volumes by Hermann and Simonutti (2011).
20. For the concept of a Radical Enlightenment, see Israel (2001) and Jacobs (1981). Jonathan Israel's many pages on these subjects find a succinct synthesis in Israel (2010).

CHAPTER I
Political Liberty

1. The bibliography is vast, but see, in particular, Pocock (1976), Skinner (1998), and Skinner (2002), 177–85. Also important in this context are Petit (1997) and Viroli (2004).

2. For the government of Florence under the Medici, see Rubenstein (1966).

3. Although the Great Council numbered about three thousand members, it has been claimed that it constituted something of a closed class, which tended to control the executive. For a history and analysis of the Great Council, see Rubenstein (1990).

4. For the nature and details of Machiavelli's active political career, see Rubenstein (1972).

5. See Skinner (1978).

6. For details of the publication of Machiavelli's *Discourses*, see Corrado Vivanti, "Nota al testo," in Machiavelli (2000), xlvii–li.

7. See "Dell'arte della guerra," in Machiavelli (1997), 1:534: "giudicò Cosimo [Rucellai], per soddisfare meglio al suo desiderio, che fusse bene, pigliando l'occasione dal fuggire il caldo, condursi nella più segreta e ombrosa parte del suo giardino. Dove pervenuti e posti a sedere, chi sopra all'erba che in quel luogo è freschissima, chi sopra a sedili in quelle parti ordinati sotto l'ombra d'altissimi arbori." The English translation in the text is my own.

8. For the much discussed problem of the exact dating of the composition of the *Discourses*, see the "Introduzione" in Machiavelli (2000), viii–xiii.

9. Machiavelli (2000), 3: "Perchè in quello io ho espresso quanto io so e quanto io ho imparato per una lunga pratica e continua lezione delle cose del mondo." All my references to Machiavelli's *Discourses* and Guicciardini's commentary on them come from this text; the English translations are my own.

10. See Landucci (1969), 61.

11. De' Nerli (1728), 138.

12. Machiavelli (2000), 234: "E veramente, quella sentenza di Cornelio Tacito è aurea che dice che gli uomini hanno ad onorare le cose passate e ad ubbidire alle presenti, e debbono desiderare i buoni principi, e comunque ei si sieno fatti tollerargli. E veramente chi fa altrimenti, il più delle volte rovina sé e la sua patria."

13. *The Prince*, like the *Discourses*, was only published in Rome, after Machiavelli's death, in 1532; see Machiavelli (1532); another edition came out the same year in Florence.

14. See chap. 15 in Machiavelli (1532); see also "Machiavelli e Vico," in Croce (1931), esp. 251–53.

15. See the introduction by Pedullà in Machiavelli (2013b), lxvi–lxx.

16. A pioneering discussion of the idea of liberty in Machiavelli's works can be found in Colish (1971).

17. On Machiavelli and Polybius, see "Polibio e Machiavelli: costituzione, potenza, conquista," in Sasso (1967), 223–80.

18. For a book-length study of this subject, see Pedullà (2011).
19. See Dante's *Purgatory*, canto 7, vv. 121–23 (slightly misquoted by Machiavelli).
20. See Machiavelli (1997), 3:33–37.
21. See Machiavelli (1997), 2:135–38; the English translations in the text are my own.
22. See Machiavelli (1997), 1:186–87.
23. See Sasso (1980), 193–205.
24. The relationship between Machiavelli and More has been much debated, going from claims that More and Erasmus were the real "moderns" because they were more aware of the social and economic problems of their time, whereas Machiavelli tended to remain within a purely political logic, to a claim that there was no such relationship. On this subject, see Sasso (1980), 267 and n. 89, and Worden (2002). A detailed analysis of "Machiavelli e *Utopia*" can be found in Barbuto (2013), 287–307.
25. See More (1963–1997), vol. 4, *Utopia*, 98–99.
26. "La moltitudine è più savia e più costante di un principe" is the title of book 1, chap. 58 of the *Discourses*. See Machiavelli (2000), 123. For the comment on corrupt cities, see Machiavelli (2000), 56: "acciocché quegli uomini i quali dalle leggi, per la loro insolenzia, non possono essere corretti, fussero da una podestà quasi regia in qualche modo frenati."
27. Machiavelli (2000), 359: "se bene in simili casi è necessario mettere mano nel sangue, sarebbe stato meglio non avere avuto necessità."
28. See More (1963–1997), vol. 6, *The Apology*, xxi.
29. Berlin's essay was originally read at a meeting of the Political Science Association at Oxford in 1953 and subsequently given as a lecture at Yale University. It was published in an integral version for the first time in 1972; see Berlin (1972).
30. See Viroli (2005), xxxiii and 3.
31. A seminal study of this subject is Baron (1966). For a detailed study of Machiavelli's rhetoric and its political implications for the early modern world, see Kahn (1994).
32. For further biographical details, see Barbuto (2013), 115–26, and Viroli (2002).
33. The letter is in Machiavelli (1997), 2:294–97.
34. See Ascoli (1993). It is interesting to note the constant reference in this essay to Antonio Gramsci's mentions of Machiavelli in his *Prison Notebooks*.
35. See, in particular, the preface to Black (2013), 1–4.
36. See Barbuto (2013), 128, and Anselmi (2013). See also Giorgio Inglese's introduction to Machiavelli (2013), viii.
37. For a detailed discussion of Machiavelli's many comments on the French, both negative and positive, see Cadoni (1974). An essential study of Machiavelli's idea of a civil principality is "Principato civile e tirannide," in Sasso (1988), 2:351–490; for Machiavelli's praise of the French monarchy as a particularly successful example of a civil principality, see 388–96.
38. An important essay on this subject is Fasano Guarini (1990).
39. See Viroli (2013), where Gramsci, Chabod, and Russo are all amply quoted and praised.

40. See Machiavelli (1997), 1:741: "Senza satisfare all'universale, non si fece mai alcuna republica stabile. Non si satisferà mai all'universale dei cittadini fiorentini, se non si riapre la sala: pero', conviene al volere fare una repubblica in Firenze, riaprire questa sala, e rendere questa distribuzione all'universale, e sappia Vostra Santità, che qualunque penserà di torle lo stato, penserà innanzi ad ogni altra cosa di riaprirla. E pero è partito migliore che quella l'apra con termini e modi sicuri, e che tolga questa occasione a chi fusse suo nemico di riaprirla con dispiacere suo, e destruzione e rovina de' suoi amici."

41. Alessandro dei Pazzi's discourse on the same subject, after he, too, was interrogated by cardinal Giulio dei Medici, can be found in Dei Pazzi (1842). In it he defined Machiavelli's proposals for Florence as "insolita a quella città e stravagante" (strange for that city, and extravagant; see 429).

42. Machiavelli (2000), 94: "per quelle medesime cagioni che nascono la maggior parte delle tirannidi nelle città: e questo è da troppo desiderio del popolo d'essere libero, e da troppo desiderio de' nobili di comandare. E quando è non convengano a fare una legge in favore della libertà, ma gettasi qualcuna delle parti a favorire uno, allora è che subito la tirannide surge."

CHAPTER 2
Liberty and Religion

1. For Savanorola's long-lasting influence on Florentine affairs, see Polizzotto (1995).
2. See Machiavelli (2000), 39 and 301.
3. See Landucci (1969), 142; see also Martines (2006).
4. See Machiavelli (2000), xliv.
5. For the sixteenth-century development of the radical Protestant movement, see the monumental Williams ([1962] 1992).
6. On this subject, see McGrath (1986), 2:16.
7. For this passage from the *Letter*, see Luther ([1520] 1947), 98. *A Treatise on Christian Liberty* can be found in Luther ([1520] 1947), 251–90.
8. See Berlin (1970), esp. 131–34, and Taylor (1979).
9. My remarks on Machiavelli here are made in the light of Skinner (1984).
10. Luther ([1520] 1947), 257.
11. Ibid., 258.
12. For the Lutheran concept of politics, see Skinner (1978), vol. 2.
13. The relevant texts can be found in Baylor (1991).
14. Luther ([1520] 1947), 258.
15. An English translation of "In Praise of Folly" can be found in Erasmus (1974–), 27:77–154.
16. Erasmus to Willibald Pirckheimer, November 29, 1521, quoted in the introduction to Erasmus (1974–), 76:li.
17. See the section "Erasmus 'A Heretic to Both Sides': Summer 1521–Winter 1523," in Erasmus (1974–), 76:xlvii–lvi.

18. See Luther (1957), 78.
19. The preface is in Erasmus (1974–),76:5–14.
20. The introduction is in Erasmus (1974–), 76:14–20.
21. For the "Brief Definition of Free Will," see Erasmus (1974), 76:21.
22. For the scholastic background to the early modern discussion of freedom of the will, see Sleigh, Chappell, and Della Rocca (1998).
23. See De Michelis Pintacuda (2001), 58–59.
24. See Erasmus (1974–), 76:87.
25. For these final arguments of the *De libero arbitrio*, see Erasmus (1974–), 76: 87. Erasmus replied to Luther with his *Hyperaspistes*, a much longer work in two volumes. It has not received frequent attention from the commentators, but for an unusually extended analysis, see Torzini (2000).
26. A classic account of Erasmus's use of scholastic sources in his defense of free will is Garin (1938), 102–46.
27. See Margolin (1986).
28. See Calvin ([1581] 2007), 155–75.
29. Ibid., 237. For a balanced account of this ambivalence of Calvin's contradictory heritage with respect to the modern world, see Peddle (2008).
30. Calvin ([1581] 2007), 171.
31. See Luther ([1520] 1947), 293–94.
32. Ibid., 73.
33. Ibid., 182.
34. See Roland Bainton's extensive "Introduction" in Castellio (1935), 12.
35. Ibid., 24–25.
36. For Castellio on Augustine, see Castellio (1935), 207.
37. See Bainton, "Introduction," in Castellio (1935), 43.
38. See Luther's texts in Castellio (1935), 143 and 145.
39. Ibid., 153.
40. On Müntzner's short and disastrous story, see Williams ([1962] 1992), 161–65.
41. For the political implications of this episode, see Skinner (1978), 2:75–81.
42. See Walzer (1965), 99.
43. John Knox, "A Godly Letter of Warning or Admonition to the Faithful in London, Newcastle and Berwick" (1554), quoted in Walzer (1965), 100.
44. See Bainton, "Introduction," in Castellio (1935) and Cantimori ([1939] 2002). Bainton and Cantimori were close friends; see Tedeschi (2002).
45. On Sebastian Frank, see Furcha (1996).
46. See Castellio (1935), 212–13.
47. Ibid., 130.
48. See, for example, Postel (1560) ; and on Postel, see Bouwsma (1957).
49. The bibliography is vast, but see, in particular, Firpo (2003), esp. chap. 10, and Rotondò ([1974] 2008).
50. On Aconcio in England, see Gabrieli (1982); for Aconcio's anti-Trinitarianism, see Rotondò ([1974] 2008), 172–80.

51. A still essential study of Aconcio is Rossi (1952), chap. 4.

52. See Simonutti (2003).

53. The English translation of *Satan's Strategems* has been reproposed in Aconcio ([1565] 1940).

54. For *De methodo*, see Aconcio ([1558] 1944), 75–179.

55. See Bodin ([1588] 1975), and Kuntz (1998); see also Remer (1996).

56. Camillo's memory theater has been much discussed in recent years. See, above all, the pages dedicated to it, which include an illustrated architectonic reconstruction, in Yates (1966).

57. See Bodin ([1588] 1975), 7.

58. The importance of Bodin's question is underlined by Vittorio Hösle in his study of four early modern works dedicated to religious liberty. See Hösle (2004).

59. For the quotations herein, see Bodin ([1588] 1975), 170–71.

60. See the closing pages of Bodin ([1588] 1975), book 6.

61. For the theory of an overlapping consensus, see Rawls ([1971] 1999).

62. See Rawls (2010), 266.

63. For some French Enlightenment considerations on Venice in this sense, see Venturi (1979).

64. A bibliography that takes account of the many studies that have surrounded the four hundredth anniversary in the year 2000 of Bruno's death is Severini (2002). There is also an ample Bruno bibliography at www.oxfordbibliographies.com, section Renaissance and Reformation. For a biography in English, see Rowland (2008).

65. See *Patristic Scholarship: The Edition of St. Jerome*, in Erasmus (1974–), 61:29.

66. Ibid., 95; this reference is in Erasmus's preface to vol. 2, part 3 of St. Jerome's works. The editors of the volume concerned have not been able to trace the quote.

67. See Tedeschi (1991), 127.

68. For the theme of early attempts at mediation by the Inquisition in Bologna, see the section "L'Inquisizione di Bologna nella prima metà del secolo e l'inquisitore Leandro Alberti" in Dall'Olio (1999), 57–64. For a more general treatment of the subject, see Seidel Menchi (1983–84).

69. See "The Organisation and Procedures of the Roman Inquisition: A Sketch," in Tedeschi (1991), 127–203.

70. See Haliczer (1987), 169–88.

71. See "The Growth of Censorship," in Grendler (1977), 118. See also "La censure catholique au XVIe siècle et l'etat des recherches," in *Index des livres Interdits* (1985–86), 1:11–18; volume 10 of this edition of the *Index* is a thesaurus of the literature forbidden in the sixteenth century.

72. This document is printed in appendix 1 in Grendler (1977), 296–301.

73. See, for example, Garin (1965). For an English translation, see Garin (1969), where Garin's statement to this effect can be found on 85.

74. For the above data, see "The Index of Paul IV" in Grendler (1977), 115–27.

75. For Bruno's contribution to the science of his time, see Gatti (1999).

76. On this much discussed issue, see Knox (2013).

77. For Bruno's concept of mathematics as an approximate rather than a certain art, see De Bernart (2002). For possible intuitions of a non-Euclidean geometry, see Gatti (2011), 91–111.

78. The Latin text of this work is in Bruno (1879–91), vol. 1, part 3, 1–118. The passages from the dedicatory letter to Rudolph II relevant to a discourse on liberty are given in Italian translation, with a now classic comment, in Calogero (1963), 1–14.

79. For Bruno's attitudes toward the discovery of the Americas, see Ricci (1990b).

80. The known documents relating to Bruno's trial are in Firpo (1993).

81. For the specific characteristics of the Venetian inquisition, see "The *Tre savi sopra Eresia 1547–1605*," in Grendler (1981), 283–340, and "Ortodossia, diversità, dissenso. Venezia e il governo della religione intorno alla metà del Cinquecento," in Prosperi (2003), 141–151.

82. My comments here on Bruno's trial and execution are based on my essay "Why Bruno's 'Tranquil Universal Philosophy' Finished in a Fire," in Gatti (2011), 309–23.

83. For the third session of the trial, see Firpo (1993), 167–68. For the much discussed subject of St. Thomas's ideas about creation, see, in particular, Aertsen (1990), 9–19, and the other essays in Wissink (1990).

84. "I have always defined my ideas philosophically and according to principles of natural reason" (io sempre ho diffinito filosoficamente et secondo li principii et lume naturale). See Firpo (1993), 166, and the commentary in Berti ([1868] 1889), 274–76. On the question of the doctrine of double truth from Boezio to the Renaissance, see Gregory (1962).

85. See Gentile (1907), 59. Gentile's assessment of Bruno's behaviour during his trial is discussed, with the relevant quotation, in Spampanato (1921), 518.

86. See Gentile (1907).

87. See Mercati (1942). The *Summary*, first published by Mercati, was later incorporated in Firpo (1993).

88. See Firpo (1993), 176: "cattolicamente parlando."

89. Firpo (1993), 299–302.

90. Mersenne's harsh critique of Bruno is discussed in Ricci (1990a), 86–90.

91. For Bruno's praise of Elizabeth I, see Bruno (1977), 119–20. For the questions asked of Bruno about such praise during his trial, see Firpo (1993), 188–89.

92. On this subject, see Sacerdoti (2002), and "The Sense of an Ending in Giordano Bruno's *Heroici furori*," in Gatti (2011), 127–39. For an English translation see Bruno (2013).

93. On this subject, see Aquilecchia (1997).

94. Abbott's famous attack on Bruno's lectures at Oxford can be found in his anti-Catholic polemic; see Abbot (1604), 87. For more on this subject, see Aquilecchia (1995), 33–36.

95. See the pages on Piermartiri Vermigli, or Peter Martyr, in MacCulloch (2005).

96. See MacCulloch (2002).

97. See the introduction and the prefaces to book 1 and book 8 in Hooker (1989).

98. See Locke (1988), 288.

99. See Peltonen (2002).
100. See the preface in Hooker (1977), 33.
101. On this subject, see Voak (2003).
102. The discussion of free will is in Hooker (1977), book 1, chapters 8.7–8.9.
103. See Locke (1988), 288.
104. See Bangs (1971), 198.
105. See Van Leewen (2009), xix.
106. On the Synod of Dort, see Bangs (1971), esp. 198.
107. On the British discussion of Arminianism, see Hoenderdaal (1975).
108. See "Human Freedom and Divine Grace," in Stanglin (2007), 84.
109. See Arminius (1975).
110. See [Featley] (1626), fol. C1v.
111. Ibid., fol. D2r.
112. See Bangs (1971), 79–80.
113. See Schmitt (1983), 11.
114. See Poppi (1972).
115. See Arminius (1825), 1:370–515.
116. Ibid., 1:376, 387, 388, 390, 409, 424–27, 441–42, 463–64, 474.
117. See Belligni (2003).
118. See Sarpi ([1619] 1974) for a modern edition of the 1619 version of Sarpi's masterpiece, together with the ample introduction by Corrado Vivanti.
119. Belligni (2003), 143.

CHAPTER 3
Libertas philosophandi, *or the Liberty of Thought*

1. See Kelley (1981), 61.
2. Ibid., 58–63; the quotation herein is on 62.
3. See the many pages on religious toleration in Williams ([1962] 1992), and the dense comment on Williams's book in Rotondò ([1974] 2008), 5–56.
4. For a comparative study of some (though not all) the parliaments of Europe as they existed at this time, see Griffiths (1968).
5. See Pocock (1976); see also Skinner (1978) and the extensive bibliography in Skinner (2002).
6. See Harrington (1992), 29.
7. Contarini's text was originally titled *De Magistratibus et Repubblica Venetorum* and was published in Paris in 1543. It was translated into English by Lewes Lewkenor in 1599 with the title *The Commonwealth and Government of Venice*. For more on this subject, see Skinner (2002), 141–42.
8. On this subject, see Kingdon (1988) and Racaut (2002).
9. See the section "Huguenot Assemblies," in Griffiths (1968), 254–62.
10. The two documents cited are given in French in Griffiths (1968), 276–79 and 280–81.

11. An English translation of Hotman's text is published in Franklin (1969), 48–96; the quotations herein can be found on 73.

12. For the *Disputes against Tyrants*, see Franklin (1969), 138–99; the quotation herein can be found on 194.

13. See Montaigne (1987), book 2, essay 19, 759–63. See also Fontana (2008), esp. chaps. 3–4.

14. For the intricate problem of the authorship of *On Voluntary Servitude,* see David Lewis Schaefer, "Montaigne and La Boétie," in Schaefer (1998), 1–30.

15. An English translation of *On Voluntary Servitude* can be found in Schaefer (1998), 191–222; the quotation herein is on 194.

16. The French version of this article is given in the section "Henri IV et la pacification religieuse (1589–1598)," in Leclerc ([1955] 1994), 499–529.

17. For details of the history and legislative measures of the edict, see Mentzer (2002).

18. On this subject, see Israel (1995).

19. See the chronological list of assemblies of the Estates-General of the Low Countries supplied in Griffiths (1968), 322–23.

20. Thorold Rogers, *Story of Holland*, quoted in Griffiths (1968), 510.

21. The declaration is given in Dutch and French in Griffiths (1968), 510–13.

22. On this subject, see the many pages on Holland in Israel (2001).

23. Henry VIII's act of proclamations is document 8 in the section "The English Parliament," in Griffiths (1968), 528–616.

24. The quotations herein are taken from the Elizabethan parliamentary documents in Griffiths (1968), 585–616.

25. See document 4, "The Petition of the Speaker of the House, Sir Thomas More, for Freedom of Speech." in Griffiths (1968), 557–58.

26. See document 11, "Peter Wentworth on Freedom of Speech," in Griffiths (1968), 593–601.

27. See Griffiths (1968), 585–616.

28. For Bruno's trial as a struggle for the freedom of philosophy, see Finocchiaro (2002). The more general case for Bruno's trial as a plea for liberty was made by Luigi Firpo in a now classic analysis that was first published in two parts in the *Rivista storica italiana* in 1948–49, and then as a single volume in Naples in 1949. It was continually revised throughout his life, and appears in its final form in Firpo (1993), 3–140.

29. See Provvidera (1998).

30. These were the *Spaccio della bestia trionfante* (1584) and the *Heroici furori* (1585), both published in London by the printer John Charlewood. For a study of Bruno's printer and his relationship to the Sidney circle, see Provvidera (2002).

31. For the Essex-Jonson connection, see Donaldson (2011).

32. The documents related to this episode are multiple and complex, and have been the subject of much discussion among Shakespearean editors of this play. For a detailed account, see the introduction by Andrew Gurr in Shakespeare (2003), 4–10.

33. For a bibliography of studies on the Bruno-Shakespeare relationship, which started in the nineteenth century, see Gatti (1989), appendix 2. For a more detailed reading of *Hamlet* in the light of Bruno's works and thought, see "Bruno and Shakespeare: Hamlet," in Gatti (2011), 140–60.
34. On Florio, see Wyatt (2005).
35. The Bruno-Florio relationship was first treated systematically in Yates (1934).
36. For the text used here see Shakespeare ([1600] 1982).
37. Ibid., 176 (act 1, scene 1).
38. For Hamlet's first monologue in the play, see Shakespeare ([1600] 1982), 187–90 (act 1, scene 2).
39. Shakespeare ([1600] 1982), 183 (act 1, scene 2).
40. Ibid., 748 (act 2, scene 2).
41. See in particular, *De l'infinito, universo et mondi,* in Bruno (2002), 2:7–167. An English translation can be found in Singer (1950).
42. See Shakespeare ([1600] 1982), 291–92 (act 3, scene 2).
43. These two often differing texts of *King Lear* are today considered by some scholars to be two distinct versions of the play; sometimes they are published separately. The text used in this comment is a composite text edited in 1972 by Kenneth Muir for the Arden Shakespeare. For the differences between the two versions, see Taylor and Warren (1983).
44. See Shakespeare ([1605?] 1972), 206 (act 5, scene 3).
45. See Pocock (1976), 98–99. See also Garin (1954); Garin et al. (1955); and Yates (1964).
46. See Yates (1984).
47. An early discussion of these problems that takes the Hermetic and magical view of the new science as a purely provisional starting point can be found in Hess (1980).
48. See Harrison (1998). For the sociology of Renaissance science, see Shapin (1998). A synthesis of these various themes is attempted in Henry (2002).
49. An English translation of this unfinished text can be found in Bruno (1998).
50. See Westman (2011), 9.
51. On Bruno's Italian dialogues written in London, see Aquilecchia (1991).
52. See *The Advancement of Learning* in Bacon (2000), esp. 8–9 for the quotations herein.
53. See "A Reformed Natural Philosophy," in Martin (1992), 171.
54. See Bacon ([1627] 1900?), 398.
55. On this subject, see Finocchiaro (2005).
56. The essential trial documents can be found in English translation, with an ample comment and bibliography, in Finocchiaro (1989).
57. See Finocchiaro (2005).
58. See "Galileo's Letter to the Grand Duchess" in Finocchiaro (1989), 87–118.
59. For an English translation, see Galileo ([1611] 1989).
60. For an English translation, see Galileo ([1633] 1962).

61. For English language versions of all the documents mentioned herein, see Finocchiaro (1989).

62. An English translation of this letter can be found in Finocchiaro (1989), 87–118. This quotation is at 91.

63. On Bruno and the Bible, see "Bruno's Use of the Bible in His Italian Philosophical dialogues," in Gatti (2011), 264–79.

64. See Finocchiaro (1989), 97.

65. See Job 9:6. For Bruno's praise, in his *Ash Wednesday Supper*, of the truths of natural philosophy to be found in Job, see Bruno (2002), 527.

66. See McMullin (1998).

67. See Pera (1998).

68. See Blackwell (1998).

69. See the pages on the Paschini case, with bibliographical references, in Finocchiaro (2005), 318–30.

70. See Feldhay (1995) and (2001).

71. For a revisionist account of Galileo's astronomical discoveries of 1610, see Biagioli (2001).

72. A major study of Jesuit science is Baldini (1992); see also Baldini (1984).

73. See Swerdlow (1998), 244.

74. See Finocchiaro (1989), 103–4.

75. See "Philosophic Freedom," in Finocchiaro (2005), 72–79.

CHAPTER 4
The Freedom of the Press

Portions of this chapter were published earlier in *The Making of the Humanities, Vol. II: From Early Modern to Modern Disciplines*, edited by Rens Bod, Jaap Maat, and Thijs Weststeijn (Amsterdam: Amsterdam University Press, 2012), 167–181.

1. See Biagioli (1993), 229.

2. See Biagioli (1993), 353–62.

3. On the Italian academies of the sixteenth and early seventeenth centuries, see Chambers (1995).

4. On the history of the de Thou family, see Harisse (1905).

5. The widespread fortune of de Thou's history up to the beginning of the nineteenth century, and its rapid decline ever afterward, are closely connected to its complicated printing history; see Kinser (1996).

6. Kinser (1966), 9: "Il y aura quelque chose de changé ou plutost adouci; car de dire autrement les choses qu'elles ne sont, ou dissimuler laschement la verité, j'en ferais conscience."

7. See Kelley (1973), 218.

8. This translation was included in the volume *Opuscules françoises des Hotmans* (Paris, 1616, reprinted 1617). As Kinser (1966), 297, notes, "Henry IV ordered this

translation made for him personally, after de Thou submitted the preface and first part of his *History* to the king for approval before publication in 1603. There are no introductions, notes, or other commentary in either of these editions."

9. All quotations from de Thou's preface are taken from the English translation in Collinson (1807); For the quotation herein, see 389.

10. For these quotations, see de Thou ([1604] 1807), 390–91.

11. Ibid., 408.

12. Ibid., 409–15.

13. See ibid., 417.

14. For a comment on the importance of de Thou's pages on the massacre, see "Le renversement de la politique royale: la Saint-Barthélemy," in Leclerc ([1955] 1994), 470–77.

15. For this paragraph and its relevant quotations, see de Thou ([1604] 1807), 418–24.

16. De Thou ([1604] 1807), 424 and 428.

17. Ibid., 430–37; capitalization in the original.

18. See Corrado Vivanti's references to Sarpi's use of de Thou in Sarpi ([1619] 1974), vol. 1, lxxiv and cxlix.

19. See Sarpi (1961), 167; the translation here is my own.

20. See Sosio (2006).

21. See Sarpi (2001), vol. 1, chap. 2.

22. For Sarpi's involvement with the Anglicanism of James I and his deep influence on Protestant cultures of the seventeenth and eighteenth centuries, see the classic Yates essay (1944).

23. A major statement to this effect can be found in the influential Chabod (1974).

24. Sarpi (2001), 218; Corrado Pin's introduction to this text can be found at 216–20, and the text itself at 220–47.

25. Sarpi's *Consultant Reports* have also been the subject of much attention from modern commentators and historians. See the widely admired reading of this particular text in Chabod (1974), 506–15.

26. Paulo Sarpi to the French Huguenot Jérôme Groslot, May 27, 1608, in Sarpi (2001), 1:56.

27. See Malcolm (1984), 38.

28. For these events, see Belligni (2003), 138–153.

29. See Malcolm (1984), 29.

30. For the London publication of Sarpi's *History*, see Rees and Wakely (2009), 101–6.

31. For some of the most recent developments in this discussion, see Trebbi (2006).

32. Micanzio's Italian-language biography can be found in Sarpi ([1619] 1974), 2:1273–1413; for the remarks referred to herein, see 1354 and 1359.

33. See *Sopra l'officio dell'inquisizione*, in Sarpi (1958), 119–212.

34. See Sarpi (1958), 189–208. In 1615, Sarpi wrote a short report for the Venetian Senate dedicated specifically to the problem of the prohibition of books. See *De vietare la stampa di libri perniciosi al buon governo*, in Sarpi (1958), 215–31.

35. Sarpi did this through a letter written to de Dominis by his friend, collaborator, and future biographer, Fulgenzio Micanzio. A copy of the letter is given in Corrado Vivanti's introduction to Sarpi ([1619] 1974), 1:xc and note 1 on the same page.

36. See Rees and Wakely (2009), 110.

37. These quotations are taken from de Dominis's letter of dedication in the English translation of 1620.

38. See Sarpi ([1619] 1974), 1:6; my translation.

39. See Macaulay (1843) and Masson (1881–94).

40. See "Milton I" [1936] and "Milton II" [1947], in Eliot (1957), 156–64 and 165–83. *Milton I* was first published in *Essays and Studies* of the English Association, Oxford University Press, 1936, while *Milton II* was delivered as a lecture at the British Academy in 1947 and first published in Eliot (1957).

41. See Kermode (1960) and Ricks (1963).

42. For a balanced attempt to defend Milton from the most extreme of such criticisms, see Lewalski (2000).

43. The text, with a detailed introduction by Maurice Kelley, can be found in Milton (1973).

44. The controversy was started in Hunter (1992); it elicited many responses in subsequent issues of the journal *Studies in English Literature* in 1992, 1993, and 1994.

45. Lewalski (2000), 415–41.

46. See Dobranski and Rumrich (1998).

47. See Armitage, Himy, and Skinner (1995). Against this thesis of Milton as a convinced classical republican, see, more recently, Walker (2009).

48. Apart from extended treatments in all the major biographies, a full-length book on the subject is Di Cesare (1991).

49. The text of the biography by Edward Phillips is in Darbishire (1932).

50. See Milton ([1644] 1959), 609.

51. Ibid., 622–23.

52. On this subject see, in particular, Worden (2002).

53. A detailed account can be found in Lewalski (2000), 120–53.

54. These two passages come from the pamphlet *On Reformation* (1641), in Milton (1953), 590–600.

55. *Julius Caesar*, in Shakespeare (2003), 681.

56. For the difference between ordinance, order, and act in the period of the Long Parliament, see Firth and Rait (1911), 3:iv.

57. It was not until December 1646 that the Westminster Assembly of Divines submitted to Parliament a "Confession of the Faith" advising the introduction of a national Presbyterian Church in England along the lines of that already in Scotland.

58. On this subject, see Gatti (2012).

59. The story of Milton's first marriage and the composition of his writings on divorce can be found in Lewalski (2000), 156–90.

60. See "Note to the Reader," in Montaigne (1987), lxiii.

61. On the importance of the Arminian controversy, see the section "Religion as Dogma or Religion as Debate? Richard Hooker and Jacobus Arminius" in chapter 2 of the present volume.

62. Milton's Arminianism, particularly as it is argued in his *De doctrina Christiana*, is examined in Lewalski (2000), 420–24.

63. The *Areopagiticus* can be found in Isocrates (1954), vol. 7. On the relationship between Isocrates and Plato, see Jaeger ([1939] 1986).

64. See Milton (1644), 3. For an extended discussion of the significance of Milton's title, see Dowling (1955).

65. The quotation is from *The Suppliant Women* and the translation is Milton's own. For a discussion of this motto, see Hale (1991).

66. See Milton (1644), 2.

67. Ibid., 3; italics in the original.

68. Ibid., 4.

69. Ibid.

70. For the *Congregazione in Trento. Libri proibiti*, see Sarpi ([1619] 1974), 2:753–59.

71. See Milton (1644), 7.

72. For Milton's sometimes critical use of Sarpi as a source, see Sirluck (1953).

73. On this subject, see the introduction by J. M. de Bujanda in de Bujanda, Higman, and Farge (1985–86), 1:30–31.

74. See Milton (1644), 8.

75. Ibid., 24.

76. *Commonplace Book*, in Milton (1953), 450.

77. For the quotations in this paragraph, see Milton (1644), 31–34.

78. For the metaphor of Isis and Osiris and Milton's comments on the slow Reformation, see Milton (1644), 29–30, and the whole final section of his pamphlet.

79. There is a considerable recent bibliography of critical assessments of Milton as a libertarian thinker, especially among American scholars. A particularly influential interpretation of Milton as ultimately not interested in liberty at all can be found in Fish (2005).

80. On the long European crisis caused by the Thirty Years' War, see MacCulloch (2005), 485–501.

81. See Hill (1972).

82. See Hill (1978).

83. See Macaulay (1843)

84. For Milton's remarkable pages on the slow construction of the temple of the Lord, and the metaphor of truth as a deeply rooted tree, see Milton (1644), 32–33.

85. For the rhetorical panegyric of London as a new version of republican Rome, see Milton (1644), 33.

86. Milton (1953), 505.
87. For this much discussed passage, see Milton (1644), 37.
88. For a previous development of this argument, see Gatti (2012).
89. The subject has been treated in the widely admired Hart (1999).
90. See Locke (2003) and Macaulay (1843).
91. Plates from these frescoes can be found in MacCulloch (2005), between pages 388 and 389.
92. See Dzelzainis (1995).
93. See Lewalski (2005), 240–41.
94. The *Observations* are in Milton (1962).
95. The *Articles of Peace*, with the relative correspondence, appeared in London as an official governmental publication in 1649, followed by Milton's *Observations*. All this material can be found in Milton (1962).
96. Milton (1953), 499.
97. Ibid., 421.
98. John Milton, *Paradise Lost,* book 6, vv. 109–10; for the parliament in hell, see book 2.

CHAPTER 5
Epilogue

1. For these quotations in the original Italian, see Machiavelli (1584), fols. 2r–4r.
2. For a detailed account of Giacomo Castelvetro's presence in Elizabethan London and of John Wolfe's contradictory attitudes toward its Italian community, see Wyatt (2005), 185–99; for the quotations herein, see 188.
3. See Harrington (1992), xv.
4. See the important work on Neville in Italy in Crinò (1952) and (1957)
5. For a modern edition, see Bruce (1999).
6. See the anonymous *Works of the Famous Nicholas Machiavel,* (1680). Usually attributed to Neville, these translations were published together with a spurious letter said to be written by Machiavelli himself. Recently it has been argued that the translations were probably not by Neville, but that the letter defending Machiavelli's thought from his already "diabolical" reputation was probably of Neville's devising; see the sections "The Machiavelli Translation" and "Nicholas Machiavel's Letter" in Mahlberg (2009), 201–15
7. Harrington (1992), xi.
8. See "Letter from the Publisher to the Reader," in [Neville] (1681); all references herein to Neville's *Plato redivivus* come from this edition.
9. See the "Nota filologica" in Marchand, Fachard, and Masi (2001), 621–23.
10. See Inglese (1985), 214.
11. See Raab (1964), 185–217.
12. For a more detailed reading of Machiavelli's *Discourses*, see chapter 1 of the present volume.

13. On Contarini, see Skinner (1978), 1:140–42.
14. See Sieur de la Haye (1671).
15. See Machiavelli (2000), 48–56.
16. The theme is a constant one in Machiavelli, and returns in other works such as *The Prince* and *The Art of War*. In the *Discourses* it is treated specifically in book 2, chap. 20; see Machiavelli (2000), 189–90.
17. See Contarini (1599), 16.
18. Sieur de la Haye (1671), 146.
19. See, in particular, the introduction by Gabriele Pedullà in Machiavelli (2013b).
20. For this quote, see Inglese (2006), 25, and also, in the same volume, the section "Uno opuscolo 'De principatibus,' " 45–89, which contains interesting comments on Machiavelli's criticism of Venetian policy in the Italian Peninsula.
21. Contarini (1599), 147.
22. Ibid., 148–49.
23. Ibid., 135.
24. See the section "English Republicans," in Robbins (1969), which contains a modern edition of Neville's *Plato redivivus*; see also Mahlberg (2009), 163–82.
25. See the "Preliminaries, Showing Principles of Government," in Harrington (1992), 25.
26. On Machiavelli's disapproval of plots against the established powers in a state, see chapter 1 of the present volume.
27. This theme recurs throughout the *Discourses*, but is also particularly emphasized in the *Discourse on the Situation in Florence*. On this subject, see the discussion in chapter 1 of the present volume.
28. Contarini (1599), 42.
29. Ibid., 78.

Bibliography

Abbot, George. (1604). *The reasons vvhich Doctour Hill hath brought, for the vpholding of papistry, which is falselie termed the Catholike religion.* Oxford: Joseph Barnes.

Aconcio, Giacomo. ([1558] 1944). *De methodo e opuscoli religiosi e filosofici.* Edited by Giorgio Radetti. Florence, Italy: Vallecchi editore.

Aconcio, Jacopo. ([1565] 1940). *Satan's Stratagems.* Edited by Charles D. O'Malley. San Francisco: California State Library.

Aertsen, J. A. (1990). "The Eternity of the World: The Believing and Philosophical Thomas." In *The Eternity of the World in the Thought of St. Thomas Aquinas and His Contemporaries*, ed. J.B.M. Wissink, 9–19. Leiden, Netherlands: Brill.

Gian Maria Anselmi. (2013). "Per leggere *Il Principe*." In *Il principe di Machiavelli e il suo tempo: 1513–2013* (exhibition catalog), 117–31. Rome: L'Enciclopedia Treccani.

Aquilecchia, Giovanni. (1991). *Le opere italiane di Giordano Bruno: critica testuale e oltre.* Naples, Italy: Bibliopolis.

Aquilecchia, Giovanni. (1995). "Giordano Bruno in Inghilterra (1583–1585): Documenti e Testimonianze." *Bruniana e Campanelliana* 1, nos. 1–2: 21–42.

Aquilecchia, Giovanni. (1997). "Giordano Bruno at Oxford." In *Giordano Bruno, 1583–1585: The English Experience*, ed. Michele Ciliberto and Nicholas Mann, 117–24. Florence, Italy: Olschki.

Arminius, Jacobus. (1825). *The Works.* 3 vols. Translated by James Nichols. London: Longman and Green.

Arminius, Jacobus. (1975). *The Auction Catalogue of the Library.* Facsimile ed. with an introduction by Carl O. Bangs. Utrecht, Netherlands: HES.

Armitage, David, Armand Himy, and Quentin Skinner, eds. (1995). *Milton and Republicanism.* Cambridge: Cambridge University Press.

Ascoli, Albert Russell. (1993). "Machiavelli's Gift of Counsel." In *Machiavelli and the Discourse of Literature*, ed. Albert Russell Ascoli and Victoria Kahn, 219–57. Ithaca, NY: Cornell University Press.

Ascoli, Albert Russell, and Victoria Kahn, eds. (1993). *Machiavelli and the Discourse of Literature.* Ithaca, NY: Cornell University Press.

Bacon, Francis. ([1627] 1900?). "The New Atlantis." In *The Works of Francis Bacon*, vol. 3, ed. James Spedding, Robert Leslie Ellis, and Douglas Denon Heath, 354–413. Boston: Houghton and Mifflin.

Bacon, Francis. (2000). *The Oxford Francis Bacon*, vol. 4. Edited by Michael Kiernan. Oxford: Oxford University Press.

Baldini, Ugo. (1984). "L'astronomia del Cardinale Bellarmino." In *Novità celesti e crisi del sapere*, ed. Paolo Galluzzi, 293–305. Florence, Italy: Annali dell'Istituto e Museo di Storia della Scienza.

Baldini, Ugo. (1992). *Legem impone subactis. Studi su filosofia e scienza dei gesuiti in Italia (1540–1632)*. Rome: Bulzoni.

Bangs, Carl O. (1971). *Arminius: A Study in the Dutch Reformation*. Nashville, TN: Abingdon.

Barbuto, Gennaro Maria. (2013). *Machiavelli*. Rome: Salerno Editrice.

Baron, Hans. (1966). *The Crisis of the Early Italian Renaissance*. Princeton, NJ: Princeton University Press.

Baylor, Michael G., ed. (1991). *The Radical Reformation*. Cambridge: Cambridge University Press.

Belligni, Eleonora. (2003). *Auctoritas e Potestas: Marcantonio de Dominis fra l'Inquisizione e Giacomo I*. Milan: Franco Angeli.

Berlin, Isaiah. (1970). *Four Essays on Liberty*. Oxford: Oxford University Press.

Berlin, Isaiah. (1972). "The Originality of Machiavelli." In *Studies on Machiavelli*, ed. Myron P. Gilmore, 149–206. Florence, Italy: Sansoni.

Berti, Domenico. ([1868] 1889). *Giordano Bruno da Nola*. 2nd enlarged ed. Turin, Italy: Paravia.

Biagioli, Mario. (1993). *Galileo Courtier: The Practice of Science in the Culture of Absolutism*. Chicago: University of Chicago Press.

Biagioli, Mario. (2001). "Replication or Monopoly? The Economics of Invention and Discovery in Galileo's Observations of 1610." In *Galileo in Context*, ed. Jürgen Renn, 277–320. Cambridge: Cambridge University Press.

Black, Robert. (2013). *Machiavelli*. London: Routledge.

Blackwell, Richard. (1998). "Could There Be Another Galileo Case?" In *The Cambridge Companion to Galileo*, ed. Peter Machamer, 348–66. Cambridge: Cambridge University Press.

Bock, Gisella, Quentin Skinner, and Maurizio Viroli, eds. (1990). *Machiavelli and Republicanism*. Cambridge: Cambridge University Press.

Bodin, Jean. ([1588] 1975). *Colloquium of the Seven about the Secrets of the Sublime*. Edited and translated by Marion Leathers Daniels Kuntz. Princeton, NJ: Princeton University Press.

Bouwsma, William J. (1957). *Concordia mundi: The Career and Thought of Guillaume Postel (1510–1581)*. Cambridge, MA: Harvard University Press.

Bruce, Susan. ed. (1999). *Three Early Modern Utopias: Thomas More: Utopia / Francis Bacon: New Atlantis / Henry Neville: The Isle of Pines*. Oxford: Oxford University Press.

BIBLIOGRAPHY

Bruno, Giordano. (1879–91). *Opera latine conscripta*. 3 vols. in 7 parts. Edited by Francesco Fiorentino, Felice Tocco, Carlo Maria Tallarigo, Vittorio Imbriani, and H. Vitelli. Naples, Italy: Le Monnier.

Bruno, Giordano. (1977). *The Ash Wednesday Supper*. Edited and translated by Edward A. Gosselin and Lawrence S. Lerner. Hamden, CT: Archon.

Bruno, Giordano. (1998). *Cause, Principle and Unity: And Texts on Magic*. Edited by Richard J. Blackwell and Robert de Lucca. Cambridge: Cambridge University Press.

Bruno, Giordano. (2013). *On the Heroic Frenzies*. Edited and translated by Ingrid Rowland. Toronto: Toronto University Press.

Bruno, Giordano. (2002). *Opere italiane*. 2 vols. Edited by Giovanni Aquilecchia and Nuccio Ordine. Turin, Italy: UTET.

Cadoni, Giorgio. (1974). *Machiavelli, regno di Francia e "principato civile."* Rome: Bulzoni.

Calogero, Guido. (1963). "La Professione di Fede di Giordano Bruno." *La cultura* 1: 1–14.

Calvin, John. ([1581] 2007). *Institutes of the Christian Religion*. Translated by Henry Beveridge. Peabody, MA: Hendrickson.

Cantimori, Delio. ([1939] 2002). *Eretici italiani del Cinquecento*. Turin, Italy: Einaudi.

Castellio, Sebastian. (1935). "Concerning Heretics." In *Concerning Heretics: Whether They Are to Be Persecuted and How They Are to Be Treated. A Collection of the Opinions of Learned Men Both Ancient and Modern*, ed. Roland H. Bainton, 119–253. New York: Columbia University Press.

Chabod, Federico. (1974). "La Politica in Paolo Sarpi." In *Scritti sul rinascimento*, 459–588. Turin, Italy: Einaudi.

Chambers, D. S., ed. (1995). *The Italian Academies of the Sixteenth Century*. London: Warburg Institute.

Colish, Marcia L. (1971). "The Idea of Liberty in Machiavelli." *Journal of the History of Ideas* 32: 323–50.

Collinson, John. (1807). *Life of Thuanus*. London: Longmans.

Contarini, Gasparo. (1599). *The Commonwealth and Government of Venice*. Translated by Lewes Lewkenor. London: John Windet for Edmund Mattes.

Crinò, Anna Maria. (1952). "Un amico inglese del Granduca Cosimo III di Toscana: Sir Henry Neville." *English Miscellany* 3: 235–47.

Crinò, Anna Maria. (1957). "Lettere inedite italiane e inglesi di Sir Henry Neville." In *Fatti e figure del Seicento Anglo-toscano*, 173–208. Florence, Italy: Olschki.

Croce, Benedetto. (1931). *Etica e politica*. Bari, Italy: Laterza.

Dall'Olio, Guido. (1999). *Eretici e inquisitori nella Bologna del Cinquecento*. Bologna, Italy: Istituto per la Storia di Bologna.

Darbishire, Helen, ed. (1932). *The Early Lives of Milton*. London: Constable.

De Bernart, Luciana. (2002). *Numerus quodammodo infinitus*. Rome: Edizioni di Storia e Letteratura.

De Bujanda, J. M., Francis M. Higman, and James K. Farge. (1985–86). *Index des livres Interdits*. 11 vols. Quebec: Editions de l'Université de Sherbrooke.

De Michelis Pintacuda, Fiorella. (2001). *Tra Erasmo e Lutero*. Rome: Edizioni di Storia e Letteratura.

De' Nerli, Filippo. (1728). *Commentarj de' Fatti Civili Occorsi dentro la Citta' di Firenze dall'anno MCCXV al MDXXXVII*. Augusta, Germany: David Raimondo Mertz and Gio. Jacopo Majer.

De Thou, Jacques Auguste. ([1604] 1807). *The Preface to His History*. Translated by John Collinson. In John Collinson, *Life of Thuanus*, 389–443. London: Longman.

Dei Pazzi, Alessandro. (1842). "Discorso sulle cose di Firenze indirizzato a Cardinale Giulio dei Medici." *Archivio storico italiano* 1: 420–32.

Descartes, René. (1996). *Meditations on First Philosophy*. Edited by John Cottingham and Bernard Williams. Cambridge: Cambridge University Press.

Di Cesare, Mario, ed. (1991). *Milton in Italy: Contexts, Images, Contradictions*. Binghamton, NY: Medieval and Renaissance Texts and Studies.

Dobranski, Stephen B., and John P. Rumrich, eds. (1998). *Milton and Heresy*. Cambridge: Cambridge University Press.

Donaldson, Ian. (2011). *Ben Jonson: A Life*. Oxford: Oxford University Press.

Dowling, Paul M. (1995). *Polite Wisdom and Heathen Rhetoric in Milton's "Areopagitica."* Lanham, MD: Rowman and Littlefield.

Dzelzainis, Martin. (1995). "Milton and the Protectorate: 1658." In *Milton and Republicanism*, ed. David Armitage, Armand Himy, and Quentin Skinner, 181–205. Cambridge: Cambridge University Press.

Eliot, T. S. (1957). *On Poetry and Poets*. New York: Farrar, Straus and Cudahy.

Erasmus, Desiderius. (1974–). *The Collected Works*. 89 vols. Toronto: Toronto University Press.

[Featley, Daniel.] (1626). *Pelagius redivivus. Or Pelagius raked out of the ashes by Arminius and his Schollers*. London: Robert Mylbourne.

Feldhay, Rivka. (1995). *Galileo and the Church: Political Inquisition or Critical Dialogue?* Cambridge: Cambridge University Press.

Feldhay, Rivka. (2001). "Recent Narratives on Galileo and the Church: Or the Three Dogmas of the Counter-Reformation." In *Galileo in Context*, ed. Jürgen Renn, 219–37. Cambridge: Cambridge University Press.

Finocchiaro, Maurice. (1989). *The Galileo Affair: A Documentary History*. Berkeley and Los Angeles: University of California Press.

Finocchiaro, Maurice. (2001). "Philosophy versus Religion and Science versus Religion: The Trials of Bruno and Galileo." In *Giordano Bruno: Philosopher of the Renaissance*, ed. Hilary Gatti, 51–96. London: Ashgate.

Finocchiaro, Maurice. (2005). *Retrying Galileo: 1633–1992*. Berkeley and Los Angeles: University of California Press.

Firpo, Luigi. (1993). *Il processo di Giordano Bruno*. Edited by Diego Quaglione. Rome: Salerno Editrice.

Firpo, Massimo. (2003). *Riforma protestante ed eresie nell'Italia del Cinquecento: un profile storico.* Rome: Laterza.

Firth, C. H., and R. S. Rait, eds. (1911). *Acts and Ordinances of the Interregnum 1642–1660*, vol. 3. London: HMSO.

Fish, Stanley. (2001). *How Milton Works.* Cambridge, MA: Harvard University Press.

Fontana, Biancamaria. (2008). *Montaigne's Politics: Authority and Governance in the "Essais."* Princeton, NJ: Princeton University Press.

Franklin, Julian H., ed and trans. (1969). *Constitutionalism and Resistance in the Sixteenth Century: Three Treatises by Hotman, Beza, and Mornay.* New York: Pegasus.

Fuhrmann, Manfred. (1992). *Cicero and the Roman Republic.* Translated by W. E. Yuill. Oxford: Blackwell.

Furcha, E. J. (1996). "'Turks and Heathen Are Our Kin': the Notion of Tolerance in the Works of Hans Denck and Sebastian Franck." In *Difference and Dissent: Theories of Toleration in Medieval and Early Modern Europe*, ed. Cary J. Nederman and John Christian Laursen, 83–99. Lanham, MD: Rowman and Littlefield.

Gabrieli, Vittorio. (1982). "Jacopo Aconcio in Inghilterra." *La Cultura* 21, no. 2: 309–40.

Galileo Galilei. ([1611] 1989). *Sidereus nuncius or the Starry Messenger.* Edited and translated by Albert Van Helden. Chicago: University of Chicago Press.

Galileo Galilei. ([1633] 1962). *Dialogue concerning the Two Chief World Systems—Ptolemaic and Copernican.* Edited and translated by Stillman Drake. Berkeley and Los Angeles: University of California Press.

Galileo Galilei. (1895). *Le opere di Galileo.* Edited by Antonio Favaro. Florence, Italy: G. Barbera.

Garin, Eugenio. ([1938] 2009). "La *dignitas hominis* e la letteratura patristica." In *Interpretazioni del rinascimento*, vol. 1, ed. Michele Ciliberto, 1–32. Rome: Storia e letteratura.

Garin, Eugenio. (1954). *Medioevo e rinascimento.* Bari, Italy: Laterza.

Garin, Eugenio. (1965). *Scienza e vita civile nel rinascimento.* Bari, Italy: Laterza.

Garin, Eugenio. (1969). *Science and Civic Life in the Italian Renaissance.* Translated by Peter Munz. Garden City, NY: Anchor.

Garin, Eugenio, Cesare Vasoli, Mirella Brini, and Paola Zambelli, eds. (1955). *Testi umanistici sull'ermetismo.* Rome: Fratelli Bocca.

Gatti, Hilary. (1989). *The Renaissance Drama of Knowledge: Giordano Bruno in England.* London: Routledge.

Gatti, Hilary. (1999). *Giordano Bruno and Renaissance Science.* Ithaca, NY: Cornell University Press.

Gatti, Hilary, ed. (2002). *Giordano Bruno: Philosopher of the Renaissance.* London: Ashgate.

Gatti, Hilary. (2011). *Essays on Giordano Bruno.* Princeton, NJ: Princeton University Press.

Gatti, Hilary. (2012). "The Humanities as the Stronghold of Freedom: John Milton's *Areopagitica* and John Stuart Mill's *On Liberty*." In *The Making of the Humanities*, vol. 2: *From Early Modern to Modern Disciplines*, ed. Rens Bod, Jaap Maat, and Thijs Weststeijn, 167–82. Amsterdam: Amsterdam University Press.

Gentile, Giovanni. (1907). *Giordano Bruno nella storia della cultura.* Milan: Remo Sandron.

Gilbert, Felix. (1965). *Machiavelli and Guicciardini: Politics and History in Sixteenth Century Florence.* Princeton NJ: Princeton University Press.

Gilmore, Myron P., ed. (1972). *Studies on Machiavelli.* Florence, Italy: Sansoni.

Gregory, Tullio. (1962). "Discussioni sulla 'Doppia verità.'" *Cultura e scuola* 2: 99–106.

Gregory, Tullio. (1998). "*Libertinisme érudit* in Seventeenth Century France: The Critique of Ethics and Religion." *British Journal of the History of Philosophy* 6, no. 3: 323–49.

Grendler, Paul. (1977). *The Roman Inquisition and the Venetian Press (1540–1605).* Princeton, NJ: Princeton University Press.

Grendler, Paul. (1981). *Culture and Censorship in Late Renaissance Italy and France.* London: Variorum Reprints.

Griffiths, Gordon. (1968). *Representative Government in Western Europe in the Sixteenth Century.* Oxford: Clarendon.

Guarini, Elena Fasano. (1990). "Machiavelli and the Crisis of the Italian Republics." In *Machiavelli and Republicanism*, ed. Gisela Bock, Quentin Skinner, and Maurizio Viroli, 17–40. Cambridge: Cambridge University Press.

Hale, John K. (1991). "Areopagitica's Euripidean Motto." *Milton Quarterly* 25, no. 1: 25–27.

Haliczer, Stephen, ed. (1987). *Inquisition and Society in Early Modern Europe.* Totowa, NJ: Barnes and Noble.

Harrington, James. (1992). *The Commonwealth of Oceana and a System of Politics.* Edited by J.G.A. Pocock. Cambridge: Cambridge University Press.

Harrison, Peter. (1998). *The Bible, Protestantism and the Rise of Natural Science.* Cambridge: Cambridge University Press.

Harrisse, Henry. (1905). *Le president de Thou et ses descendents.* Paris: Henri Leclerc.

Hart, H.L.A. (1999). "Rawls on Liberty and Its Priority." In *The Two Principles and Their Justification*, ed. Henry S. Richardson, 2–23. New York: Garland.

Henry, John. (2002). *The Scientific Revolution and the Origins of Modern Science.* New York: Palgrave.

Hermann, Camilla, and Luisa Simonutti, eds. (2011). *La centralità del dubbio: un progetto di Antonio Rotondò.* 2 vols. Florence, Italy: Olschki.

Hesse, Mary. (1980). *Revolutions and Reconstructions in the Philosophy of Science.* Bloomington: Indiana University Press.

Hill, Christopher. (1940). *The English Revolution 1640.* London: Lawrence and Wishart.

Hill, Christopher. (1972). *The World Turned Upside Down: Radical Ideas during the English Revolution.* London: Maurice Temple Smith.

Hill, Christopher. (1978). *Milton and the English Revolution.* New York: Viking.

Hobbes, Thomas. (2008). *Leviathan*. Edited by J.C.A. Gaskin. Oxford: Oxford University Press.

Hoenderdaal, G. J. (1975). "The Debate about Arminius outside the Netherlands." In *Leiden University in the Seventeenth Century: An Exchange of Learning*, ed. T. H. Lunsingh Scheurleer and G.H.M. Posthumus Meyjes, 136–59. Leiden, Netherlands: Brill.

Hooker, Richard. (1977). *Of the Laws of Ecclesiastical Polity*. Edited by Georges Edelen. Cambridge, MA: Harvard University Press.

Hooker, Richard. (1989). *Of the Laws of Ecclesiastical Polity*. Edited by Arthur Stephen McGrade. Cambridge: Cambridge University Press.

Hösle, Vittorio. (2004). "Interreligious Dialogues during the Middle Ages and Early Modernity." In *Educating for Democracy:* Paideia *in an Age of Uncertainty*, ed. A. M. Olson, D. M. Steiner, and I. S. Tuuli, 59–83. Lanham, MD: Rowman and Littlefield.

Hunter, William B. (1992). "The Provenance of the *Christian Doctrine*." *Studies in English Literature* 32: 129–42.

Inglese, Giorgio. (1985). "Il *Discursus florentinarum rerum* di Niccolò Machiavelli." *La cultura* 33: 203–28.

Inglese, Giorgio. (2006). *Per Machiavelli: L'arte dello stato, la cognizione delle storie*. Rome: Carocci.

Israel, Jonathan. (1995). *The Dutch Republic: Its Rise, Greatness and Fall: 1477–1806*. Oxford: Oxford University Press.

Israel, Jonathan. (2001). *Radical Enlightenment: Philosophy and the Making of Modernity 1650–1750*. Oxford: Oxford University Press.

Israel, Jonathan. (2010). *A Revolution of the Mind: Radical Enlightenment and the Intellectual Origins of Modern Democracy*. Princeton, NJ: Princeton University Press.

Isocrates. (1954). *Isocrates*. Translated by George Norlin. 3 vols. Cambridge, MA: Harvard University Press.

Jacobs, Margaret. (1981). *The Radical Enlightenment*. London: Allen and Unwin.

Jaeger, Werner. ([1939] 1986). *Paideia: The Ideals of Greek Culture: Archaic Greece and the Mind of Athens*. Oxford: Oxford University Press.

Kahn, Victoria. (1994). *Machiavellian Rhetoric: From the Counter-Reformation to Milton*. Princeton, NJ: Princeton University Press.

Kelley, Donald R. (1973). *François Hotman: A Revolutionary's Ordeal*. Princeton, NJ: Princeton University Press.

Kelley, Donald R. (1981). *The Beginning of Ideology: Consciousness and Society in the French Reformation*. Cambridge: Cambridge University Press.

Kermode, Frank, ed. (1960). *The Living Milton*. London: Routledge and Kegan Paul.

Kingdon, Robert M. (1988). *Myths about the St. Bartholomew's Day Massacres 1572–1576*. Cambridge, MA: Harvard University Press.

Kinser, Samuel. (1966). *The Works of Jacques-Auguste de Thou*. The Hague: Martinus Nijoff.

Knox, Dilwyn. (2013). "Bruno: Immanence and Transcendence in *De la causa, principio et uno*, Dialogue II." *Bruniana e campanelliana* 19, no. 2: 463–82.
Kuntz, Marion Leathers. (1998). "The Concept of Toleration in the *Colloquim Heptaplomeres*." In *Beyond the Persecuting Society*, ed. John Christian Laursen and Cary J. Nederman, 125–44. Philadelphia: University of Pennsylvania Press.
Landucci, Luca. (1969). *A Florentine Diary from 1450 to 1516*. Translated by A. De Rosen Jervis. London: Dent and Dutton.
Laursen, John Christian, and Cary J. Nederman, eds. (1998). *Beyond the Persecuting Society: Religious Toleration before the Enlightenment*. Philadelphia: University of Pennsylvania Press.
Leclerc, Joseph. ([1955] 1994). *Histoire de la tolerance au siècle de la Réforme*. Paris: Albin Michel.
Lewalski, Barbara K. (2000). *The Life of John Milton*. Oxford: Blackwell.
Locke, John. (1988). *The Second Treatise of Civil Government (1690)*. In *Two Treatises of Government*, ed. Peter Laslett, 265–429. Cambridge: Cambridge University Press.
Locke, John. (2003). *Two Treatises on Government and A Letter concerning Toleration*. Edited by Ian Shapiro. New Haven, CT: Yale University Press.
Luther, Martin. ([1520] 1947). *Three Treatises*. Edited by C. M. Jacobs, A.T.W. Steinhauser, and W. A. Lambert. Philadelphia: Muhlenberg Press. Texts reprinted from the *Works of Martin Luther*, 6 vols., Philadelphia.
Luther, Martin. (1957). *The Bondage of the Will*. Translated and edited by J. I. Packer and O. R. Johnston. Grand Rapids, MI: Fleming H. Revell.
Macaulay, Thomas Babington. (1843). "Milton." In *Critical and Historical Essays Contributed to the Edinburgh Review*, vol. 1, 1–61. London: Longmans.
Machamer, Peter, ed. (1998). *The Cambridge Companion to Galileo*. Cambridge: Cambridge University Press.
MacCulloch, Diarmaid. (2002). "Richard Hooker's Reputation." *English Historical Review* 473: 773–812.
MacCulloch, Diarmaid. (2005). *The Reformation: A History*. Oxford: Oxford University Press.
Machiavelli, Niccolò. (1532). *Il principe*. Rome: Blado.
Machiavelli, Niccolò. (1584). *I discorsi di Niccolò Machiavelli sopra la prima deca di Tito Livio*. Palermo, Italy: Antoniello degli Antonielli (actually London: John Wolfe).
Machiavelli, Niccolò. (1997). *Opere*. 3 vols. Edited by Corrado Vivanti. Turin, Italy: Einaudi.
Machiavelli, Niccolò. (2000). *Discorsi sopra la prima deca di Tito Livio, seguiti dale Considerazioni del Machiavelli di Francesco Guicciardini*. Edited by Corrado Vivanti. Turin, Italy: Einaudi.
Machiavelli, Niccolò. (2013a). *Il principe: Edizione del cinquecentennale*, with introduction and commentary by Gabriele Pedullà. Rome: Donzelli.
Machiavelli, Niccolò. (2013b). *Il principe: Nuova edizione*. Edited by Giorgio Inglese. Turin, Italy: Einaudi.

Mahlberg, Gaby. (2009). *Henry Neville and English Republican Culture in the Seventeenth Century.* Manchester, England: Manchester University Press.

Malcolm, Noel. (1984). *De Dominis 1560–1624: Venetian, Anglican, Ecumenist and Relapsed Heretic.* London: Strickland and Scott.

Marchand, Jean-Jacques, Denis Fachard, and Giorgio Masi, eds. (2001). *Niccolò Machiavelli:* L'arte della guerra e Scritti Politici Minori. Rome: Salerno Editrice.

Margolin, Jean-Claude. (1986). "La notion de la dignité humaine selon Erasme." In *Erasme: le prix des mots et de l'homme,* 205–19. London: Variorum Reprints.

Martin, Julian. (1992). *Francis Bacon, the State and the Reform of Natural Philosophy.* Cambridge: Cambridge University Press.

Martines, Lauro. (2006). *Scourge and Fire: Savonarola and Renaissance Florence.* London: Cape.

Masson, David. (1881–94). *The Life of John Milton: Narrated in Connection with the Political, Ecclesiastical and Literary History of his Time.* 7 vols. London: Macmillan.

McGrath, Alistair. (1986). *Iustitia dei.* 2 vols. Cambridge: Cambridge University Press.

McMullin, Ernan. (1998). "Galileo on Science and Scripture." In *The Cambridge Companion to Galileo,* ed. Peter Machamer, 271–347. Cambridge: Cambridge University Press.

Mentzer, Raymond A. (2002). "The Edict of Nantes and Its Institution." In *Society and Culture in the Huguenot World: 1559–1685,* ed. Raymond A. Mentzer and Andrew Spicer, 98–116. Cambridge: Cambridge University Press.

Mentzer, Raymond A., and Andrew Spicer, eds. (2002). *Society and Culture in the Huguenot World: 1559–1685.* Cambridge: Cambridge University Press.

Mercati, Angelo. (1942). *Il sommario del processo di Giordano Bruno.* Vatican City: Biblioteca Apostolica Vaticana.

Milton, John. (1644). *Areopagitica: A Speech to the Parliament of England.* London: n.p. Held by the British Library in the Thomason Tracts, 4:E.18[9].

Milton, John. ([1644] 1959). *Areopagitica.* In *Complete Prose Works of John Milton,* vol. 2, ed. Ernest Sirluck, 486–570. New Haven, CT: Yale University Press.

Milton, John. (1953). *Complete Prose Works of John Milton,* vol. 1. Edited by Don M. Wolfe. New Haven, CT: Yale University Press.

Milton, John. (1962). *Complete Prose Works of John Milton,* vol. 3. Edited by Merritt Y. Hughes. New Haven, CT: Yale University Press.

Milton, John. (1973). *Complete Prose Works of John Milton,* vol. 6. Edited by Maurice Kelley. New Haven, CT: Yale University Press.

Montaigne, Michel de. (1987). *The Complete Essays.* Translated by Michael A. Screech London: Penguin.

More, Thomas. (1963–1997). *The Complete Works of St. Thomas More.* 15 vols. New Haven, CT: Yale University Press.

Murphy, Andrew R. (2001). *Conscience and Community: Revisiting Toleration and Religious Dissent in Early Modern England and America.* University Park: Pennsylvania State University Press.

Nederman, Cary J., and John Christian Laursen, eds. (1996). *Difference and Dissent:*

Theories of Toleration in Medieval and Early Modern Europe. Lanham, MD: Rowman and Littlefield.

[Neville, Henry.] (1681). *Plato redivivus, or a Dialogue concerning Government.* 2nd ed. London: R. Dew.

Peddle, David. (2008). "Intimations of Modernity, Freedom and Equality in Calvin's *Institutes.*" *Animus* 12: 3–14.

Pedullà, Gabriele. (2011). *Machiavelli in tumulto: Conquista, cittadinanza e conflitto in Discorsi sopra la prima deca di Tito Livio.* Rome: Bulzoni.

Peltonen, Harkku. (2002). "Citizenship and Republicanism in Elizabethan England." *Republicanism* 2: 85–106.

Pera, Marcello. (1998). "The God of Theologians and the God of Astronomers: An Apology of Bellarmine." In *The Cambridge Companion to Galileo*, ed. Peter Machamer, 367–87. Cambridge: Cambridge University Press.

Petit, Philip. (1997). *Republicanism: A Theory of Freedom and Government.* Oxford: Clarendon.

Pintard, René. (1943). *Le libertinisme érudit.* Paris: Boivin.

Pocock, J.G.A. (1976). *The Machiavellian Moment: Florentine Political Thought and the Atlantic Republican Tradition.* Princeton, NJ: Princeton University Press.

Polizzotto, Lorenzo. (1995). *The Savonarolan Movement in Florence 1494–1545.* Oxford: Oxford University Press.

Poppi, Antonino. (1972). *La dottrina della scienza in Giacomo Zabarella.* Padua, Italy: Antenore.

Postel, Guillaume. (1560). *De la republique des turcs, et là ou l'occasion s'offrira, des meurs et loy de tous Muhamedistes.* Poitiers, France: Enguilbert de Marinef.

Il principe di Machiavelli e il suo tempo: 1513–2013. (2013). Exhibition catalog. Rome: L'Enciclopedia Treccani.

Prosperi, Adriano. (2003). *L'inquisizione romana: Letture e ricerche.* Rome: Edizioni di Storia e di Letteratura.

Provvidera, Tiziana. (1998). "Essex e il *Nolanus*. Un nuovo documento inglese su Bruno." *Bruniana e Campanelliana* 4, no. 2: 437–48.

Provvidera, Tiziana. (2002). "John Charlewood, Printer of Giordano Bruno's Italian Dialogues, and His Book Production." In *Giordano Bruno: Philosopher of the Renaissance*, ed. Hilary Gatti, 167–86. London: Ashgate.

Raab, Felix. (1964). *The English Face of Machiavelli: A Changing Interpretation 1500–1700.* London: Routledge and Kegan Paul.

Racaut, Luc. (2002). "Religious Polemic and Huguenot Self-Perception and Identity, 1554–1619." In *Society and Culture in the Huguenot World: 1559–1685*, ed. Raymond A. Mentzer and Andrew Spicer, 29–43. Cambridge: Cambridge University Press.

Rawls, John. ([1971] 1999). *A Theory of Justice.* Cambridge, MA: Harvard University Press.

Rawls, John. (2010). *A Brief Enquiry into the Meaning of Sin and Faith, with "On My Religion."* Edited by Thomas Nagel, Joshua Cohen, and Robert Adams Merrihew. Cambridge, MA: Harvard University Press.

Rees, Graham, and Maria Wakely. (2009). *Publishing, Politics, and Culture: The King's Printers in the Reign of James I and VI*. Oxford: Oxford University Press.
Remer, Gary. (1996). "Bodin's Pluralistic Theory of Toleration." In *Difference and Dissent: Theories of Toleration in Medieval and Early Modern Europe*, ed. Cary J. Nederman and John Christian Laursen, 119–37. Lanham, MD: Rowman and Littlefield.
Ricci, Saverio. (1990a). *La fortuna del pensiero di Giordano Bruno (1600–1750)*. Florence, Italy: Le Lettere.
Ricci, Saverio. (1990b). "Infiniti mondi e mondo nuovo. Conquista dell'America e critica della civiltà europea in Giordano Bruno." *Giornale Critico della Filosofia Italiana*, fascimile ed. 2: 204–22.
Ricks, Christopher B. (1963). *Milton's Grand Style*. Oxford: Clarendon.
Robbins, Caroline, ed. (1969). *Two English Republican Tracts*. Cambridge: Cambridge University Press.
Rossi, Paolo. (1952). *Giacomo Acconcio*. Milan: Fratelli Bocca.
Rotondò, Antonio. ([1974] 2008). *Studi e ricerche di storia ereticale del Cinquecento*. Florence, Italy: Olschki.
Rowland, Ingrid. (2008). *Giordano Bruno: Philosopher and Heretic*. New York: Farrar, Straus and Giroux.
Rubenstein, Nicolai. (1966). *The Government of Florence under the Medici (1434–1494)*. Oxford: Oxford University Press.
Rubenstein, Nicolai. (1972). "Machiavelli and Florentine Politics." In *Studies on Machiavelli*, ed. Myron P. Gilmore, 5–28. Florence, Italy: Sansoni.
Rubenstein, Nicolai. (1986). "Libertas fiorentina." *Il rinascimento*, 2nd series, 26: 3–26.
Rubenstein, Nicolai. (1990). "Machiavelli and Florentine Republican Experience." In *Machiavelli and Republicanism*, ed. Gisela Bock, Quentin Skinner, and Maurizio Viroli, 3–16. Cambridge: Cambridge University Press.
Sacerdoti, Gilberto. (2002). *Sacrificio e sovranità: teologia e politica nell'Europa di Shakespeare e Bruno*. Turin, Italy: Einaudi.
Sarpi, Paolo. ([1619] 1974). *Istoria del concilio di Trento*. 2 vols. Edited by Corrado Vivanti. Turin, Italy: Einaudi.
Sarpi, Paolo. (1958). *Scritti giurisdizionalistici*. Edited by Giovanni Gambarin. Bari, Italy: Laterza.
Sarpi, Paolo. (1961). *Lettere ai Gallicani*. Edited by Boris Ulianich. Wiesbaden, Germany: Franz Steiner Verlag.
Sarpi, Paolo. (2001). *Consulti*. 2 vols. Edited by Corrado Pin. Pisa, Italy: Istituti editoriali e poligrafici internazionali.
Sasso, Gennaro. (1967). *Studi su Machiavelli*. Naples, Italy: Morano.
Sasso, Gennaro. (1980). *Niccolò Machiavelli: Storia del suo pensiero politico*. Bologna, Italy: Il Mulino.
Sasso, Gennaro. (1988). *Machiavelli e gli antichi, e altri saggi*. 3 vols. Milan: Riccardo Ricciardi.
Schaefer, David Lewis, ed. (1998). *Freedom over Servitude: Montaigne, La Boétie, and On Voluntary Servitude*. Westport, CT: Greenwood.

Schmitt, Charles B. (1983). *Aristotle in the Renaissance.* Cambridge, MA: Harvard University Press.

Seidel Menchi, Silvana. (1983–84). "Inquisizione come repressione o Inquisizione come mediazione? Una proposta di periodizzazione." *Annuario dell'Istituto Storico Italiano per l'Età Moderna e Contemporanea* 35–36: 53–77.

Severini, Maria Elena. (2002). *Bibliografia di Giordano Bruno: 1951–2000.* Rome: Edizioni di Storia e Letteratura.

Shakespeare, William. ([1600] 1982). *Hamlet.* The Arden Edition, edited by Harold Jenkins. London: Methuen.

Shakespeare, William ([1605?] 1972). *King Lear.* The Arden Edition, edited by Kenneth Muir. London: Methuen.

Shakespeare, William. (2003). *Richard II.* Edited by Andrew Gurr. Cambridge: Cambridge University Press.

Shapin, Steven (1998). *The Scientific Revolution.* Chicago: University of Chicago Press.

Sieur de la Haye. (1671). *The Policy and Government of Venice, Englished.* London: John Starkey.

Silvestrini, Virgilio. (1958). *Bibliografia di Giordano Bruno (1582–1950).* Edited by Luigi Firpo. Florence, Italy: Sansoni.

Simonutti, Luisa. (2003). "Scepticism and the Theory of Toleration: Human Fallibility and 'Adiaphora'." In *The Return of Scepticism: From Hobbes and Descartes to Bayle*, ed. Gianni Paganini, 283–304. International Archives of the History of Ideas 184. Dordrecht, Netherlands: Kluwer Academic.

Singer, Dorothea. (1950). *Giordano Bruno: His Life and Thought.* New York: Shuman.

Sirluck, Ernest. (1953). "Milton's Use of Historical Sources: An Illustration." *Modern Philology* 50: 226–31.

Skinner, Quentin. (1978). *The Foundations of Modern Political Thought.* 2 vols. Cambridge: Cambridge University Press.

Skinner, Quentin. (1984). "The Idea of Negative Liberty: Philosophical and Historical Perspectives." In *Philosophy in History*, ed. Richard Rorty, J. B. Schneewind, and Quentin Skinner, 193–221. Cambridge: Cambridge University Press.

Skinner, Quentin. (1998). *Liberty before Liberalism.* Cambridge: Cambridge University Press.

Skinner, Quentin. (2002). *Visions of Politics*, vol. 2: *Renaissance Virtues.* Cambridge: Cambridge University Press.

Sleigh, Robert, Jr., Vere Chappell, and Michael della Rocca. (1998). "Determinism and Human Freedom." In *The Cambridge History of Seventeenth Century Philosophy*, vol. 2, ed. Daniel Garber and Michael Ayers, 1195–1206. Cambridge: Cambridge University Press.

Sosio, Libero. (2006). "Paolo Sarpi, un frate nella rivoluzione scientifica." In *Ripensando Paolo Sarpi*, ed. Corrado Pin, 183–236. Venice: Ateneo veneto.

Spampanato, Vincenzo. (1921). *Vita di Giordano Bruno.* Messina, Italy: Principato.

Stanglin, Keith D. (2007). *Arminius on the Assurance of Salvation.* Leiden, Netherlands: Brill.

Swerdlow, Noel M. (1998). "Galileo's Discoveries with the Telescope and Their Evidence for the Copernican Theory." In *The Cambridge Companion to Galileo*, ed. Peter Machamer, 244–70. Cambridge: Cambridge University Press.

Taylor, Charles. (1979). "What's Wrong with Negative Liberty?" In *The Idea of Freedom,* ed. Alan Ryan, 175–93. Oxford: Oxford University Press.

Taylor, Gary, and Michael Warren, eds. (1983). *The Division of the Kingdoms: Shakespeare's Two Versions of "King Lear."* Oxford: Oxford University Press.

Tedeschi, John. (1991). *The Prosecution of Heresy: Collected Studies on the Inquisition in Early Modern Italy.* Binghamton, NY: Medieval and Renaissance Texts and Studies.

Tedeschi, John, ed. (2002). *The Correspondence of Roland H. Bainton and Delio Cantimori (1932–1966): An Enduring Transatlantic Friendship between Two Historians of Religious Toleration.* Florence, Italy: Olschki.

Torzini, Roberto. (2000). *I labirinti del libero arbitrio: La discussione tra Erasmo e Lutero.* Florence, Italy: Olschki.

Trebbi, Giuseppe. (2006). "Paolo Sarpi in alcune recenti interpretazioni." In *Ripensando Paolo Sarpi*, ed. Corrado Pin, 651–95. Venice: Ateneo veneto.

Van Gelderen, Martin, and Quentin Skinner, eds. (2002). *Republicanism: A Shared European Heritage.* 2 vols. Cambridge: Cambridge University Press.

Van Leewen, T. Marius. (2009). "Introduction." In *Arminius, Arminianism, and Europe*, ed. Th. Marius van Leewen, Keith D. Stanglin, Marijke Tolsma, ix–xxii. Leiden, Netherlands: Brill.

Venturi, Franco. (1979). "Venise et, par occasion, de la liberté." In *The Idea of Freedom*, ed. Alan Ryan, 195–210. Oxford: Oxford University Press.

Viroli, Maurizio. (2002). *Niccolò's Smile: A Biography of Machiavelli.* New York: Hill and Wang.

Viroli, Maurizio. (2004). "Il repubblicanesimo di Machiavelli." In *Libertà politica e virtù civile*, ed. Maurizio Viroli, 1–29. Turin, Italy: Edizioni Fondazione Giovanni Agnelli.

Viroli, Maurizio. (2005). *Il Dio di Machiavelli e il problema morale dell'Italia.* Rome: Laterza.

Viroli, Maurizio. (2013). *Redeeming The Prince: The Meaning of Machiavelli's Masterpiece.* Princeton, NJ: Princeton University Press.

Voak, Nigel. (2003). *Richard Hooker and Reformed Theology: A Study of Reason, Will and Grace.* Oxford: Oxford University Press.

Walker, William. (2009). *"Paradise Lost" and Republican Tradition from Aristotle to Machiavelli.* Turnhout, Belgium: Brepols.

Walzer, Michael. (1965). *The Revolution of the Saints: A Study in the Origins of Radical Politics.* Cambridge, MA: Harvard University Press.

Westman, Robert. (2011). *The Copernican Question: Prognostication, Skepticism, and Celestial Order.* Berkeley and Los Angeles: University of California Press.

Williams, George Huntston. ([1962] 1992). *The Radical Reformation.* Kirksville, MO: Sixteenth Century Journal Publishers/Northeast Missouri State University.

Wissink, J.B.M., ed. (1990). *The Eternity of the World in the Thought of St. Thomas Aquinas and His Contemporaries.* Leiden, Netherlands: Brill.

Worden, Blair. (2002). "Republicanism, Regicide and Republic: The English Experience." In *Republicanism: A Shared European Heritage*, vol. 1, ed. Martin van Gelderen and Quentin Skinner, 307–27. Cambridge: Cambridge University Press.

Works of the Famous Nicholas Machiavel. (1680). London: John Starkey.

Wyatt, Michael. (2005). *The Italian Encounter with Tudor England: A Cultural Politics of Translation.* Cambridge: Cambridge University Press.

Yates, Frances A. (1934). *John Florio: The Life of an Italian in Shakespeare's England.* Cambridge: Cambridge University Press.

Yates, Frances A. (1944). "Paolo Sarpi's History of the Council of Trent." *Journal of the Warburg and Courtauld Institutes* 7: 123–43.

Yates, Frances A. (1964). *Giordano Bruno and the Hermetic Tradition.* London: Routledge and Kegan Paul.

Yates, Frances A. (1984). "The Hermetic Tradition and Renaissance Science." In *Ideas and Ideals in the North European Renaissance: Collected Essays*, vol. 3, 227–46. London: Routledge and Kegan Paul.

Index

Abbot, George (Archbishop of Canterbury). 77, 128, 131, 183n94; critique of Bruno by, 66

Aconcio, Jacopo, 75, 77, 181n50; *On Method*, 51; pre-enlightenment optimism of, 51; *Satan's Strategems*, 50

Alva, Duke of (Fernando Álvarez of Toledo): persecutor of Protestantism in the Netherlands, 121–22

America, 1, 6–8, 40, 183n79; North, 2, 6, 47, 83, 89, 134, 141, 159, 176; South, 61

Amsterdam (Netherlands), 72, 133

Anabaptists, 82–83; occupation of Münster by, 46. *See also* radical Protestants

Anglican settlement, 153; Bruno's praise of, 66; Hooker's apology for, 66–71

Aquinas. *See* Thomas Aquinas (Saint)

Areopagus, the (ancient Greek parliament), 19

Aretino, Pietro, 59

Ariosto, Ludovico: *Orlando Furioso*, 75, 118

Aristotle, 58, 60–61, 63, 66, 71, 76, 107, 114; *Politics*, 6

Arminius, Jacobus (Jacob Harmensz), 40, 65, 71, 78, 143, 176; critique of Calvin's doctrine of predestination by, 71–74; followers of called Remonstrants, 72; library of, 75; *On Reconciling Religious Dissensions among Christians*, 76–77

Ascoli, Albert Russell, 24, 179n34

Athens (ancient Greece), 15, 144

Augustine (Saint) 53, 55, 108; *In Genesim ad literam (On the Literal Interpretation of Genesis)*, 109–111; and the Pelagian heresy, 41–44

Bacon, Francis, 76, 99, 114, 117; *The Advancement of Learning*, 64; and the liberty of the new science, 102–3; *The New Atlantis*, 103; *A Wise and Moderate Discourse Concerning Church-Affaires*, 147

Bainton, Roland, 43–44, 47–48, 181n44

Barbuto, Gennaro Maria, 25, 179n24

Bellarmino, Roberto (Cardinal and Inquisitor), 63–64, 105, 112, 129

Bellius Martin, 47. *See also* Castellio, Sebastian

Bentivoglio, Giovanni, 18

Berlin, Sir Isaiah, 2–4, 21, 33; as admirer of John Stuart Mill, 3; *Two Concepts of Liberty*, 2

Berti, Domenico: biographer of Bruno, 63

Beza, Theodore, 7, 40, 71–72; doctrine of double predestination of, 142–43

INDEX

Biagioli, Mario: *Galileo Courtier*, 118, 187n71
Bill, John: the King's printer, 78, 129; printing of Sarpi's *History of the Council of Trent* by, 131–33
Blackwell, Richard, 113
Blake, William, 139
Bodin, Jean, 86; *Colloquium of the Seven about Secrets of the Sublime*, 51–54, 61–62
Boccaccio, Giovanni: *Decameron*, 59
Bolinbroke, Henry (later King Henry IV of England), 93
bondage of the will: Calvin on, 40, 71; Luther on, 36, 42–43, 74
Borgia, Cesare, 14
Brent, Nathaniel: English agent in Venice, 131
Brenz, John, 45–46, 48, 82
Broughton, Hugh, 66
Bruccioli, Antonio, 59
Brucioli, Francesco, 59
Bruni, Leonardo, 5, 11
Bruno, Giordano, 50, 54–55, 59, 65, 83, 131, 182n64; *The Ash Wednesday Supper*, 65; burnt at the stake, 50, 65, 92; concept of liberty of, 59–62; and the new science, 101, 107, 110, 114, 117; *On the Heroic Frenzies*, 65; and Shakespeare, 93–94; trial of, 62–64
Buckley, Samuel, 120
Buondelmonti, Zanobi, 12, 24
Buonmattei, Benedetto, 136

Calvin, John (Calvinism, Calvinists), 7, 46–48, 51–52, 57, 68–74, 77, 79, 83, 85, 134, 138, 142–43, 149, 181n29; *Institutes of the Christian Religion*, 40–42
Camillo, Giulio: *Memory Theatre*, 52, 182n56
Campion, Edmund (Jesuit priest): torture and death of, 153

Canaye de Fresne, Philippe, 124
Cantimori, Delio, 7, 48–49, 181n44
Cardano, Girolamo, 75
Carlton, Sir Dudley, 73
Castelli Benedetto (pupil of Galileo Galilei), 106, 111
Castellio, Sebastian, 48–49; *Concerning Heretics, Whether They Are to Be Prosecuted and How They Are to Be Treated*, 44–45, 47
Castelnau, Michel de (Lord of Mauvissière), 65
Castelvetro, Giacomo, 159, 191n2
Castelvetro, Ludovico, 159
Cesi, Federico: and the Accademia dei Lincei, 118. *See also* Galileo Galilei
Chabod, Federico, 27, 179n39
Charles I (King of England, Scotland, and Ireland), 5, 133, 136, 138, 140–41, 146, 149, 153, 170
Charles II (King of England, Scotland, and Ireland), 5, 133, 152, 154, 156, 161–62, 168, 170–71
Charles V (Holy Roman Emperor), 121
Charles IX (King of France), 85, 121–22
Charlewood, John, 65, 185n30
Christina of Lorena (Grand Duchess of Tuscany): Galileo's letter to, 64, 104–6, 111–15, 147
Christophe of Württemberg (Duke), 48
Cicero, 6, 21, 37, 108; *De officiis* (*On Moral Obligations*), 69
Circignani, Niccolò, 153
Clement VII (Pope): and Erasmus of Rotterdam, 36, 55; *and* Machiavelli, 22
Clement VIII (Pope): and Bruno, 62
Colet John, 135
Constantine (Roman Emperor), 43
Contarini, Gasparrini: *Commonwealth and Government of Venice*, 84, 164–66, 171, 184n7. *See also* Venetian republicanism

INDEX

Coornhert, Dirck Volckertsz, 83; anti-Calvinist polemic of, 72, 143

Collinson, John: *Life of Thuanus,* 120, 188n9. *See also* Thou, Jacques Auguste de

Commonwealth of England (1649–1653, known as the Protectorate, 1653–1659), 6, 133, 138, 144, 149–50, 153–54, 156, 160–61

Copernicus, Nicholaus: Copernican theory and the cosmology of the bible, 105, 107–9; *On the Heavenly Revolutions,* 101, 112, 114. *See also* Galileo Galilei

Cosimo dei Medici (Cosimo il Vecchio), 5, 11

Cosimo II (Grand Duke of Tuscany), 104, 106

Cosimo III (Grand Duke of Tuscany), 161

Council of Trent (1544–63), 56–57, 78–79, 110, 121, 127, 129, 132, 146, 152, 174. *See also* Sarpi, Paolo

Counter-Reformation, 32, 54, 58–59, 75, 127, 129–30, 132, 152

Cranmer, Thomas (Archbishop of Canterbury), 67

Croce, Benedetto, 14

Cromwell, Oliver, 5–6, 84, 133, 138, 160–61, 163; and Milton, 150, 153–156

Curione, Celio Secundo, 47–48, 50, 75

Cusa, Nicholas of (Cardinal), 53, 60, 71

Dante, Alighieri, 16, 18, 23

Dati, Carlo, 136

Descartes, René, 51, 62, 89, 142; *Meditations on First Philosophy,* 4–5

Diderot, Denis, 8

Diggers and Levellers (radical underground movements), 6, 149–51

Diodati, Charles: friend of Milton, 135, 137

Diodati, Elio: translator of Galileo, 115

Dominis, Marcantonio de: abandonment of Catholic church by, 77–79; involvement of with the London publication of Sarpi's *History of the Council of Trent,* 128–32, 189n35. *See also* Sarpi, Paolo

Du Plessis-Mornay, Philippe: *Vindiciae contra Tyrannos (Disputes against Tyrants),* 86

Edict of Beaulieu, 83, 86–87, 122. *See also* Henri III (French king)

Edict of Nantes, 70, 88, 119, 123–24. *See also* Henri IV (French king)

Eliot, T. S.: critique and rehabilitation of Milton by, 134, 189n40

Elizabeth I (Queen of England), 65–69, 71, 89–91, 93–95, 98, 146, 153, 156, 159–60

Enlightenment, 2, 7, 50, 52. *See also* Descartes, René; Hobbes, Thomas; Spinoza, Benedict de

Epicurus: philosophy of, 52

Episcopius (Simon Bischop), 73

Erasmus of Rotterdam, 19, 31, 57–58; *Discussion of Free Will* (dispute with Luther), 36–43; *Hyperaspistes: A Warrior Shielding a Discussion of the Enslaved Will of Martin Luther,* 36, 74; *In Praise of Folly,* 35; *Life of Jerome,* 55

Essex, Earl of (Robert Devereux): abortive coup attempt by, 93; and the order for a drama of Richard II, 93–95

Euripides: *The Suppliant Women,* 144

Featley, Daniel, 74–75. *See also* Arminius Jacobus; Pelagius (Pelagian heresy)

Ferdinand I (Holy Roman Emperor): and religion as peaceful debate, 121

Ficino, Marsilio, 39, 60, 71

INDEX

Finocchiaro, Maurice, 185n28; Galileo's *Dialogue* translated into Latin in Geneva by, 115; and historical repetition of "the Galileo affair," 104

Fish, Stanley, 190n79

Florence, 6, 16, 18, 22–24, 27, 31, 57, 118, 125, 136, 162, 180n41

Florentine republican liberty, 5, 11–12, 14–15, 17, 25, 54, 84–85, 151, 169, 171. *See also* Machiavelli, Niccolò

Florentine Great Council, 13, 28, 167

Florio, John, 94–95

fortuna: Machiavelli and, 16–18, 135

Foucault, Léon, 112

Franck, Sebastian, 48–49

Frederick V (Elector Palatine), 128

freedom. *See* liberty

freedom of the will, 4, 17, 142, 181n22; Arminius on, 73–75; Erasmus, Luther, and Calvin on, 31–42; Hooker on, 71

freedom of the press, 92, 117–157. *See also* Milton, John, *Areopagitica*

Gaddi, Jacopo: admirer of Milton, 136; library of, 162

Galilei, Galileo: Copernicanism of, 103–105; *Dialogue on the Two Major World Systems*, 101, 115; *Letter to Madama Christina Lorena*, 64, 108–12, 114; recent discussion of, 112–14

Geneva (Switzerland), 7, 46–48, 57, 69, 71, 75, 120, 123, 131, 135

Gentile, Giovanni: defender of Bruno, 63, 183n85

Ghislieri, Michele (Cardinal), 58–59

Giannotti, Donato, 164

Giovanni di Lorenzo dei Medici (Pope Leo X), 23, 27

Giulio dei Medici (Cardinal, later Pope Clement VII), 13, 22, 27; global culture (globalization), 1

Gramsci, Antonio, 27, 179n34

Greece: ancient, 14, 35, 49, 81, 84, 92, 144; modern, 136–38

Grendler, Paul, 58, 182n71

Grotius, Hugo: *The Law in War and Peace* (*De jure belli ac pacis*), 72–73

Guicciardini, Francesco, 20

Hales, John (British delegate at the Synod of Dort), 73

Hannibal (ancient Roman general), 18

Harmenz, Jacob. *See* Arminius, Jacobus

Harrington, James: *Commonwealth of Oceana*, 84, 160–64, 171

Hartlib, Samuel, 141

Hathloday, Raphael, 19. *See also* More, Sir Thomas: *Utopia*

Henry III (French king), 65, 83, 85–86, 88, 119, 122

Henry IV (French king, previously Henry of Navarre), 88, 93, 119–125, 187n8

Henry VIII (King of England), 19, 21, 55, 67–68, 89–91, 166

heresy, 40–44, 48–49, 57, 65, 74, 141

Hermes Trismegistus, 52; doctrine of and the new science, 99

Hill, Christopher:; and the radical underground movements, 149–50; studies of Cromwell's republic by, 6. *See also* Diggers and Levellers

Hobbes, Thomas: *Leviathan*, 4, 51, 163, 167

Holbach, Paul Henri Thiery d', 8

Holland (The Netherlands), 5, 48, 50, 71, 89, 121

Hooker, John, alias Vowell, 67

Hooker, Richard, 65–69; *Laws of Ecclesiastical Polity*, 69–71

Hotman de Villiers, Jean, 120. *See also* Thou, Jacques Auguste de

individual conscience: liberty of Hotman, Francis, 120; *Francogallia*, 86

Huguenots (French Protestants), 82, 85–

210

INDEX

86, 88, 120, 123. *See also* St. Bartholomew's Night Massacre
human rights, 1, 9
Huss, Jan: early Protestantism of oppressed by Catholic church, 146

Index of Prohibited Books, 57–59, 62, 78, 85, 105, 109, 120–21, 128, 130,142, 146, 172, 182n71; Congregation of, 57, 118, 124
individual conscience: liberty of, 8–9, 11, 33, 39, 43, 46–47, 63, 73, 77, 81–82, 85–86, 88, 97, 120, 126–27, 139, 142–43, 146, 150 155–56
Inglese, Giorgio, 25
Inquisition (Roman Catholic), 7, 44, 50, 54, 78, 85, 95,106, 121, 131, 146–47, 155, 182n68; and Bruno, 56–58, 62–63; and Galileo, 103–6; and Sarpi, 129–30
inquisition(s), 8, 45, 51, 121
Islam, 49, 51, 174
Isocrates (ancient Greek rhetorician): *Areopagiticus*, 144, 190n63
Israel, Jonathan, 7, 177n20

Jacobs, Margaret, 177n20
James I (King of England, Scotland, and Ireland), 64, 73, 78, 94–95, 98, 102, 125, 128, 131, 133, 135, 147, 149
James II (King of England, Scotland, and Ireland), 5, 152–53, 162
Jews, 1, 31, 48, 52–53, 56, 103. *See also* Kabbalah
Jewel, Bishop of Salisbury, 67
John Paul II (Pope): rehabilitation of Galileo by, 104, 113
John the Evangelist (Saint), 33, 39
Jonson, Ben, 93
Joshua (Biblical book): Galileo on, 106, 111–12
Julius II (Pope), 17, 22, 165–66

Kabbalah, 58
Kahn, Victoria, 7
Kelley, Donald R, 82
Kermode, Frank: *The Living Milton*, 134
Kinser, Samuel, 187n5
Knox, John, 47, 181n43
Kuntz, Marion Leather, 51

La Boétie, Etienne de: *On Voluntary Servitude*, 87. *See also* Montaigne, Michel de
La Haye, Sieur, 164–65
Landucci, Luca, 13, 31
Laud, William (Archbishop of Canterbury): as oppressor of radical Protestants, 136, 138–39
Laursen, John Christian, 177n17
League of Cambrai, 165–66
Leicester, Earl of (Robert Dudley), 93
Leiden, University of, 72, 76
Lewalski, Barbara K: *Life of John Milton*, 134–35
Lewkenor, Lewes, 164, 184n7. *See also* Contarini, Gasparro
L'Hospital, Michel de: Councilor of the French *Parlement*, 121
liberalism, 1–2, 5, 46, 65, 82–83, 92, 142, 150, 152, 164
libertarianism, 1
libertinism (philosophic), 1–2. *See also* Gregory, Tullio; Pintard, René
liberty: of conscience, 8–9, 11, 82; and the law, 11–16, 123–24; definitions of, 2; and the new science, 101–115; "negative" form of, 2–4; and Parliament, 90–92; "positive" form of, 2–4. *See also* freedom of the will; individual conscience, liberty of
Livy, Titus, 6, 12–13, 20–21, 24, 27, 84, 160–62
Loredan, Leonardo, 166
Locke John, 50; *Letter on Toleration*, 152; *Second Treatise of Government*, 68, 71

INDEX

London (Great Britain), 19, 35, 50, 59, 65–67, 69, 74, 77–79, 89–90, 94–95, 101, 120, 128, 131, 133, 135–37, 140–41, 151, 154–56, 159–62, 164

Long Parliament (the), 5–6, 138, 141–43, 145–46, 150, 154–55

Lorenzo dei Medici (junior, Duke of Urbino), 12, 24, 27, 162

Lorenzo dei Medici ("Il Magnifico"), 5, 11–13, 18, 23, 27

Louis XIV (French king), 88, 168

Luther, Martin, 11, 21, 31–32, 40–43, 45–46, 48, 51–52, 55, 57–59, 67, 73–74, 82–83, 129, 142, 148–49; *The Bondage of the Will*, 36, 42–43, 74; dispute with Erasmus on the freedom of the will, 32–35, 38–39; doctrine of the elect of, 70–71; *An Open Letter to the Christian Nobility of the German Nation concerning the Reform of the Christian Estate*, 32; *A Treatise on Christian Liberty*, 32. *See also* Protestant Reformation

Macaulay, Thomas Babbington, 133, 150, 152–53

MacCulloch, Diarmaid, 153

Machiavelli, Niccolò, 4, 7–8, 11, 31–33, 40, 59, 63–64, 66, 69, 82–85, 88, 93, 97, 99, 104, 117–18, 149, 151, 154–55, 157, 161, 163–66, 168–69, 173, 175; *Art of War*, 12; *Discourse on the Situation in Florence* 27–29, 162–63, 171; and *fortuna*, 17–19, 135; *The Prince*, 14, 22–27; republicanism of (*Discourses on the first Ten Books of Titus Livy*), 6, 12–16, 29, 135, 159–60, 162–63; as the Satanic Machiavel, 7, 32, 172 and Sir Thomas More, 19–22

Magna Carta, 170

Malcolm, Noel, 128

Manso, Giovanni Battista, 136–37

Margolin, Jean-Claude, 39, 74

Marlowe, Christopher, 114

Martin, Julian, 102

Mary, Queen of Scots, 94

Maurice of Nassau (Dutch Calvinist prince), 73

McGrade, Arthur Steven, 67–68

McMullin, Ernan, 112

Melanchthon, Philipp, 34–35, 46, 58

Methodism, 73. *See also* Wesley, John

Micanzio, Fulgenzio, 78, 129–30, 188n32. *See also* Sarpi, Paolo

Michelis Pintacuda, Fiorella de, 38

Mill, John Stuart: *On Liberty*, 3, 152, 177n5

Milton, John, 133–57, 161–63, 170, 173, 189n40, 190n79; *Areopagitica: a Speech of Mr John Milton for the Liberty of Unlicens'd Printing*, 141–42, 144–53; Arminianism of, 143; *On Christian Doctrine*, 134; *Commonplace Book*, 133, 151; on the Irish question, 153–56; *Paradise Lost*, 156–57

Mocenigo, Giovanni, 62. *See also* Bruno, Giordano, trial of

Montaigne de, Michel, 61, 88, 92, 119, 142; *Essays*, 75, 95; "On Freedom of Conscience", 86–87; "On Friendship," 86. *See also* La Boétie, Etienne de

More, Sir Thomas, 21, 35, 58, 179n24; and freedom of speech in Parliament, 90–91; *Utopia* 19–20, 22, 163

Müntzner, Thomas: *Sermon Before the Princes*, 45–46, 181n40

natural philosophy: ancient, 58; modern, 59, 76, 102, 108, 110, 117, 119, 125, 175

Nederman, Cary, 177n17

neoplatonism (neoplatonists, neoplatonic), 39, 52, 59–60, 71, 101

Nerli, Filippo de': *Commentary on the Civil Events that took place in the City of Florence*, 13

INDEX

Neville, Henry, 159; admiration of Machiavelli, 162–63, 170–72; *Plato redivivus,* 161, 164–72; and Venetian republicanism, 165–66
Nichols, James, 76. *See also* Arminius, Jacobus

Ochino, Bernardino, 50, 75
Oldenbarnsveldt, Johan von, 72
Oxford: University of, 3, 50, 60, 66–67, 101, 179n29, 183n94

Padua: University of, 63, 75–76, 125
Paine, Thomas, 8
Paris (France), 5, 57, 59–60, 65, 72, 85, 119–20, 122–23
Parlements (French), 26, 85–86, 88, 121–22
Parliament (Dutch), 88; and the American *Declaration of Independence,* 89
Parliament (English), 5, 68–70, 89–90, 133–34, 136, 140, 153, 160–62,169, 171, 175; and freedom of speech, 90–92. *See also* Long Parliament (the)
parliaments (parliamentary democracy), 8, 15, 71, 83–84, 86, 139, 141, 144, 148, 156–57, 159, 163, 167–68, 175
Patrizi, Francesco, 75
Paul (Saint), 33, 37, 39, 126, 135
Paul III (Pope), 56, 107, 132
Paul IV (Giampietro Carafa, Pope), 57–59
Pazzi, Alessandro dei, 28, 162, 180n41
Peace of Westphalia, 79
Peasants' War, the, 45
Pedullà, Gabriele, 14
Pelagius (Pelagian heresy), 41–42, 74–75
Peltonen, Harkku, 68–69
Perkins, William, 71
Petit, Philip, 6, 177n13
Petrarca, Francesco, 75
Phillips, Edward (nephew and first biographer of John Milton), 136

Pico della Mirandola, Giovanni: *Oration on the Dignity of Man,* 39, 42, 74, 100
Pintard, René: *Le libertinisme érudit,* 177n3
Plato, 52, 60, 108, 160–61, 190n63: approval of censorship, 144; dialogue form of works, 163 *See also* Neville, Henry; *Plato redivivus*; and neoplatonism
Pliny, the Younger, 55–56, 182n66
Pocock, J.G.A., 6–7; editor of Harrington's *Oceana,* 160–61, 163; *The Machiavellian Moment,* 84, 99–101, 177n13
Poliziano, Angelo, 75
Polybius: *Histories,* 6, 15, 161, 178n17
Pomponazzi, Pietro: theory of double truth, 63
Popkin, Richard, 7
Postel, Guillaume, 49
Protestant Reformation, 11, 21, 32, 34–35, 43, 48–49, 56–57, 81, 85, 149,173. *See also* Luther, Martin; Calvin, John
Pucci, Francesco, 50
Pythagoras: Pythagorean harmony, 53; Pythagorean natural philosophy,63, 108

Raab, Felix, 160–61, 163
Rabelais, François, 59
radical enlightenment (*philosophes*), 2, 8–9, 89, 133, 176 *See also* Israel, Jonathan; Jacobs, Margaret
radical Protestants and Protestantism (Radical Reformation), 6–7, 32, 34, 41, 45, 47, 50, 66–67, 69, 70, 73, 82, 94, 169; John Milton and,134, 136–37, 143, 149–50. *See also* Williams, George Huntston
Rainolds, John, 66–67
Rawls, John, 54, 152, 182n61
Rees, Graham, 132
Remonstrants (Dutch), 72–73, 76, 78. *See also* Arminius, Jacobus

INDEX

republicanism, 5–8, 24–25, 27, 64, 68–69, 133, 135, 155, 160–61, 164, 171,175, 177n13. *See also* Florentine republican liberty; Venetian republican liberty

Roman Catholic Church, 7, 22, 32, 65, 74, 83, 85, 94, 112, 120, 152–53

Rome: ancient, 6, 13–16, 19–20, 35, 49, 81, 84, 92, 151, 156, 171; modern, 7, 12, 22–23, 27, 50, 54–58, 62, 66, 69, 75–78, 85, 90, 92, 105–6, 118–20, 124–32, 136, 153, 174

Rotondò, Antonio, 7, 83, 177n19

Rubenstein, Nicolai, 5

Rudolph II (Holy Roman Emperor), 183n78

Sallust, 6

Salutati, Coluccio, 5, 11

Sarpi, Paolo, 119, 125, 128, 145–46; attempted assassination of, 129–30; *Consultant Reports (Consulti)*, 126–27; *History of the Council of Trent*, 78–79,124, 129, 131–33, 184n118; and the Venetian interdict, 125, 128–29

Sasso, Gennaro, 18–19, 179n37

Savonarola, Girolamo, 31–32, 75

Schmitt, Charles, 76. *See also* Zabarella, Giacomo

Servetus, Miguel: anti-trinitarianism of, 47; burnt at the stake in Geneva,47–48

Shakespeare, William, 92; involvement of in the abortive *coup* by the Earl of Essex, 93–94; liberty in *Hamlet*, 95–97; liberty in *King Lear*, 98–99

Sidney, Sir Philip, 86, 93, 101

Skinner, Quentin, 3–4, 6, 135, 160

Smith, Thomas: *On the English Republic (De republica anglorum)*, 68–69

Socrates (death of), 52

Soderini, Giovan Battista, 17

Soderini, Piero, 17

Sozzini, Lelio, 47–48, 50

Spinoza, Benedict de: *Tractatus Philosophico-politicus*, 7

Stanglin, Keith D, 73. *See also* Arminius, Jacobus

Star Chamber, the, 141

Statius (ancient Roman poet): *Sylvae*, 122

St. Bartholomew's Night Massacre, 85, 122

Synod of Dort, 72–73, 77–79, 143

Tacitus, Cornelius, 14, 19, 147

Taylor, Charles, 177n6

Tedeschi, John, 56, 181n44

Temple Church (The), 67, 90

Thirty Years' War, 8, 79, 149–50, 153, 190n80

Thomas Aquinas (Saint), 38, 42, 44, 48, 63, 71, 110, 183n83

Thou, Christophe de: president of the French *Parlement*, 119, 122

Thou, Jacques Auguste de, 117, 133, 156, 176; *The History of His Own Time*, 119, 120–24

Tocqueville, Alexis de, 141

Toland, John, 133, 161

Travers, Walter, 67, 69

Ubaldis, Baldus de, 86

Urban VIII (Maffeo Barberini, Pope): and Galileo, 118, 131

utopia (utopian), 19–22, 84, 103, 160, 163, 171, 174. *See also* More, Sir Thomas

Vanini, Giulio Cesare, 50

Venice, 22, 52, 58–59, 62–63, 78, 124, 133, 137

Venetian interdict, 125–31. *See also* Sarpi, Paolo

Venetian republican liberty, 14, 51, 54, 84–85, 164–71

Vermigli, Peter Martyr, 67

INDEX

Vettori, Francesco, 23, 166
Viroli, Maurizio, 6–7, 21, 27, 160, 179n39
Vivanti, Corrado, 32, 178n6

Walzer, Michael, 47
Wentworth, Peter: and freedom of speech in Parliament, 91
Wesley, John (founder of Methodism), 73
Westminister Assembly of Divines, 140–41, 150, 154, 189n57
William III of Orange (King of Holland and England, Scotland, and Ireland), 5, 83
Williams, George Huntston, 83. *See also* radical Protestants
Williams, Roger, 141

Wittenberg (Germany), 36, 46, 59, 83, 96. *See also* Luther, Martin
Whittinton, Robert, 69
Wolfe, John: English publisher of Machiavelli, 159–60, 191n2
Wolsey, Thomas (Cardinal and Lord Chancellor of England), 21
Wooton, David: and Sarpi's religion, 126
Worden, Blair, 135, 160
Wotton, Henry (British ambassador to Venice): letter to Milton by, 137
Wyclif, John: early Protestantism of, oppressed by Catholic church, 146

Yates, Frances, 99–100. *See also* Hermes Trismegistus

Zabarella, Giacomo, 75–76

GPSR Authorized Representative: Easy Access System Europe - Mustamäe tee 50, 10621 Tallinn, Estonia, gpsr.requests@easproject.com

www.ingramcontent.com/pod-product-compliance
Lightning Source LLC
Chambersburg PA
CBHW021855230426
43671CB00006B/403